THE HISTORY
OF
ꙍORKINGTON

From 1866 to 1955

BY

Richard L. M. Byers

RICHARD BYERS
Bookseller & Publisher
Workington

First published in May 2003 by

Richard Byers
PO Box 45, Workington
Cumbria. CA14 3GP

www.richardbyers.co.uk

ISBN 0 9529812 5 4 (softback)

British Library Cataloguing in Publication Data
A catalogue record for this book is available from the British Library

Design and typeset by Pages & Pages
Printed and Bound in Great Britian

Also available in this series

Sugden's History of Arlecdon & Frizington
(ISBN 0952981211)
History of Workington (Earliest times to 1865)
(ISBN 095298122X)

Also from the same publishers

Bessemer Steel - A Pictorial Archive of Steelmaking at Workington
(ISBN 0953844714)
Workington War Heroes
(ISBN 0 953844 76 5)
Dickinson's Cumberland Dialect Dictionary
(ISBN 0 953844 77 3)

❧ AUTHORS PREFACE ❧

THIS BOOK charts Workington's history from the stern and industrial Victorian times, through the dramatic events of two World Wars and the harsh depressions of the 1920s and 30s. It follows on from my earlier volume, but can certainly be read and clearly understood, without the need to constantly refer back to the previous book.

The reader is taken back in time with a detailed walk through the streets of Old Workington. Looking at the communities and prominent buildings that have long since disappeared. Do you remember the St. John's School, the Drill Hall, Tuscan Villa or Central Station?

The chapter structure of this book is very similar to the last, with Workington's once prominent industrial past being carefully detailed. The history of each of the town's churches, schools and prominent landmarks are also explored.

I would like to give my thanks to all those listed below, for their kind assistance and selfless provision of facts and information. Without whom the task of writing this book would have been almost impossible.

"History is like a massive irregular shaped jigsaw puzzle, more often than not complicated by missing pieces. The true task of the historian is to complete as much of the jigsaw as possible, without reaching for a pair of sissors."

Richard L. M. Byers   April 2003

This is a special first edition of the book, personally signed by the author. No signature will appear here in later reprints or any subsequent editions. ∎

ACKNOWLEDGMENTS
Jo E. Byers, Frank Manders (Sunderland), Thomas A. Hickey (Ontario, Canada), Gavin Beattie (National Film Archive), James Kearney (Film Images), Lisa Bond (Northern Region Film and Television Archive), Alan J. Stein (Kirkland, Washington County, USA), Joyce Byers, Andy Byers, Kerry Evans (Kalgoorlie, Western Australia), Fiona Leslie (Victoria & Albert Museum), Eldred Christian Curwen (Kendal), Joy Tracey (Western Australia), City Managers Office (Kirkland, Washington County, USA.), Albert Brown (Harrington), Michael Burridge (Workington), Steve Durham (Workington AFC.), Derek Ellwood (Hampshire), Mike Faulkner (Allerdale Borough Council), Janet Thompson (Workington), Trevor Jones (Workington Library), Eleanor Gawne (RIBA Library and Archives), Jed Holmes (Workington), Philip Crouch, Harold Martin, Pat Evans (Helena Thompson Museum), Kenneth Mulcaster (Workington), Eric Hutton (Workington), Rebecca Walker (Marks & Spencer, London), Sherry Steel (Castle Museum, York), Chris Munroe (Guildford Public Library), Jane Tombe (Surrey History Centre), David Powell, Fergus McManus (Workington), Rosie Allen (Beamish Museum and Resource Centre), Whitehaven Record Office, Kendal Record Office, Carlisle Record Office, Carlisle Public Library, Tyne and Wear Archive Service, Newcastle upon Tyne City Library Service, Gateshead Library Service, Public Record Office, Kew, Durham Mining Museum. ∎

In Memory of my father
John Albert Byers (May 1919 - May 2000)

An octogenarian Workingtonian who witnessed so much history.
Thank you for sharing your memories with me.

RB 2003

READERS NOTES

The main text of this book is set in area **A** of the page layout (see right) With further additional notes and references to guide the reader through the work, being provided in area **B**. A reference number in brackets, is used to link these notes to the appropriate point in the text - eg. [03]

As many members of the influential **CURWEN** family shared the same Christian name, in order that each can be properly identified, a reference is provided after each name - eg **Henry [iii] Curwen**, refers to **Henry Curwen** (1661-1725).

ABBREVIATIONS

C&WA&AS	- Cumberland and Westmorland Archaeological and Antiquarian Society
C&WJR	- Cleator & Workington Junction Railway
C&WR	- Cockermouth and Workington Railway
WI&SCo.	- Workington Iron and Steel Company
LNWR	- London North Western Railway
M&CR	- Maryport and Carlisle Railway
M&S	- Marks and Spencer
OS	- Ordnance Survey
RIBA	-Royal Institute of British Architects
WJR	- Whitehaven Junction Railway

CONTENTS

LIST OF SUBSCRIBERS

Jeffrey Armstrong, Workington
Rees L. Banton, Flimby, Maryport
A. Barnes, Egremont
Edward Batty, Harrington, Workington
Miss Audrey Bell, Workington
Colin R. Bell, Workington
David Bell, Welshman Reef, Victoria, Australia
Lawrence & Jean Berwick, Harrington, Workington
John I. Bethwaite, Workington
S. E. Bignell, Workington
Mrs Freda Bode, Workington
Mike Borthwick, High Harrington, Workington
Margaret Brennan, Workington
Dicky Briggs, Kirklinton, Carlisle
J. Brown, Workington
J. Burr, Workington
Ann Bradley, Allonby, Maryport
Douglas Bridgewater, Henley-in-Arden
Joan Breen, Great Clifton, Workington
Mr J. H. Brelsford, Harrington, Workington
Margaret Bremner (nee Colling), Blennerhasset, Wigton
Jos. Brown, Workington
Josephine Buckley (nee Sowerby), Grange-over-Sands
Michael Burridge, Workington
Alison L. Cottier, Workington
P. & J.B. Cowman Seaton, Workington
S.M. Clifford, Little Clifton, Workington
Sheila Coles, Workington
Mark Coles, Dagenham, Essex
P.G.C. Cowman, Whitehaven
W. L. Carruthers, Workington
David Harvey Chambers, Workington
J. Cunningham, Siddick, Workington
Mrs A. Cross, Workington
Joan Crellin, High Harrington, Workington
Bill Currie, Harrington, Workington
F. Campbell, Scotland
J. Dolan, Chester-le-Street
Alastair Duncan, High Harrington
Pat Evans, Workington
Maureen Fisher, Lamplugh, Workington
Danny Ferris, Workington
Jim Fleming, Workington
Michael Faulkner, Broughton Moor
Malcolm Fee, Great Clifton, Workington
Colonel George K. Gillberry, Ambrosden, Oxon
Pauline Gregory, York
Denis Greenop, Workington
Eric Greenop, Sydney, Australia
Mr D. Vernon Hooke, Maryport
D. Holliday, Workington
Gordon Hodgson, Workington
Janet & John Hetherington, Seaton, Workington
Judith Harris Bridgefoot, Workington
L. P. & F. Hall Beccles, Suffolk
Mrs Ethel Heathcote, Moss Bay, Workington
Mr & Mrs John Heron, Workington
John Harrison, Workington
Len Harvey, Workington
G. K. Holliday, Workington
Norman Hyde, Seaton, Workington
Sue Hiscock, Oxford
Tess Hamblin, Workington
Edgar Iredale
James Harris Jones, Workington
Mr B. Jenkinson, Flimby, Maryport
Malcolm Jackson, Frizington
Len Johnston, Dearham, Maryport
T. N. Jackson, Workington
John Kelly, Workington
Mr M. Kilgour, Seaton, Workington

Stanley Kane, Workington
John Lace, Devon
Mr A. Lawson, Sheffield
Miss Mary Ann Lancaster, Whitehaven
Jack Lancaster, Northside, Workington
Jørgen & Muriel Madsen, Workington
Cliff & Joyce Martin, Whitehaven
Douglas Murray, Retford, Notts.
Ronald McAllister, Workington
A. Moncrieff, Workington
Elaine McDonald, Workington
Stephen Martin, Workington
Mrs I. A. Messenger, Workington
David Messenger, Cheltenham, Glos.
D. Maginnis, Seaton
M. Mansergh, Workington
Mrs Emily Mitchell, Seaton, Workington
E. Martin, Seaton, Workington
Ted Matear, Workington
R. McGinn, Workington
Sylvia Martin, Harrington, Workington
Cynthia McFarland, High Harrington, Workington
R. V. Martin, Distington, Workington
Mrs Joan Minto, Westfield, Workington
David T. Morton, Lowca, Whitehaven
Mary Morgan, Burnley
Pat Martin, Workington
Mary Morgan (nee Bond), Workington
K. P. Nicholson, Workington
Arthur Orton, Workington
Mrs H. Ostle, Low Seaton, Workington
A. B. Old, Flimby, Maryport
Sheila Ostle, Seaton, Workington
Roger A. Park, Atlanta, Georgia, USA
Sheila Pearson, Workington
C. Preston, Motherwell
Alan Pooley, Workington
John George Pearson, Workington
Dino Pardini, Workington
Michael Palmer, Hinckley, Leics.
Mr D. Rawding, Wansford, Peterborough
Colette Riddle, Workington
Kenneth Reed, Workington
E. Routledge, High Harrington, Workington
Denis Roper, Whitehaven
J. A. Relph, Workington
E. Carole Rael, Cockermouth
G. B. Routledge, Whitehaven
Alan Russell Turner, Paris, Illinois USA
Ian Smith, Alnwick
Mary Stringer, Workington
Ian & Margaret Smith, High Harrington, Workington
Ron Smith, Chesterfield
Anne Stephenson, Workington
Mr A. Sewell, Workington
Glynn Scurr, Seaton, Workington
Kathleen Smithson, Biloxi, Mississippi, USA
Lorraine Sydney, Stainburn, Workington
E. Tugman, Workington
Mrs J. E. Tuke, Seaton, Workington
Jennifer Tinnion, Leeds, West Yorkshire
Dennis Thompson, Great Clifton, Workington
Dr. A. Tognarelli, Seaton, Workington
Gordon & Marion Turrell, Workington
Mrs M.E. Watson, Workington
John Hodgson Wilson, High Harrington, Workington
Richard Wilson, Cockermouth
Mr L. White, Workington
Mr J. H. Watson, Workington
Oliver Woolcock, Seaton, Workington
Mrs L. Young, Workington

CHAPTER ONE

LOCAL GOVERNMENT

AS DETAILED IN the earlier volume of this history, Workington first obtained self government in May 1840. Initially the town's affairs were managed and controlled by a group of elected trustees. But following the adoption of the Local Government Act of 1858, they became more commonly known as the Local Board. Thirty years later, the town was granted a *"Charter of Incorporation"* [01] and the first municipal elections were held *"amid great rejoicing"* on the 1 November 1888. A week or so later, the old Town Council was formally replaced with the new Borough Council (or Corporation - as it was often called locally). As one local newspaper reported *"the first Municipal elections showed that the burgesses took a lively and healthy interest in their affairs, every ward was hotly contested"*. Very fittingly, Henry Fraser Curwen (of Workington Hall) was unanimously elected as the town's first Mayor, and John Warwick was appointed as town clerk.

One of the first tasks of the new Borough Council was to commission a Municipal Coat of Arms. (see illustration overleaf) Records suggest that it may have been designed by local painter John Snowdon Armstrong, who lived in Fisher Street. He is said to have copied the blast furnace from Oldside Ironworks, and the unicorn from those which once adorned the gates of Workington Hall. One of the ships was said to be the clipper *"Alaska"*, which he described as the *"greyhound of the Atlantic"*. The area of interlaced stranded plait-work, seems to have been adopted from the Curwen family coat of arms. Although many believe that this fretwork like design has its origins in the Viking stones found at St. Michaels church. This coat of arms served the town for almost 78 years, until the Corporation decided to commission a new one.

Exactly, why the town needed a new coat of arms is not too clear. One can surmise that it was around the time of the 1951 Festival of Britain. A period when the whole country was striving to lift itself from the "post-war doldrums" of rationing and shortages. Approved in July 1950, the new Borough of Workington coat of arms in heraldic terms is *"sable between two piles or billetee azure a garb of the second and for the crest on a wreath*

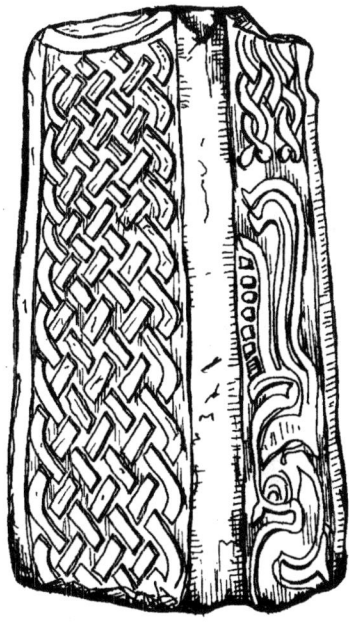

ABOVE - One of the Viking stones found at St. Michaels church. See page 27 of *History of Workington (Earliest times to 1865)* for more details of the origins of the interlaced stranded plait-work. ■

[01] The charter of incorporation was granted by Her Majesty Queen Victoria on 6 September 1888. The first elected councillors were for St. Michaels Ward; Joseph Harding, Lancelot Ward, Richard Harrison Hodgson, John Milburn, Charles McKerrow, and James Fletcher. St. Johns Ward; Thomas Iredale, Charles James Valentine, William Wilson, James Duffield, John Hen-ry Howe, and Alfred Peile. South Ward; John Paterson, Edwin Carlisle, Samuel Warren Bradbury, John Yeowart, Edwin Loach and Richard Robinson.

On 23 November 1888, John Milburn, Thomas Iredale, James Duffield, Alfred Peile, John Paterson, Samuel Warren Bradbury were elected the town's first Aldermen. Their places on the Borough Council were taken by James Whitfield, George John Smith, William Paisley, Henry McAleer, Joseph Eden and Frank Unwin. ■

ABOVE TOP - The original 1888 municipal coat of arms, described on the previous page. ■

[01] See page 22 of *History of Workington (Earliest times to 1865)* for details of the orgins of the name "Workington". ■

azure a garb of the second and for the crest on a wreath of the colours issuant from a mural crown or a unicorn's head argent in the mouth an anchor in bend sable", the supporters on the dexter side a representation of Vulcan and on the sinister side a representation of Themis both proper."* More simply, the shield is black, the two inverted triangles, the piles, are gold and the small rectangular figures or billets are blue. The garb or wheatsheaf is gold and represents the town's agricultural past. The silver unicorn's head, again taken from the Curwen family arms, has in its mouth an anchor which represents shipping. The figure of Vulcan to the right, was the Roman god of metal workers, obviously appropriate due to the town's rich iron and steel history. Themis is the other figure, the Greek goddess who personified justice, and is intended to symbolise good local government.

Originally, it was first proposed to use the motto *"Floreat oppidum laborans"* or *"May the working town flourish"*. This was intended as a play on the name "Workington". However, it was later thought by many to be quite inappropriate, as the origins of the town name certainly had nothing to do with "working".[01] In the summer of 1951, Canon Croft's suggestion to use *"Levavi oculus meos in montes"* or *"I will lift up mine eyes unto the hills"* (from Psalm 121) was adopted as a more acceptable alternative. Obviously, this refers to the close proximity of the Lakeland hills, and a suggestion that the townspeople should always strive for highest standards. The new coat of arms was reproduced for the first time in the official programme of the Workington Shopping Week, part of the town's Festival of Britain celebrations of September 1951.

After the introduction of the new coat of arms, the original 1888 design was removed from most public buildings. However, an example that still exists and can be seen today, is carved in red sandstone and built into the wall of the old gasworks building on the south side of Stanley Street. Some mystery surrounds the much larger example that was erected on the Oxford Street facade of the relatively new, Electricity Showrooms (opposite the top end of Gray Street). We know it was removed intact in 1950, but where is it now?

Following his death in 1945, Sir John Scurrah Randles left the town the sum of £1000 for *"some useful memorial to his memory"*. Although the legacy was received by the council within a few months, it would be nine years before the money was eventually used to purchase a new set of Civic Regalia. During Queen Elizabeth's coronation year, the Borough Council resolved to renew the mace and mayor's chain. This new civic regalia was funded by the residue of Sir John Randles bequest to the Council. The original mayoral chain of office, which dated back to 1888, was in urgent need of renovation.[01] The original mace, presented to the town by brewer Thomas Iredale in 1890, also required extensive repairs. In addition, the official coat of arms on both pieces needed updated. The 1890 mace is currently displayed at Helena Thompson Museum. [02]

The boundaries of the town were extended in 1882, when the Cloffolks was added to urban area. Seventeen years later, the boundaries of the Borough of Workington were subsequently extended north, to include both Siddick and Northside, previously part of West Seaton. Oldside and Barepot then also became part of the Borough. [03] With this boundary change came the opportunity to build a new road bridge over the River Derwent at Northside. Much of the cost being principally funded by the County Council. By the Cumberland review Act of 1934 the boundaries were further extended, with the absorption of the old Harrington Urban District Council, to the south of the town. Harrington now became a new additional ward of the Borough of Workington.

In 1865, the Local Board were known to have met in their offices in Udale Street. Around a decade or so later, they also held their meetings in the Board Room of the Good Templars Hall. When the Borough Council was formed in 1888, they rented premises on the west side of Washington Street from Mr. Brouch for their *"town hall"*.[04] Although this was adequate in the early years, the ambitious new local authority soon out grew the basic facilities. The Council minutes of December 1892 reveal that the Washington Street premises were *"an old building....the council chamber, for instance, was made out of three bedrooms belonging to two cottages"*. The building also needed constant, sometimes expensive maintenance. Although they rented the premises for £52 10s per annum, any alterations would be at the council's cost and not recoverable when the lease expired. In addition due to lack of office space, they needed to rent other properties in the town for the Gas Manager's office and Nuisances Office. As *"considerable sums of money were being paid in rent, repairs and alterations without the chance of the Corporation ever possessing a brick in the buildings they now or may occupy"*, it was resolved to look into the possibility of acquiring new larger premises.

But it was January 1899, before the Borough Council eventually purchased an alternative building. They

The boundaries of the town were extended in 1882, when the Cloffolks was added to urban area.

[01] Henry Fraser Curwen (of Workington Hall) is recorded as providing the towns first *"Municipal or Civic Regalia"*. ▪
[02] The new Civic Regalia was formally presented to the town on 28 Sept 1954, by the niece of Sir John Scurrah Randles, Mrs. Doris H. Ellis. Sir John had the honour of being made Workington's first Freeman of the Borough, on 27 July 1916. ▪
[03] This extension of the boundaries was authorised under the Workington Corporation Act of 1899, and came into operation on 9 Nov 1899. ▪
[04] Thomas Holliday, estate agent and auctioneer is known to have had his offices within the *"Old Town Hall"* in Washington Street around 1911. Council minutes show us that plans were approved for alterations to the same building in Feb 1920, for Mr J. Smith. ▪

Up to 1907, the regular full council meetings were often held in the Albert Hall, in Fisher Street. Then they were transferred to the committee room at the Carnegie Library.

[01] Richard Harrison Hodgson was first elected to the old Local Board in 1879, and to the Borough Council in 1888, became Mayor in 1898 and an Alderman in 1901. He was a building contractor and served as chairman of the Bank of Whitehaven in 1915-16. Hodgson was also a Lieutenant in the 1st. Cumberland Artillery Volunteers and a member of Workington Cricket Club. He died in the autumn of 1932. ■

[02] Copies of the competition instructions, conditions and plans of Field House are stored in the RIBA archives. ■

£2,300 for the property. This included all the gardens and stables and other outbuildings. It was the former home of Richard H. Hodgson. [01] By April, the Corporation announced an open competition for architects to adapt Field House to a Town Hall. Offering a top prize of £40 to *"the authors of the design placed first in order of merit"* [02]. The competition was won by architects Oliver and Dodgson of Carlisle and Leeds. And G. D. Oliver was appointed as site architect for the works. The Borough Council then sought approval to borrow £11,750 to complete the purchase of Field House and carry out the conversion work. It appears that the government would not sanction the funding for the work and the Council had to review the extent of the work to reduce costs.

In November 1900, a much less ambitious scheme was proposed to now convert Field House to provide 10 offices, committee rooms, and a council chamber. In addition, the old coach house would be used as a fire station, and the stables converted to a caretaker's cottage. The estimated costs was now around £4,400, and again the Council applied to the Local Government Board to borrow the necessary funds. Again there appears to have been problems funding the project and it was shelved. By the autumn of 1904, much of Field House still lay vacant and was only occupied by the Council's *"Inspector of Nuisances"*. Earlier in the year, it had been one of those properties offered to the County Council for it's proposed new Technical College. As plans for the new school were delayed until at least the next spring, the Corporation decided to carry out only minor work to the building. They created offices for the Town Clerk and a committee room. The Corporation's Treasurers department also moved to Field House in the spring of 1905.

Soon after the purchase of Field House, the Borough Council vacated the rented premises in Washington Street. They moved to new offices in Finkle Street, often also known then as the *"municipal buildings"*. This was only a temporary arrangement as the Finkle Street property had been earmarked for demolition, in order to widen the street. Up to 1907, the regular full council meetings were often held in the Albert Hall, in Fisher Street. Then they were transferred to the committee room at the Carnegie Library. This council chamber was located at the front of the building, immediately to the left of the Finkle Street entrance. All council and their subcommittee meetings were subsequently held here for many years.

Again in December 1935, the Corporation considered once more the question of completing the conversion of Field House into a Town Hall. And in the ensuing years,

Field House into a Town Hall. And in the ensuing years, they also enthusiastically proposed altering Bankfield, the former mansion of the prominent Kirk and Iredale families. In addition from 1947 after the town was gifted Workington Hall, a great deal of time and funds were spent on a scheme to also convert this ancient building into a *"town hall and municipal offices"*. [01]

Exactly when the poorhouse or workhouse at Ellerbeck was closed is not quite clear. The national census of 1841 showed just over 100 *"paupers"* were then accommodated in the building. Whilst a decade later, the 1851 census lists the premises as being *"uninhabited"*. Workington by then was part of the Cockermouth Union, formed under the Poor Law Amendment Act of 1834. The Union encompassed much of West Cumberland and catered for the needs of *"poor, less fortunate and orphaned"* in Cockermouth, Keswick, Maryport and Workington. By 1843, a new workhouse had been built in Cockermouth's Gallowbarrow, and thereafter Workington's paupers were accommodated there. Although the cost of which was still bourne by the Workington townspeople.

This was when the vacant Ellerbeck was first sold, as there is certainly references to the money received being invested *"for the use of the poor"* in the town. The buildings are then known to have passed through various hands. And by 1861, the *"Old Poor House"* was now referred to as *Ellerbeck Hall*. It appears that at least part of the building remained a dwelling until the property was eventually sold by Joseph Smith Peel to Workington Borough Council in 1888. For a Thomas Berry (a quarryman and farmer) and his family are recorded in both the 1871 and 1881 census, as living there.

Ellerbeck was purchased by the Borough Council, for conversion into an isolation hospital. Throughout Victorian Britain, frequent epidemics of cholera, small pox, typhoid, scarlet fever and diphtheria occurred and the townspeople of Workington certainly didn't escape from these highly infectious and potentially fatal diseases. Then of course there was no preventative vaccinations, nor antibiotics to treat victims. Isolation away from the rest of the community was the only way to prevent major epidemics.

Small pox was particularly prevalent in the town between 1861-1880. This was a highly infectious and contagious viral fever. The first symptoms of which were usually a headache, back pain and fever. Followed by a major rash, culminating in severe purulent or weeping

The townspeople of Workington certainly didn't escape from these highly infectious and potentially fatal diseases.

[01] See chapter seven for more details about the gift and proposals to convert it to a town hall. ■

blisters to the arms, legs and face. In it's most severe forms a high proportion of cases were fatal. Those that did survive often suffered long term complications such as paralysis, blindness or hearing problems.

Another small pox epidemic spread throughout the north of England during the spring of 1893. The first case in the town occurring in March, was William Carruthers, a *"tripe dresser"* of Washington Street. He was immediately admitted to Ellerbeck, and all his bedding was destroyed.

During the period 1861-80, we know up to 25 of every 1000 cases in children up to 4 years old were fatal. But by the turn of the century virtually no child died of the disease in the town. Between 1902-04 there was still a constant stream of small pox cases in Workington, all of which were generally accommodated at Ellerbeck.

When an outbreak occurred in 1902, one of the first victims was George Harwood, a steelworker, who lived with his family at 137 Harrington Road. He was diagnosed with the disease soon after returning to the town from a trip to London. He was actually sent to the Merchants Quay Isolation hospital [01], and was joined a few days later by his sons George and Charles Harwood. It appears that the Harwoods were sent to the Merchants Quay to avoid mixing other infectious diseases in the same hospital. Whenever possible, it was often the policy at Ellerbeck to not mix patients suffering from smallpox, typhoid, scarlet fever, diphtheria etc. and to keep them separated. When Merchants Quay was not available, often patients had to be accommodated in two timber buildings within the grounds of Ellerbeck. Although only basic temporary structures they remained in place until the spring of 1932, when the council disposed of them.

Small pox was again prevalent in the town in March 1924, with 29 cases reported. A month later this had risen to 67 cases, all of which were sent to Ellerbeck, as it was almost free of other patients. The epidemic peaked in May at 94 cases, by which time the libraries, schools and cinemas had all been closed for several weeks, in an effort to contain the outbreak. Because of the highly contagious nature of small pox, any cases of typhoid, scarlet fever etc. which occurred in the town during the epidemic were now sent to the Galemire Hospital at Moor Row. It would be almost a year before Ellerbeck was clear of small pox cases, and after being *"entirely and thoroughly disinfected"*, these other patients could be admitted once more.

In July 1884, a report in the *Maryport and Workington Advertiser* states *"there is typhoid fever in King Street,*

Once I had a fever,
I won't forget it soon,
I was hot as a basted-turkey,
and crazy as a loon.
    author unknown (c.1905)

[01] The Merchants Quay Isolation hospital, operated by the Port Sanitary Authority, was little more than a wooden hut, erected to "isolate any suffers" who usually entered the port aboard a ship. Occasionally it would also be used to keep different diseases apart, as an alternative to Ellerbeck. ∎

Cavendish Street, Udale Street, South Watt Street, Longdale, Church Street, Clifton Terrace, Botany Street and Devonshire Street". Typhoid fever is usually contracted by swallowing a specific bacillus when drinking water was polluted with urine or faeces, or may also be conveyed by flies. Frequent other cases occurred in the town throughout the next twenty years or so. Some were isolated, whilst others developed into epidemics, virtually all were admitted to Ellerbeck.

During the epidemic of 1906-08, Esmé Violette Curwen was highly commended by the Borough Council for dealing with the typhoid cases at Ellerbeck. Her desire to nurse the typhoid cases was quite remarkable, as her own sister Margaret Fairfax Curwen (1866-1876) had died of typhus fever whilst attending school, in the Normandy town of Caen. Both girls where the daughters of Rev. Alfred Francis Curwen (1835-1920) and Laura Naomi Smith. Their brother was the solicitor John Neville St. George Curwen (1879-1967) and uncle was Henry Fraser Curwen (1834-1900).

We know from the 1896 writings of Rev. Saunders Greene that *"Scarlet Fever has been more or less prevalent in town for at least three years"*. During the winter of 1895, there was a particularly large number of admissions. With over one hundred and forty cases reported in a single month. Dr. John Highet,[01] the towns medical officer of health, blamed the inadequate sanitary conditions as a principle cause. A disinfection chamber was subsequently installed at the hospital in order that cases could receive *"proper treatment"*.

This particular epidemic of scarlet fever lasted many months, public schools and sunday schools being closed *"twice within a short period"* by order of the Town Clerk. Each building was later fumigated and disinfected before the pupils were allowed to return. Rev. Greene also tells us that *"trade was suffering as people are not entering the town"*. A new report on the town's sewers suggests that their structure was considered *"generally satisfactory"*, but highlighted some problems with flushing and ventilation. [02] Whilst the Borough Council addressed these problems, information posters were printed and posted throughout the town to educate the townspeople on avoiding the disease. They also stressed the need for the *"cordial co-operation of the inhabitants of the borough"* inorder to contain and combat the epidemic.

By mid February 1896, after a Margaret Elliot [03] was discharged from Ellerbeck, the hospital was reported to be *"now clear of fever-infected patients"*. Although

[01] In 1896, Dr. John Highet was paid £120 per annum by the Borough Council to act as the town's Medical Officer of Health.■

[02] Data from this 1896 report tells us that the total length of the town's sewers was then 15.5 miles (or 26987 linear yards). It also records that there was 170 or so streets and lanes.■

[03] Margaret Elliot had spent 44 days at Ellerbeck Isolation hospital, being discharged on the 3rd February 1896.■

Between 1861-70, scarlet fever accounted for over 15% of childhood mortality (aged 1-4). By 1871-1900, this had drop-ped significantly but was still almost 1 in 10.

that month 96 cases were still reported, with Clay Street and Bromley Street *"most affected"* with seventeen cases. This suggests that not all scarlet fever victims were actually removed to Ellerbeck. Others seem to have taken to their beds and stayed at home. During this particular epidemic lasting around six months, some 369 cases were reported by *"the nine doctors of the Borough"*. It did eventually subside, but was not totally eliminated, for two years later there was still over twenty cases reported in the town each month. Between 1861-70, scarlet fever accounted for over 15% of childhood mortality (aged 1-4). By 1871-1900, this had dropped significantly but was still almost 1 in 10. Further outbreaks of scarlet fever in the town continued to cause concern until well after WW1.

In 1901-2, the isolation hospital was once again extensively refurbished and formally re-opened on 25 September 1902. The work included construction of the new administration block, a small mortuary, wash house, drying and ironing rooms. The builders contractor was J. I. Wilson, working along side joiners, G. H. Chambers. The hospital was now capable of holding about fifty patients.

Extracts from 1896 "Objects and Rules" of
The Ellerbeck "Infectious Hospital or Sanatorium" in Workington, Cumberland.

Object to prevent dangerous infectious diseases, by means of isolation, with medical treatment and nursing for all classes, dealing with Cholera, Diphtheria, Scarlet Fever, Small Pox, Typhoid and Typhus Fever.

The Medical Superintendent shall prescribe the diet of each patient and keep all records of all cases. The Caretaker will have charge of the Hospital, acting as *"Messenger, Porter and General Attendant, assisting the Nurse or Nurses"* and shall "disinfect and bury all excreta, burn or otherwise destroy infected articles, and conduct all processes of disinfection in the hospital"

Patients, must reside in Urban District and are only admitted with signed certificate of Chairman of Committee and the MOH., not allowed to leave without written permission. Visitor, including clergy, by special permission in writing. When patients dangerously ill, notice is sent to relatives, *"with an Intimation that a patient may be visited"*. Fees - Free if under 20 shillings a week income and in receipt of parochial relief. 7 shillings a week for other Working Classes (income under 20 shillings), 15 shillings a week for Domestic Servants, Fees for members of Families depended on the ratable value of the family home and varied between 10s 6d to £1.1s per week.

During 1906-8, the town suffered further severe epidemics of both scarlet fever and typhoid. Many of the scarlet fever cases, mostly children, were accommodated within the isolation hospital. While typhoid patients were housed in three large *"make shift"* marquees, erected in the grounds of Ellerbeck. By March 1908, there had been 645 cases in the town, with 28 fatalities. The source of this typhoid epidemic was never really found, some suspected the town's water supply from Crummock, but tests proved it was not contaminated. Infected patients could usually expect to stay in the hospital for on average 7½ weeks. The cost of their care was estimated (in 1909) to be £2.16s.11½d (£2.85) each. By August 1908, Ellerbeck was *"almost clear"* of typhoid cases, but at least one new case of scarlet fever occurred each week until 1910. A further outbreak of typhoid did occur in 1914, with around forty cases. This being traced to bacteria discovered in mussels, then quite commonly eaten in the town. Until the 1920's, Ellerbeck could expect to deal with around six new typhoid patients annually.

Between 1919-20, the hospital had to deal with around 273 cases of Diphtheria. That particular epidemic peaking at 41 cases in March 1920, but further cases of the disease were common over the next twenty years. Diphtheria is an acute infectious disease and highly contiguous. Although transmitted by direct contact with a *"drop of saliva"*, the organism responsible also grows freely in milk, and infection is often conveyed in this way. It was particularly prevalent in this country during the post war years. With a death rate of more than 1 in 10. The majority of cases occurred in children up to 13 years old, with those aged 2 to 7 being most susceptible.

The hospital in December 1935 was still receiving around six to eight diphtheria or scarlet fever cases per month, together with the odd couple of typhoid cases, from ships visiting the harbour. Two years later, Diphtheria accounted for 75% of all cases admitted to the hospital. In March 1940, Ellerbeck also had to handle a minor epidemic of cerebro-spinal meningitis amongst the soldiers stationed at Workington Hall and the Drill Hall. These patients were amongst the last nursed by hospital matron, Miss E. G. Robnett who retired the following month. She had held the post at Ellerbeck for around 37 years and cared for hundreds of extremely sick people, suffering from a wide array of highly infectious diseases. In 1942 during WW2, the Borough Council began a Diphtheria *"immunisation"* program amongst the children of the town. This effectively eliminated the disease in the ensuing years.

Around this time, immunisation against other diseases was also gradually introduced, but we know from Dr. Ronald Grant's biography [01] that even in the 1950's, *"epidemics of measles, mumps, whooping cough, German measles, hepatitis and poliomyelitis"* were still quite common. Poliomyelitis (or Polio) is an infectious viral

Between 1919-20, the hospital had to deal with around 273 cases of Diphtheria. That particular epidemic peaking at 41 cases in March 1920.

[01] Dr. Ronald Napier Robertson Grant (b.1919), son of Doctors George O. and Jessie N. R. Grant (who had a General Practise in Carlisle). Qualified in 1943 and moved to Workington in September 1953 - taking over the practise of Dr. H.A.K. Rowland in John Street. (Dr. Rowland was later struck off by the British Medical Council for prescription fraud). ■

In 1920, visiting days at Ellerbeck were each Sunday and Thursday, between 2 - 4 pm only. Then only two adults were allowed to visit each patient, no children were allowed.

disease affecting the spinal cord and the brain, and often resulted in some permanent paralysis. Children are most susceptible, but it can also occur in young adults. Today of course all babies are immunised against Polio when very young. The recommended treatment being *"total and complete bed rest"* at the first signs of the disease. and isolation from others. Although the first case of polio in this country was recorded in 1912, outbreaks were rare until after WW2. Dr. Grant recorded that the most severe epidemic in Workington occurred during the winter of 1953.

Up until the mid 1950s, Ellerbeck continued to be used as a isolation hospital, particularly for treatment of tuberculosis of the lungs. Then as Dr. Grant later wrote *"antibiotics for tuberculosis were developed and those wards full of seriously ill patients disappeared"*. Soon after the main buildings of Ellerbeck were converted to house a geriatric unit, with the annexe or adjoining buildings being used as a convalescent ward. These patients requiring comparatively long periods of bed rest and recuperation.

After the new maternity ward was opened at Workington Infirmary, the older maternity ward was converted into a new geriatric unit. Elderly patients were now transferred to the new unit and Ellerbeck was subsequently closed. The redundant hospital buildings were later purchased by the Nicholson family, who later demolished much of the dilapidated property. The site is now a small secluded private housing estate, known as Ellerbeck Close. Apart from the old red brick *"administration"* block (which is now also a dwelling) little remains to remind us of the original complex. Except perhaps the condition of the very uneven and narrow roadway leading down to the site, from Ellerbeck Lane. For in October 1899, the always articulate Dr. John Highet (the town's medical officer of health) wrote *"complaints have been made by my medical confers with regards to the state of the road. It is at present time a chronic source of revenue to carriage builders and bicycle repairers, bearing somewhat hard on the limited incomes of my self-sacrificing profession"*. Although minor repairs must have been carried out to the road, a century later, nothing has really changed as the occupants and visitors of Ellerbeck Close will no doubt confirm.

Apart from the somewhat ambitious proposal to erect a *"cottage"* hospital in the town to the memory of Dr. Anthony Peat. [01] It appears the idea for an infirmary or hospital in the town was first seriously raised by the management of the Charles Cammell works, shortly after they moved to Workington in 1883. They offered a one-off donation of £500 to build the hospital, or £100 per annum. On the condition *"other similar establishments do similar"*. But it was eighteen months later, before the subject was addressed once more. At that time if anyone had been involved in an accident or was seriously ill, they had to be taken to either Whitehaven or Carlisle, by train or horse-drawn carriage. In 1882, the number of patients sent from the town to Carlisle was 56, whilst 26 were conveyed to Whitehaven.

In July 1884, a report in the *Maryport and Workington Advertiser*, tells of an influential and well-attended inaugural meeting in the Portland Square's Assemby Rooms. Where it was resolved that *"an infirmary be built in the town for both surgical and medical cases"*. A large committee under the direction of Henry F. Curwen was formed, this included Doctors Douglas, Ormrod, Highet, McKerrow, Lowe and Hodgson. Lord of the Manor, Henry Fraser Curwen gifted the land for the new hospital (said to be valued at £400) and the building was designed by Workington architect, George. D. Oliver. It is thought the design was based on a similar new infirmary in Middlesborough, which had cost around £3000.

In August 1885, the foundation stone for the new infirmary was laid by Edward Darcy Curwen and construction work took almost fifteen months. The infirmary was formally opened on 29 November 1886 by Mrs. A. Wilson of Sheffield. [01] The new building consisting of three wards, Curwen, George Wilson Ward and another unnamed. There was initially 12 male and 4 female beds and a nursing staff consisting of a matron, assisted by a day and night nurse. The first patient was admitted on 31 Dec. 1886. It is believed that Robert Armstrong, aged 29 was the first person to die in the new infirmary. He was employed as a pig lifter at the New Yard Works, when a badly stacked quantity of pig iron fell on him. His fellow workers worked frantically to free him and rushed him to the infirmary, but he died a few hours later never regaining consciousness. Such industrial accidents were very common place at the time, as the coroners records and many of the gravestones in the town's cemeteries will confirm.

In these early years, Workington Infirmary was supported entirely by voluntary contributions, the workers of the district became some of the first in the country to make these regular weekly contributions from their wages. Most agreeing to pay *"1 old penny a week"* to maintain the hospital. This was long before the statutory deductions we have today and the creation of the National

The infirmary was formally opened on 29 November 1886 by Mrs. A. Wilson of Sheffield.

[01] She was the wife of George Wilson the former managing director of the Charles Cammell works, and a driving force behind the establishment of the Infirmary. He had died in Dec 1885, before the building was completed. ∎

Health Service. The success of the hospital was also due to the frequent subscriptions and donations from the more affluent townspeople. Even the local doctors gave there services voluntarily. Dr. Charles McKerrow was appointed the first medical officer at the infirmary. It was also administered and managed by a *"tireless and dedicated"* committee.

Over the next half century, Workington Infirmary was altered and enlarged on a number of occasions. In 1901, a childrens ward was built and a new operating theatre added during WW1. The hospital eventually acquired an X-ray unit in 1925, some six years after Dr. Thompson (the town's medical officer of health) expressed great concern that the Infirmary still didn't have this facility. And emphasized *"what a godsend this would be to the medical staff"*. In Jan. 1930, Miss Helena Thompson (of Park End) gifted the Infirmary the sum of £500 to build a new maternity ward.

In July 1948 (under the National Health Act of 1946) Workington Infirmary like others across the country was handed over to be administered by the Regional Health Boards. A new 30 bed maternity unit was added in 1956, on the Mason Street side of the old C&WJ Railway line next to the existing hospital.

In June 1902, the Hospital Committee of the Borough Council purchased a *Brougham* ambulance for £95, from Wallace Bros. (of Ramsey Brow). This horse-drawn vehicle was shared by Ellerbeck Isolation Hospital and also used to transport accidents to the infirmary. Records suggest it was still in use until at least the end of WW1. In September 1920, the town's first *"motor ambulance"* was acquired for the infirmary. This vehicle was replaced twelve years later, when Mrs. N. G. Barrowclough purchased a new ambulance, in memory of her mother Mrs. Hugh Barbar (the daughter of James Duffield). Her only stipulation of the *"gift"* being that the vehicle be used only within the Borough of Workington. The Council agreed to this condition and a new small garage was built in their Vulcans Lane yard (behind the Carnegie Library), to house the ambulance. This was completed in February 1933, at a cost of £200. Later, that year it was agreed that a member of the local St. Johns Ambulance Brigade should accompany the town's ambulance when called out to an incident.

In October 1936, Workington's ambulance was integrated into a new county wide ambulance service. And during WW2, it was stationed at Padua House, in Washington Street. The Corporation's ambulance station

Dr. Charles McKerrow was appointed the first medical officer at the infirmary.

and under the control of Cumberland County Council. There was still no full-time ambulance staff, drivers were simply supplied by local motor engineers, Dunn and Sons. In return for being willing to turn out whenever required, they were paid a retainer of 10/- (50p) per week, plus the costs of the *"call-out"*. Each ambulance journey was then charged to the patient at "half a crown" or 2/6 (12.5p), with an additional 4d (1½p) per mile outside the district.

In September 1943, the Council ordered a new motor ambulance. It was an *Austin* 2-ton limousine chassis, fitted with a modern ambulance body. This vehicle supplied by Wadham Brothers, cost £1200 and was delivered in May 1945. This long delay in delivery arose because manufacturers were then of course, severely restricted in their allocation of steel and other materials due to WW2. This new vehicle was housed once more at the Vulcans Lane ambulance station, having now been vacated by the ARP warden's. Messrs. Dunn and Sons again supplied the drivers for the new vehicle, receiving £450 per year, to cover both round the clock call-outs and general maintenance of the ambulance. The older ambulance was stored at the Old Paper Mill building, before being sold at auction in February 1946.

With the implementation of the National Health Act 1946, the ambulance service in Cumberland was now permanently administered by the County Council [01]. Workington's 1944 Austin ambulance being transferred to their fleet and thereafter stationed at the new fire station at Francis Croft. The Corporation's old ambulance station behind the library on Vulcans Lane ceased to be used and was later used by the highway's department. In 1953, their was still no full-time ambulance staff, the emphasis was on running a service that was as economical as possible. Then it was not uncommon for the ambulance driver to have very little knowledge of first-aid, his main role being to merely collect and transport patients to hospital. So very different from the highly trained paramedic ambulance crews of today.

Before 1882, it is thought that there was no real provision for a fire brigade in Workington. The nearest appliance was located at Cockermouth, with another housed at the *Fletcher Jennings* locomotive works, near Lowca. If there was a major fire, it was initially simply fought unaided by the local townspeople. By April 1882, a detachment of the police were recruited by the Local Board and drilled as a temporary fire brigade, to be called upon whenever required. In February 1884, the leader of this brigade was Sergeant Reed of the towns police force.

In September 1943, the Council ordered a new motor ambulance. It was an *Austin* 2-ton limousine chassis, fitted with a modern ambulance body.

[01] The National Health Act of 1946 became effective from 5 July 1948. Workington's ambulance service was formerly transferred to the County Council on 31 March 1949.■

By January 1894, the hand-powered fire engine was now considered unsatisfactory and the Borough Council invested in a horse-drawn Merryweather steam fire engine soon after.

[01] Several photographs exist of this 1913 Merryweather Fire engine (400 gallon pump), undergoing trials on the Cloffolks. It can be identified by it's thin wheels and solid tyres. ∎

Exactly what equipment was used to fight fires in these early days is not quite clear, although in October 1886, the Local Board agreed to borrow £350 for it's fire brigade. It is likely they then purchased a hand-powered fire engine, which would have been drawn through the streets by the brigade members themselves.

A decade or so later, it appears that the volunteer town's fire brigade now also included some non-police personnel, again under the direction of the local Super-intendent of Police. But following the decision by the Fire Brigade Committee (of the Local Board) to pay the constables, with no provision being made to also pay the volunteers, the volunteers eventually resigned on mass. By the end of 1893, the local police again took full control of all the duties of operating Workington's fire service, being only formed from members of the police force stationed in the town. Supt. J. Hope accepted the position of *"Captain of the Brigade"*, and three sergeants and fifteen constables made up the remainder of the brigade. For the next ten years, they *"kept both law and order and dealt with 84 outbreaks of fire"*.

In January 1894, it is recorded that this hand-powered fire engine was then quite unsatisfactory and the Borough Council invested in a horse-drawn Merryweather steam fire engine soon after. In 1904, *"two of the Corporation's horses in double harness"* were still being used to pull the town's fire-engine. Horses were then considered less temperamental than the early petrol engines, although very much slower when the brigade was called to any out-of-town fires. On one such occasion it took 1¼ hours to reach a blaze at Castlerigg farm, near Moresby. But rapid advances in the design and reliability of petrol-powered vehicles would soon render the horse obsolete in fire-fighting. By August 1913, the Fire Brigade had acquired a new Merryweather Motor Fire Engine [01] to replace it's antiquated horse-drawn pump. Fire fighter, Joseph Wilkinson was appointed "motor driver", with Thomas Wilkinson his assistant. The response time to incidents improved dramatically. When called to the 1917 fire at Whitehaven's Wellington Pit, they arrived in just 25 minutes.

Further problems with manning the brigade arose again in March 1903, when Workington's police Supt. Hope was replaced by Supt. George Cheeseman. He refused to also take charge of the town's fire brigade nor allow his men to serve as firemen. The Borough Council was now forced to assemble a totally new 14 man brigade from their employees, Councillor John McMullen was appointed it's new captain. [01] On 30 September 1903, his new brigade, having been trained by the police, formally took charge. New "caps, tunics and trousers" for the men, were then ordered from local tailor, Joseph Thompson of Pow Street. [02]

In 1904-5, anxious for better accommodation for it's new Fire Brigade, the Borough Council built a new fire station on a *"vacant"* site next to it's slaughter house and stables in Harrington Road.[03] They also invested in a *"Shand-Mason Curricle fire-escape"*, to extend the reach of it's ladders to 45 feet (13.7 m). The Council Minutes of February 1911, tend to indicate that the Corporation's Fire Brigade underwent a degree of reorganisation, with at least five new members being recruited from staff at the town's Gasworks.[04] At this time a new uniform and boots were again issued to its members. By 1919, the charges for calling out the town's fire brigade was *"two guineas per hour"* (£2.10), plus 4/- per hour for the Chief Officer, 3/6 for 2nd Officer, 3/6 for the Driver and 2/6 for each Fireman. Between 1906-1926, the well drilled Fire Brigade won several annual Northern District Fire Brigade Competitions, including three in a row from 1920.

In September 1927, the Borough Council agreed to purchase a new *"Dennis"* light type, 250 gallon turbine fire engine from Messrs Dennis Brothers of Guildford.[05] The new pump appears to have been delivered in July 1926, and may have been initially supplied on a trial basis, pending approval. The famous Guildford based Dennis business was started by John and Raymond Dennis, and produced it's first fire engine in 1908. This new fire engine was a vast improvement on the old Merryweather engine, which still continued in use up until 1932. It had pneumatic tyres and brakes on all four wheels as standard. Fire appliances were still of normal control layout with a protruding bonnet, as of course, were most lorries of the time. So that fire crews could get on and off their engines in the minimum amount of time, there was no enclosed cab. Depending on the number of crew members, they sat alongside the driver or on a bench along the body-side, clinging to grab rails. The use of brass fittings was still very much in vogue. The practice of specifying hard-wearing brass, a feature of earlier horse-drawn fire engines, had been carried over to these new motorised machines. It would be late in the 1930s, before the majority of brigades would accept that brass-finished radiator shells and headlamp casings were something of an unnecessary luxury.

In 1929, the Workington brigade still only had 8-10 members and records show that they were often called

In March 1923, W. Charters and R. E. Jones completed 10 years service with the Fire Brigade.

[01] Corporation employees' Joseph Stephenson, William Pape, Robinson James, John McCall, Joseph Pelter, Simon Douglas, John Bowness, William Wilson, Henry Jackson, Thomas Harrison, James Kenyon, Thomas Hird, Joshua Jenkinson and James Hall joined the Fire Brigade in April 1903. For each drill they attended they received "one shilling" (5p) and were also paid for attending fires. Later that year, Mr H. Skidmore was appointed captain, Mr T. Hinde (lieutenant), Mr M. Holliday (engineer) and Joseph Stephenson (secretary). ■
[02] These uniforms cost the Borough Council £1.19s.6d each with caps 3s. extra - today this would total under £2.12 per uniform.■
[03] The site of this "new" fire station was opposite the present St. Jos-ephs School in Harrington Road. The Charters Close housing dev-elopment now occupies the site of both the old slaughterhouse and the fire station.■
[04] The five new recruits were Joseph King, Joseph Mark, Thomas Dodgson, John Booth and John Bowness. All were also employees of the Borough Council at it's Gasworks. ■
[05] During the 1930's, Workington Iron and Steel Co and Workington Docks also purchased Dennis Fire Engines.■

In the early hours of Sunday 21 January 1940, the Workington brig-ade also sent their two appliances and ten men to assist the Whitehaven Fire Brigade, fighting the disasterous fire at the Globe Hotel.

Brigades throughout the country were re-organised into 32 new regional areas. Workington became part of the much larger Cumberland Fire Service.

out as far a field as Keswick, Allonby, Cockermouth and Whitehaven. Captain D. C. Davy who had joined the Brigade in 1910, resigned from the brigade due to ill health in October 1929, and was replaced by Lieut. William Charters. Who would later become captain of the brigade himself. Charters completed 25 years service in October 1938. In February 1932, the old Merryweather Fire Engine (400 gallon pump) needed extensive repairs. Spare parts for the aged vehicle, which still ran on solid rubber tyres, were proving hard to acquire. In September the Borough Council decided to purchase a new 400 gallon Leyland fire engine and to dispose of the 1913 Merryweather engine. The Leyland vehicle costing £870, had the Corporation's coat of arms painted on each side.

Records show that even in 1935, there was still only around ten major call outs per year for the town's fire brigade which was still manned by part-time volunteers. Many of the town and villages adjoining the town, continued to pay the Borough Council an annual *"retaining"* fee, in order that the Workington Brigade would be available to attend any fires in their areas. Perhaps the furthest they would be required to travel was to Caldbeck.

By the outbreak of WW2, the brigade, and its Leyland and Dennis appliances, were enlarged in preparation for enemy air raid attacks. By March 1940, an additional sixty local men were enrolled and trained by the permanent brigade. Proposals were also prepared to extend the fire station, to cater for this larger contingent. In the meantime, a new 50 feet (15.2 metres) wheeled escape ladder was fitted to the Leyland Fire Engine. From May 1941 as the WW2 continued, and with the very real threat of incendiary bombs, it was thought essential to centralise control of the fire service under the Secretary of State. Brigades throughout the country were re-organised into 32 new regional areas. Workington became part of the much larger Cumberland Fire Service. At the time, this temporary arrangement was effectively the beginnings of a National Fire Service, with the exchequer assuming financial responsibility and control from 1 July 1941. Just months later, Captain W. Charters, the former chief officer at Workington resigned from the newly reorganized brigade. This highly experienced firefighter who had completed nearly 28 years service in the town's brigade, is thought to have felt aggrieved at *"the unfair treatment"* received since the transfer of command to a regional level.

During the war, the fire service now temporarily occupied Gordon's Garage, close to the corner of

Washington Street and Jane Street. The Corporation's old fire station being considered far too small to accommodate the greatly expanded brigade. By July 1944, as the Borough Council anticipated that control of its brigade would soon be returned, they prepared plans for a new fire station. It was to be built on Francis Croft at the top of Guard Street. This site was owned by the Borough Council, and then laid out as allotment gardens. However within a few months, Whitehall decided that the temporary wartime control of the fire service would now be made permanent. This arrangement *"outraged"* the Corporation who *"viewed with alarm"* the loss of it's brigade. They appear to have been justifiably very proud of their well-drilled fire service, a service it had formed nearly sixty years earlier, and funded every year since. They requested and received some compensation for the land at Francis Croft (on which the new fire station had been built), together with the return of their old Harrington Road fire station. The Drill Tower was later added to the King Street fire station in 1952.

In the early 1870s, it became obvious there was a shortage of new burial plots within the town's existing graveyards.

In the early 1870s, as it became obvious there was a shortage of new burial plots within the town's existing graveyards, the Burial Board began planning a new municipal cemetery. Over many months, several sites were considered including Castle Field (Burrow Walls), Fawcett's field near the Tannery (off Stainburn Road) and at Westfield (now Moss Bay). Finally after much debate, the Harrington 'Lane' or Road site was selected for the town's new burial ground. The only major objections arose from H K Spark (of Darlington), the lessee of mineral rights close to Jane and Annie Pit. He feared the proposed cemetery might interfere with the workings, but after several meetings matters were resolved.

In 1878, two *"mortuary"* chapels were built upon the hill within the centre of this burial ground. One was set aside for Anglican funeral services whilst the other served the nonconformist burials. Prior to an interment, short services were often conducted in these chapels. I remember the latter being quite plain and unadorned, whilst the Anglican chapel was really much more ornate and attractive. These chapels were linked by a covered archway, above which was a bell tower and a tall four sided spire. This arrangement was quite similar to the mortuary chapels which still exists today at Cockermouth. The cost of laying out Workington's nine-acre cemetery and building the chapels was in the region of £10,000.

The chapels were linked by a covered archway, above which was a bell tower and a tall four sided spire.

The first interment within the Harrington Road cemetery was the late Charles Litt (aged 65), and took

Salterbeck cemetery was laid out on the 25 acre site. The cemetery was officially consecrated on 4 July 1924.

[01] In November 1945, the Corporation considered the further development of Salterbeck Cemetery. The quite ambitious proposals, involved forming a new entrance with a broad "carriage" drive, lined with beech hedges on either side. At the head of the driveway, it was intended to construct a chapel "design-ed on simple lines", built of brickwork with stone window and door surrounds. The chapel was to accommodate 200 mourners within it's nave, seated on oak pews. It was also planned to incorporate cloisters adjacent to the chapel, which may form part of a crematorium at a later date. Although the scheme was "agreed in principle", it was obviously never implemented. ■

[02] Control of the sewerage system was transferred to the North West Water Authority in 1989. ■

place on 19 February 1879. The layout of the cemetery itself is also thought to have contained at least two designated religious areas. With the Roman Catholics in particular generally being interred either side of the pathway along the northern boundary.

Over forty years later and following the rapid expansion of the town's population, even Harrington Road cemetery was now considered inadequate for future generations. So the Local Burial Board began planning a further municipal cemetery. In September 1921, the Borough Council first offered the burial board around 20 acres of land at Salterbeck (close to Mountain View). This land was part of that acquired by the Corporation in 1919, originally being earmarked for new housing. Unfortunately after examinations of the site, it was shown to be "unsuitable for burials". Suitable land closer to the town was eventually found, again this was part of Salterbeck Farm. Salterbeck Cemetery was later laid out on the 25 acre site. Much of the work was carried out using unemployed labour, in the difficult and austere post WW1 years. The Cemetery was consecrated on 4 July 1924. [01]

The Borough Council was also responsible for the drainage and sewerage system in the town. Workington was provided with its first sewerage system in 1864, designed by John Lawson of Westminster. An original plan of which still exists at Workington Library. It's highest point was then in High Street, from there it fell through Cross Hill and down into the town along King Street. Initially, there was just a single outlet discharging into the sea at St. Johns Pier. Then Workington had just 7,000 homes, by 1907 this number had grown to over 28,000. As the town grew further, additional outlets discharging into the sea, were also installed from Westfield (Moss Bay), Salterbeck and Victoria Road.

Today, much of these original 1864 brick sewers are still in use, particularly in the Washington Street area and from Church Street to the St. Johns Pier outfall. Michael Faulkner (of Allerdale Borough Council) the engineer formerly responsible for the sewage system [02] comments that "the original egg-shaped brick sewers were designed to be extremely strong, and even today are in remarkable condition". Records show that this old sewer varied in size from 2'0" x 1' 4" (600 x 400mm) in King Street, to 2'6" x 2'0" (750 x 600mm) at the outlet. Around the turn of the century (1900), the Corporation were constantly concerned that the slag waste tipped from the town's Iron and Steel works, was "very much *interfering"* with the sewer outfall at St. Johns Pier. A great proportion of this waste was being carried by the tide, northwards and often blocking the discharge pipe. So much so that the outfall was extended out to sea several times, in an effort to alleviate the problem.

The Corporation also maintained a slaughter house on Harrington Road, backing on to Peter Street. It occupied much of the old gasworks site and was located almost immediately opposite St. Joseph's School, near to where Charters Close now stands. Exactly when it was constructed is not quite clear, but we know it certainly existed before 1884. As a report in the *Maryport and Workington Advertiser* states *"the slaughter house is in a filthy state"*. Waste liquids from the buildings were apparently finding their way into the small tarn that existed close to where Tarn Street now stands. One can only imagine the polluted state of this pond and the *"abominable nuisance"* it caused. This report alone vividly records one aspect of the towns poor sewerage system in Victorian times, which no doubt aided the spread of typhoid and other diseases.

By September 1893, The Borough Council had erected new twenty-five slaughter sheds on the site. These appear to have been let to the various local butchers at a cost of around £4.00 per annum. Despite any pollution problems, by establishing one municipal slaughter house, the Corporation did at the very least now centralise *"the killing and butcher"* of animals. Previously, this would have occurred in the *"small back-yards or outbuildings"* behind the butchers shop. Often these areas were *"filthy and dirty without drainage"* and totally unsuitable. There close proximity to dwellings caused a major problem. At Harrington Road, tripe dressers also used the slaughter house premises. There was also a caretakers house on the site.

The Corporation continued to run the slaughter house until WW2. Although abortive attempts were made to let the premises to the *West Cumberland Farmers Trading Society* in November 1920. The Ministry of Food using it's emergency powers took over control of the premises in January 1940. Just two years later, despite strong objections from the Corporation, they closed the Workington slaughter house and transferred the *"slaughtering and distribution of meat"* to Whitehaven and Maryport. In 1946 as wartime food control was relaxed, *Workington Master Butchers Association* and the *Chamber of Trade* petitioned the Borough Council to provide a new slaughter house in the town. A site was

"The original egg-shaped brick sewers were designed to be extremely strong, and even today are still in remarkable condition".

Michael Faulkner
Allerdale District Council

selected for a new slaughter house to be built at Northside, but the plans were subsequently dropped.

In July 1954 as the wartime control of meat production finally ceased, the Corporation attempted to re-open it's slaughterhouse as a *"public abattoir"*. The aged buildings were then being used by the Highways Department. After much debate, these plans were also eventually dropped as it was felt the premises were *"really far too close to dwellings"*. There was also concern over the high costs involved and the *"general unsuitability of the old buildings"*. Local farmers and butchers would now have to continue to use the abattoir at Whitehaven.

As well as the Borough Council run slaughter house, there was a private one in Elizabeth Street. The town's 1925 traffic Census suggests that the Elizabeth Street slaughterhouse may still have been in operation as 220 sheep or pigs and 3 herds of cattle are recorded as being driven down King Street. Very little further is known about this particular establishment.

One further task of the Corporation was the collection and disposal of refuge. The Borough Council originally made all household refuge collections using horse-drawn carts. In 1894, they kept and stabled six horses for this purpose. All were aged from 6-14 years, with names such as *Charlie, Briton, Tom, Sally, Bod* and *Boxer*. They were generally kept at the Corporation's stables in Harrington Road, and cared for by a full-time horsekeeper. Around the turn of the century, this was Joseph Pelter who lived close-by in Peter Street. Pelter was also a member of the town's Fire Brigade, the pumps of which were *"drawn"* by the Corporation horses until around 1913. The horses needed to be regularly re-shoed, and the blacksmith work was usually done at the Gas Works.

It was July 1920, before the Borough Council acquired it's first Ford *"tip-up"* motor truck, to be used for it's refuse collections. Subsequently in October 1931, they also purchased an *"S&D freighter"* wagon. But some horses were still used to haul the *"dustcarts"* for at least another eighteen years. In July 1949, the Corporation disposed of it's horses, which were no longer required. Some were retained and used for other Council duties, but by 1951, having invested in other motor vehicles they decided to sell their last horse. If in the future they ever needed a horse, it was decided that they could always hire one for around £2 a day, including the driver. ∎

The Ministry of Food using it's emergency powers took over control of the Workington's slaughterhouse in January 1940.

On 28 September 1938, the town celebrated the *"golden jubilee of the Town Council"*. Many of the streets and municipal buildings were *"gayly"* decorated with bunting and flags. A celebration dance was also held in the Drill Hall in Edkin Street. Confectioner Mrs. M. Hinde supp-lying a light supper for those who atten-ded at 1/- (or 5p) per head. Preston North End AFC., the current FA Cup holders also agreed to play Work-ington Reds, at the newly opened Borough Park. n

PEOPLE AND PLACES IN THE TOWN

THE DEVELOPMENT of the early town is detailed up to 1865 in the earlier volume of the town's history. This chapter continues our journey through time along the streets and down the lanes of old Workington. Highlighting the many people and places that have now disappeared and been long forgotten. We begin our journey outside the LNWR Low Railway station, at the foot of what we now know as Station Road. Station Road was once very much narrower than today and was called Cooke Lane, and originally only lead up to Hagg Hill. The new street name was only adopted in the autumn of 1883, when the it was first proposed to extend the road up to Central Square and Jane Street. It received the new name by virtue of there being a railway station at each end of the street. However, when the road was nearing completion, it's central section became more commonly known as Oxford Street.

The earliest OS plan of the town published in 1863, tells us that the area around the railway station was by no means the busy thoroughfare we know today. The principle route from the town down to Low station was along Brow Top, Derwent Street and through Church Street. In these early days, the houses on Belle Isle Place extended from the railway station around to the foot of Cooke Lane. Belle Isle Street was a cul-de-sac extending only as far as Hawksley Terrace. At 7 Belle Isle Place lived Maryport born William Liddle Eaglesfield (1834-1909). The prominent engineer, architect and surveyor moved to Workington around 1865 and was appointed Borough Surveyor in 1874. His son Charles William Eaglesfield (1866-1935) also trained as an architect and designed several buildings in the town, notably the Presbyterian Church in Sanderson Street.

The Station Hotel was located at the western end of Belle Isle Place, probably built not long after the arrival of the Whitehaven Junction Railway in 1846. The Station Hotel was then one of the principle hotels in the town, and it's meeting room once played host to several prominent meetings. Perhaps one of the most important was held in October 1875, when the iron and coal traders of West Cumberland formulated the plans to build the new

Station Road received its new name by virtue of there being a railway station at each end of the street.

railway from Cleator Moor to Workington. Significantly, the meeting was held only yards from the tracks of their rivals, the London North Western Railway. Who had up until then controlled the railways in and around the town, enjoying something of a monopoly and insisted on quite excessive transport charges. From around 1876, the hotel was ran by James Cowan, who originated in Carlisle. After the turn of the century it became known as *"Bennett's Station Hotel"* ran by John Pearson Bennett. In 1909, he later also purchased Crosthwaites wine and spirit stores in Ramsey Brow, and subsequently became a director of the Workington Brewery Company.

"The elegant ballroom at the Commercial Hotel is a playground for merrymakers that had no equal in the district".
Alderman F. W. Iredale

Around 1870, a large new hotel was built on the east corner of Station Road and Belle Isle Place. Originally, it was called the Commercial Hotel, much later it was renamed the Cumberland Arms Hotel. Records suggest it was built by the Iredale Bros. who ran the High Brewery in Ladies Walk. It was certainly, included in their 1891 prospectus when the family brewery was converted into a limited company. Attached to the hotel was a dwelling house, a cottage and five offices. One of which served as the headquarters of the *Cleator and Workington Junction Railway*, before the extensions to Central Station. In 1934, the billiard room at the Commercial was converted to an elegant ballroom, then described by Alderman F. W. Iredale as *"a playground for merrymakers that had no equal in the district"*. One interesting feature of this new ballroom was the *"ingenious murals"* painted by Ambrose Palmer and Son. They were said to have depicted an Italian lake through a window, *"modern cubist in style and very attractive"*.

Behind the hotel was the Commercial stables, in 1902 they were operated by Thomas James. Here you could hire horse drawn open or closed carriages or just a single horse. James also arranged regular weekend outings for groups, into the Lake District. These carriages or wagonettes were fitted with rows of seats, very similar to a modern bus, but far less comfortable. Some carrying as many as twenty passengers and hauled by two large horses. Prior to WW1, motor buses or charabancs were introduced, gradually replacing the horse-drawn wagonettes.

Directly, opposite the Commercial Hotel on the opposite corner of Station Road was the premises of J. Huntrods and Co., ships chandlers and mill furnishers. Although the business was founded by Joseph Huntrods in 1873, this shop with dwelling above was not built until 1882. David Burrand Smith, in his *Huntrod Family History* tells us that Joseph Huntrods (1852-1923), was *"a typical self made Yorkshire man with vision"*. He was also chairman of the *Workington Bridge and Boiler Company*, a director of the *Whitehaven Iron and Steel Co.*, and at one time in charge of the New Yard foundry. Interestingly, Huntrods, a *"much travelled man"* who made several business trips to the USA and Canada is also known to have once acted as the managing director of Kirk Bros. and Co. Records suggesting that he may have given some assistance to Peter Kirk's attempts to build a new steelworks in Seattle. On his death, he still held shares in the American companies, *New States Areas Limited* and *West Springs Limited*. In 1942, some years after the ceasation of *J. Huntrods and Co.*, the *North British Engineers' Supplies Limited* operated a very similar *"mill furnishers and hardware"* factors business from the same premises. Although there appears to be no formal links between each concern.

Long before the viaduct was erected, much of the west side of Falcon Street was the shipyard of the Falcon family, hence its street name.

Prior to the turn of the century, Falcon Street which runs from the bottom of Church Street to the foot of Station Road was considerably narrower than today. And even after the present viaduct was built in the late 1880s, at it's north end by the Railway Hotel the street was barely fifteen feet wide. It was 1899, before the Borough Council reached an agreement with its owners, the Cleator Moor Brewery Company to widen the street to around 33 feet. This involved demolishing the large sections of the hotel and the two adjoining cottages. Long before the viaduct was erected, much of the west side of the street was the shipyard of the Falcon family, hence its street name. In 1881, directly opposite at 15 Falcon Street was a temperance hotel ran by William Stirling. This building would eventually became known as the Viaduct Hotel. Around 1937, it was extensively renovation and modernised when managed by William B. Murray. It had remained an *"alcohol free establishment"* and would continue to do so until well into the 1940s.

As the 1880s progressed, to the south of Station Road was built Milburn Street, Lonsdale Street and Clay Street. These long streets of small *"two up, two down"* terraced houses extended through to Gladstone Street. At this time, these rows of little houses were considered quite modern, each having a small *"scullery"* and it's own toilet located outside in the backyard. Gladstone Street, named after the Prime Minister of the day William Ewart Gladstone (1809-98) was formed when the south end of Belle Isle Street was opened up, and a new road laid out through to Senhouse Street.

At 20 Gladstone Street lived Peter Heenan (1875-

By a strange coincidence in the summer of 1927, Peter Heenan the ex.Workington man personally accompanied Edward, Prince of Wales during his tour of Kenora, whilst on a visit to Canada. This was only a few weeks after the future king had opened Workington's new Prince of Wales Dock. One wonders if his home town was discussed during their meeting.

1948), a Workingtonian who emigrated to Canada in 1902. Heenan settled in Kenora (Ontario) and was first employed as a locomotive engineer with the Canadian Pacific Railway, before pursuing a career in politics and achieving remarkable success. He eventually rose from humble beginnings to hold prominent cabinet posts with both the Provincial and Dominion Governments. From 1926-30, when serving as Canadian Minister of Labour, he is credited with settling over 160 industrial disputes through his understanding and conciliatory approach. An achievement that earned him the title *"Peter the Peacemaker"*. In 1927, the popular hard-working politician, also successfully introduced the Old Age Pensions Bill into the Canadian Parliament. Later described as *"the most human and most progressive social legislation ever enacted in Canada"*. Heenan himself regarding this as the most significant event in his political career.

He was actually born in County Down, and moved with his family to Workington when he was only seven years old. His parents were Peter and Margaret (nee Rodgers) Heenan, and the family lived in a small terraced house at 20 Galdstone Street. Peter (the younger) began his working life at St. Helens Colliery and later *"learnt locomotive engineering"*. We know he was also later employed as a lift engineman, at the Charles Cammell works. As in May 1899, Daniel Bowie (of the Blast Furnace Department) wrote a particularly glowing reference for the future Canadian politician. He described the young twenty-four year old as *"a very sober, quiet, obliging, trustworthy, and capable man"*. We can surmise that this was perhaps the time Heenan was about to leave the town to seek work in Costa Rica.

In 1928, after he was selected as Canada's representative to the International Labour Conference in Geneva. He seized the opportunity to return to Workington, accompanied by his Canadian wife and children. A very proud Borough Council invited their guest to a civic reception to honour his political achievements. During this visit to Europe, Heenan is also believed to have had an audience with Pope Pius XI. He returned to England again in May 1937, to attend the Coronation of King George VI representing the Ontario Government. Prior to the Coronation, both he and his wife were presented at Court. During this trip he returned for the last time to Workington, visiting relatives and friends.

On 12 May 1948, Peter Heenan died in Toronto, after a *"lengthy illness"*, aged 72. After his funeral, he was buried in the City's Mount Hope Cemetery. He was survived by his wife Annie, five children and six grandchildren. Sadly I learnt from one of those grandchildren that the once revered politician who influenced such significant social legislation *"is now almost totally forgotten, even in Kenora"*. Every day hundreds of vehicles pass along the picturesque main road from Kenora to Fort Frances, the majority oblivious to the fact that it was named *'Heenan Highway"* (in 1936). As a tribute to the endeavours of their hard-working Canadian Minister. [01]

In December 1897, the *Workington and District Industrial and Provident Co-operative Society* opened it's first branch shop in Station Road. Two years later, they enlarged the store on the corner of Lonsdale Street. Several other *"grocers, tea, and provision dealers"* also opened shops in this area. Infact there was usually more than one *"corner shop"* in each and every street. There was also a number of other kinds of shops along Station Road. Around the turn of the century, there was Archibald's chemist, John Bell's cloggers and shoe shop, Smiths and Walker's confectioners and the drapers shops of Edwards, Lycett and Mulcaster. In addition, there was also the tailors shops of Harkness, and Prior Bros., Kennedy's and Robinson's greengrocers, and Ogilvie's tobacconist. With upwards of five hundred new terraced houses being built in this part of the town in little less than a decade, Station Road developed into a flourishing shopping street.

Not all businesses were successful, David Knowles opened a new watchmakers business at 18 Station Road in 1880. All did not go well for Mr. Knowles, for within two years his business failed and went into liquidation. Business failure and bankruptcy held far more of a stigma and disgrace than today and Knowles is thought to have moved away from the town. His shop premises were eventually taken over by Archibald Edgar, who opened a grocers shop.

On its north side, at the west end of Fletcher Street (off Milburn Street) was the *"cordial and mineral water"* factory of Brothwell and Mills. The business was established in 1884, by George Henry Brothwell (1844-1928) who came to the town from Dronfield and James Mills (a herbalist, who ran a temperance hotel in Stanley Street). The concern lasted almost a century and many older readers must remember their lemonade and cream soda, sold in almost every corner shop throughout the town. Like Mills, Brothwell was a staunch believer in the *"temperance"* movement, whose primary aim was to curb the drinking of alcohol. But he had originally been just a simple labourer at the steelworks. The Fletcher

Every day, many hundreds of vehicles pass along the picturesque main road from Kenora to Fort Frances, the majority oblivious to the fact that they are travelling along the *'Heenan Highway"*.

[01] The author is indebted to Thomas A. Hickey and his wife Leslie Ann (nee Heenan) of Ontario, for supplying much of this Peter Heenan biographical information. Their extensive file sent from Canada will eventually be deposited at the Whitehaven Record Office. ∎

Hag or Hagg Hill derives its name from the old Cumberland word for a *"wooded green hillock"*.

Street premises which were first extended in 1893, with a new cordial factory was added in 1901. The business which also sold flour and other baking products, erected a new flour warehouse in 1947.

In the 1860s, Hag or Hagg Hill (later known as Falcon Place) was simply an open space used as a stone depot, with just a single dwelling close to St. Michaels school. Yet by the 1880s, like the surrounding areas it had become developed. At its corner with Station Road was Whitfield's Arcade, officially opened on 8 May 1886. The building owned by builders merchant James Whitfield,[01] could be likened to a *"market hall"* with permanent stallholders. It's entrance looked towards the gable end of St. Michael's school and the rear of the building extended through to South Watt Street. Here it connected to a large public hall which occupied most of the west side of South Watt Street. Part of the building was used mainly as an auction room, and eventually became the Hippodrome cinema. Above the Hagg Hill entrance to the arcade was a clock projecting into the street.

In 1893, Whitfield offered the use of the arcade and it's adjoining hall to the Borough Council for a covered market. He wrote to the Corporation saying *"having been approached by several of the stall holders of Hagg Hill market, with view of securing a covered place in which to hold the market.... I have been requested by them to offer the Arcade and room adjoining (now used as an auction room) for sum of £60 per annum. ....or for half the receipts of market tolls"*. Although the council subsequently considered the offer, it is not known if markets were eventually held there. However, we do know that twice weekly open air markets were held on Falcon Place and continued until the 1980s. They are thought to have commenced sometime around 1883, under the direction of Henry Fraser Curwen, then Lord of the Manor and holder of the market rights in the town. He subsequently sold these rights to the newly formed Workington Borough Council in 1889, who became responsible for all markets thereafter.

At the junction of Falcon Place and Fisher Street was the premises of optician, Kenneth Byers. Nearly all the front window of the shop was painted black, with attractive gilt lettering. Kenneth Byers who lived at 9 Lawrence Street, was once an active member of the town's lifeboat crew. In August 1953, he rescued a drowning Walter Dodsworth from the harbour. Later receiving a parchment testimonial from the Royal Humane Society.

Park Lane extends from the end of William Street, south across Oxford Street and along the west side of

[01] In 1875, James Whitfield had a small brickworks at the end of Senhouse Street where clay from Clay Flatts was made into bricks. He was also a slate merchant and had a compound on the South Quay. Records suggest he shipped vast quantities of roof slates into the town, from South Wales. These were a dark blue colour, quite different from the green slate found in the Lake District. ■

Vulcans Park. The 1860s OS plan of the town reveals that it follows much the same line as a narrow thoroughfare called Lowsa Lane, which ran alongside the gardens of Shrub Hill (later known as Field House). As previously mentioned in chapter one, Field House was the property purchased by the Borough Council for conversion to a Town Hall. The extensive gardens of Shrub Hill once covered quite a large area, the house was reached down a long drive which began almost at the junction of Fisher Street and South William Street. A closer look at the existing property here today, reveals a quite strange little single storey dwelling to the west side of the road, behind the Waverley Hotel. It is thought this structure was the former gatehouse of Shrub Hill. By glancing back towards the old Town Hall, the true extent of the gardens to Shrub Hill is revealed. By 1900, Gordon Street had been laid out over this area and around eight of it's large houses were now completed.

The extensive gardens of Shrub Hill covered quite a large area, the house itself was reached along a long drive which began almost at the junction of Fisher Street and South William Street.

The 1881 census reveals Richard Harrison Hodgson as living at Field House. His occupation was listed as Railway Contractor and we know he was responsible for building much of the additions to the C&WJR. Richard Hodgson was the son of Harrison Hodgson, also a building contractor and engineer. In August 1882, Field House was advertised to let. The sale particulars reveal the large six bedroomed property had an elegant drawing and dining rooms, and also a large library. With the servant quarters on the second floor level. Close to the house there was also a stable block, a coach house and harness rooms. Within the grounds were extensive gardens, with numerous fruit trees, including a *"grapery"* with vines *"in a fruitful condition"*.

Outside Field House the gradient of Oxford Street was once very much steeper than today. In 1909, this incline down towards Station Road was very much reduced. Up until 1935, the Town Hall was also surrounded by quite a tall wall. In 1910 on the opposite side of the street, to the west corner of Gordon Street and Oxford Street was built the Masonic or Freemasons Hall. The substantial dressed red sandstone building was erected by the *Workington Masons' Hall Company Limited* and originally used for meetings of the *"Sun and Sector, Curwen and Eden"* masonic lodges. For many years, William A. Hunt & Son (Auctioneers, Estate and Travel agents) also had their offices within the building. A curious 1951 advertisement suggests that this business was established in 1882. Perhaps it's proprietor William Albert Hunt (1883-1941) took over an existing business with a long history, the identity of which has yet to be discovered.

However, we do know that after his death the concern was continued by his son R. E. Hunt.

On the east side of Park Lane are the narrow little streets known as Yeowartville. Completed in 1903, these rows of red brick terraced properties were built by John L. Yeowart [01], hence their name. Prior to 1943, there were several *"now quite mature"* trees growing in each of the quiet cul-de-sacs. Probably planted soon after the houses were completed they were now *"causing a nuisance"* and were felled by the Borough Council. As we cross Oxford Street and continue towards the south part of Park Lane, it easy to forget that this area even in the 1880s was still open and undeveloped farm land. Crops of wheat and oats would have been cultivated here. Cattle and sheep would have been put out to graze in these fields. A scene so much different from today.

During the early 1930s, local authorities throughout the country were encouraged to tackle the problems of infant mortality, adopt a much greater awareness of maternity needs and the care of babies and younger children. In October 1930, the Borough Council built a new welfare clinic or *"maternity and child care"* centre. It was situated behind the town hall building on the west side of Park lane. Five years later work began on extending the building to provide a school clinic which was completed in November 1936.

As a result of the 1951 Festival of Britain, the Borough Council proposed building a *"Festival Hall"* for the town. The trustees of the late Helena Thompson actively supported the scheme, offering the balance of her memorial fund to help finance the project. This is thought to have been around £4,500. But in these early post war years, local authority spending of this type was still carefully scrutinized by central government. The Chancellor of the Exchequer banning all *"building projects over £5,000 for the purposes of entertainment"*. Despite this setback the Corporation discussed a number of sites for their new public hall. These included the grounds of Workington Hall, land at the top of Gray Street alongside Black path, and Infirmary Road. But their first choice was the Park Lane allotments, next to the Welfare Clinic, and facing Vulcans Park. Three years later the Corporation still believed the scheme should proceed, but also admitted that *"it might be some years before"* the hall will actually be built. Their ambitious plans failed to materialise, and the site is still used for allotment gardens.

Opposite the site of the Festival Hall is Vulcans Park. It was December 1904, when the Borough Council first proposed to acquire the "Glebe" land between Field

[01] John L. Yeowart (b.1844) was also a member of Workington's first Town Council (elected in 1888). The Council minutes reveal that in later life he moved to Middlewich in Cheshire, and celebrated his 100th birthday there on 7 January 1944. ■

House and Vulcans Lane, for the purposes of a park for *"public pleasure"*. But the actual purchase from the Rector of Workington was not completed until the summer of 1908. The total cost was £5,000, but a piece of the land was later transferred to the County Council for the site of the new Technical College. Previously, the site was simply open fields and formed part of *"Teasdales Farm"*, on what was often referred to as Patterson Hill.

Despite the Council preparing ambitious plans to create it's new park to commemorate the Coronation of King George V, in 1910. It would now be another fifteen years before it was formally laid out. Up until the start of the First World War, it had continued as farm land. Then it accommodated eighty five allotments until the spring of 1924. Work now began on laying out the new park, with tennis courts and a bowling green. The Corporation utilized the town's unemployed to carry out much of the works

Prior to April 1925 when the Council formally adopted it's present name, Vulcans Park was originally

LEFT - The Bandstand which stood in Vulcans Park. This eight-sided oak structure, with a green Borrowdale slate roof was built by local contractor Joseph W. Douglas. ■

ABOVE - The War Memorial in Vulcans Park, unveiled on 24 June 1928 by Mrs. Catherine Norman. During WW1, she had tragically lost four sons - George, Timperan, William and Robert Norman, together with her brother William Stewart. ■

[01] Brass band competitions, had also been held in the town since at least 1872. They also hosted the Great Northern Brass Band Competition in 1874 and 1878. Many of the local works had brass bands, including the Derwent Tin Plate works (at Barepot) and Charles Cammell & Co. ■

referred to simply as the Central or Public Park . On Thursday 4 June 1925 the park was completed, being officially opened by the Mayor Alderman J. McMullen. In its early years, it attracted an amazing number of visitors, and not just those who regularly enjoyed a Sunday afternoon walk. In 1925-6, a remarkable 25,413 rounds were played on the putting green, generating over £317 in revenue alone. A further £218 was also received from tennis, bowling and croquet. Clearly today, the park only attracts a fraction of this number of visitors.

In June 1924, the Borough Council approved the Borough Surveyor's design for a new bandstand in Vulcans Park. Mr. Williams' eight-sided oak structure, with green Borrowdale slate roof was built by local contractor Joseph W. Douglas and officially opened on 27 July 1929. Previously, despite not having a covered stage, local brass bands had regularly played each Sunday afternoon in the park. Occasionally, a military band such as the Royal Inniskilling Fusiliers and the 4th Northumberland Fusiliers would also entertain the large crowds.[01]

In December 1936, the Council accepted the offer from Miss. Helena Thompson of Park End, to fund the building of a *"shelter for aged men"* within Vulcans park. This structure is located close to the Princess Street side of the park. It was formally opened by Miss Thompson on 12 May 1937. To commemorate the event the Corporation presented her with a silver key, incorporating their coat of arms. This key survives and is currently displayed at the town's Park End Road museum, named in her honour.

Initially Oxford Street was first extended east through from Station Road, only as far as Field House. But by the turn of the century, the new road had been laid up to Vulcans Lane. The remaining section between Vulcans Lane and Central Square was completed much later, hence this last part is officially known as New Oxford Street. Although quite difficult to imagine today, this section connecting both parts of the top and bottom areas of the town, simply crossed open fields and allotments. In the centre of which was a bowling green and small pavilion. Walking down Murray Road, this old bowling green would have been located virtually at the street's midpoint.

In 1899 on the west side of Vulcans Lane, opposite the entrance to the Bus Station was built the premises of the *Workington Beehive Co-operative Society*. This society was formerly established on 20 September 1884, principally by a group of employees of the *Derwent Iron and*

Steel works. Including Allen Stainton, Edward Duffield, Jonathan Fretwell, James Brierley and Thomas Rouse, who were all former Dronfield steelworkers. At least eighty people expressed an interest at the initial meeting held in July 1884, and membership grew rapidly. Exactly where their first shop was located is not quite clear, but we know they acquired premises at 60 Peter Street in July 1888. The society continued to expand and by 1924, had a membership exceeding 4,200 and annual sales of £116,000. With branches at Napier Street, Southey Street, Harrington Road, 54 Senhouse Street, Westfield, Siddick, Bridgefoot, Harrington and Seaton. By 1938, they also operated further shops at 248 Moss Bay Road and Broughton Moor.

In the 1920s they expanded further, building additional new premises on the south east corner of Oxford Street and Vulcans Lane. The large building presently occupied by Workington Library. Together with their shops almost immediately opposite, the society now had grocery, boot and shoe, drapery, butchery, hardware, furnishings, gents outfitters, fruit, fish and confectionery departments, all within a short distance of each other. A once familiar feature of the Oxford Street elevation of this building was its large projecting *"electric clock"* added during the autumn of 1937. Above their earlier premises (built on the site of the present Simon House) was the Beehive cafe and function hall. During the war years, it was very common for wedding receptions and other events to be held here. One interesting feature of this building was a large stone beehive built into the facade, almost at roof level.

In January 1945, a major fire occurred here in the furnishing department. It started at lunchtime when it was traditional for most shops to close between 12.30 and 1.30pm. Everything was in order when the shop was closed, but within half an hour the interior was well ablaze. Flames were leaping from both the ground and first floor windows. Then it broke through into the hall, which occupied the upper floor. Fire brigades from Carlisle, Maryport, Whitehaven and Cockermouth were called and took around three hours to bring the blaze under control. Only the walls remained, with the *"blackened rafters standing out stark against the darkening sky"*.

Although the furniture department and it's contents were completely lost, the boot and grocery shops on either side were emptied of stock by a human chain of volunteers. Albert Byers (an employee of the Beehive) recalled that whilst helping clear the boot and shoe shop,

The *Workington Beehive Co-operative Society* was formerly established on 20 September 1884, principally by a group of employees of the *Derwent Iron and Steel*.

"all the kids in the universe were streaming out of the smoke laden shop with shoes in armfuls. Some we believe went straight through the crowd and neither them nor the shoes were seen again". On the other side of the inferno, "sides of bacon, butter, sugar and jams and the like" were also removed from the grocers department.

The Beehive offered each member free life assurance, based on their total yearly purchases. If a household spent on average around £2 a week in any of the Beehive branches, they would receive life assurance of up to £20 on the death of the man of the house. The Jane Street Co-operative Society offered a similar scheme.

The rows of terraced houses in Gray Street, Brown Street, Brayton Street, Hunter Street, Darcy Street and Hartington Street were not completed after the turn of the century. Although many had been built by the late 1890s, when the roads were first "metalled" or tarmaced. Then Gray Street did not extend all the way upto Oxford Street, it was a cul-de-sac terminating at the end of the existing older terraced properties (located below the present telephone exchange). Here on it's east side was a dairy ran by Ellis Martin from the 1930s. Behind his shop and house were the dairy's byres and milking sheds, which still exist today. His herd of cows were kept in the adjacent field, next to the railway line. Exactly, when the dairy was established is unclear, but it must have been around 1890. After Ellis Martin retired, the business was continued by his daughter, assisted by her husband Eric Hutton. Aerial photographs of the site in 1951, reveal that Gray Street had still to be extended through to Oxford Street.

The Oldfield family also lived in Gray Street. Henry "Harry" Oldfield (1872-1963) was only eleven years old when he moved with his family from Dronfield. He trained under prominent town architect William Graham Scott (1837-1905) who had his office in William Street. Eventually, Oldfield would establish his own practice in the chambers, above the National Provincial Bank [01], on the corner of John Street and Pow Street. Where he was joined by Robert Simpson and Jonathan Saul. The practice becoming known as *Oldfield, Simpson and Saul*. In his latter years, Harry Oldfield retired to a tiny village near Folkestone. His home then was a sixteenth century tudor cottage, with traditional oak panelling. Here during the summer of 1934, he and his wife entertained the King and Queen of Siam, who were anxious to see inside the *"classic English cottage"*.

Before the bridge was built to carry Oxford Street over the C&WJR line above Central Station, pedestrians

---

"The speed of the blaze was quite remarkable and stuns you to think. The shop was alight by 12.35pm and in total ruins by 3.30pm".

Albert Byers
Beehive Co-operative Society

[01] This bank now trades as the National Westminster Bank. ■

crossed the line by a footbridge, reached by a narrow lane rising up from infront of the Central Hotel. Throughout the early 1890s the Borough Council were constantly receiving complaints alleging this area was particularly unsafe for *"a female to traverse the place after dark...Men for want of a better accommodation are using the place as a urinal and for other purposes"*. Apparently the nearby gas street light was only then lit once a week on a Saturday, and there was no proper urinal or toilet facilities. Eventually, the Corporation built a urinal on Central Square, *"at the terminus of Jane Street"*.

In 1876, prior to the building of the Central Hotel, upon the site was a dwelling, joiners shop and timber yard. It was William Coulthard who acquired and first converted the buildings to a hotel. Without doubt it was established here as a direct result of the opening of nearby Central Station. The 1881 census lists William Coulthard living in the square, being described simply as a joiner. In August 1883 before all the alterations to the large hotel were completed, James Coward (of Keswick) had taken over the running of the Central Hotel. We know ownership later subsequently passed to Workington Brewery Company. In January 1922, plans were approved by the Borough Council for further alterations to Central Hotel. At this time the hotel was ran by Joseph Wall (1870-23). After his death, Hannah Wall (1868-1941), his wife continued to manage the premises.

One feature of this once prominent Workington hotel was it's elaborate cast iron glazed porch which extended over the pavement, at the front entrance. This was erected around 1903, and the hotel owners had to pay the

CENTRAL STATION HEADQUARTERS OF THE CLEATOR & WORKINGTON JUNCTION RAILWAY

Each New Years Eve, it was was once quite traditional for hundreds of people to gather in Central Square, and await the chimes of midnight.

"The bells then rang out some merry touches and performances by chiming Abide with Me, Rock of Ages and the National Anthem....The steam horns at the various ironworks also kept up a steady din".

Albert Byers
1944

Borough Council 5/- (or 25p) per year *"for easement"*. This porch was almost square in plan and supported at each corner by large and decorative cast iron columns. The narrow pitched roof was also glazed and hipped to the centre. Around the upper edge of the structure, the name of the hotel was also picked out in stained and coloured glass. This type of glazed porch was a particular feature of Victorian architecture. Several other's existed in the town, notably at the entrances to the Hippodrome Cinema, the Station Hotel and the Commercial Hotel.

Each New Years Eve, it was was once quite traditional for hundreds of people to gather in Central Square, and await the chimes of midnight. The origins of this celebration seem to have began with party-goers from the Central Hotel spilling out into the street. There was always lots of dancing and community singing *"around the lamp"* in the Square.

Albert Byers recalled *"People coming from all over the town to watch and sing, which stopped at midnight after the traditional Auld Lang Sye."* But long before this custom began, *"there was always plenty of people in the streets about midnight, and the church bells; works hooters and ship's horns were rang and sounded"*. A 1894 report in the West Cumberland Times also reveals *"the closing hours of the old year and the ushering in of the new was marked in the usual way.....A little before midnight the bells of the Parish Church rang out mournful cadences the dying peal for the old year. The hour of midnight was marked by firing volleys (which is the bringing down of the bells in grand clashes). The bells then rang out some merry touches and performances by chiming Abide with Me, Rock of Ages and the National Anthem....The steam horns at the various ironworks also kept up a steady din"*.

Large crowds also congregated at other parts of the town *"to let in the new year"*. During the 1890s, it was traditional for people to gather at the foot of Wilson Street to watch the illuminated clock. At the stroke of midnight they *"passed handshakes and hearty good wishes for the New Year"*. Similar scenes occurred annually beneath the clock outside Whitfield's Arcade on Hagg Hill.

In February 1905, the Borough Council approved an application from the *Derwent Engineering Company* to build a *"motor car depot"* on the corner of John Street and Central Square. These premises were designed by local architect W. G. Scott. The Derwent Engineering Company ran by the Quirk family, built and sold motor vehicles. Motoring was then very much in its infancy and developing in popularity. Cars and motor bikes were still very much a rare sight on the streets of the town.

As the 1903 *Motor Car Act* required the County Council to register all motor vehicles, these records reveal some details of Workington's early motoring history. Although it is unclear who had the very first motor car in the town, Thomas Iredale (of Workington Brewery) had the first registered vehicle in Workington. It was a 10 hp. 16 cwt. De Dion Bouton, painted light green with fine white coachlines, its registration number was AO 48. The Workington brewer and magistrate must have had quite a passion for motoring, as within less than six months he had purchased a second vehicle. Another De Dion Bouton, a little more powerful at 12 hp, painted olive green with black mouldings and red coachlines. Gladstone Street grocer, Robert Kinnear had one of the earliest registered Argyll motor cars in the town. The 10 hp, 13½ cwt. vehicle was painted dark green, with red and black coachlines. Kinnear retained this car for almost a decade, before selling it to a Mr. J. Gollock (also of Workington).

In September 1913, the Quirk family are believed to have sold their motor engineering business to John Fletcher Stout (1866-1933). And in August 1915, the Borough Council approved plans to extend the Central Square premises. A further *"wooden garage"* was also added in 1919. Several published photographs exist of these premises, showing the old vehicles displayed outside the building facing on to Central Square. When J. F. Stout died in February 1933, the company which then traded as *Stouts Garages Limited* was described as *"the largest motor engineering company in the North West".* In 1924, we know they had branches in Whitehaven and Egremont.

In 1902, a new Conservative Club was built on the north side of the approaches to the Oxford Street bridge over the C&WJR. at Central Square. The attractive three storey red-ashlar sandstone building replaced their previous premises in Pow Street. These were located opposite the present Woolworths store and opened in April 1890. After the Conservative Association relocated to their new Oxford Street building, the Pow Street premises were demolished and replaced with *"two new shops and houses, with one additional lock-up shop".* Later these red sandstone fronted shops were occupied by W. H. Moss stationery and printing business, and more recently by Reas confectioners.

Unlike today, John Street originally crossed over the east side of Central Square, and ran from Pow Street all the way down to Harrington Road. The upper section of

this street disappeared in the late 1960s when St. Johns Shopping Precinct was built. On it's east side was St. Johns Church of England Infant and Junior Schools, whilst the Primitive Methodist church was located opposite, flanked by terraced properties. In 1884, a new post office was built next to St. Johns School, behind the Pow Street *"boot and shoe premises of Mr. McAleer"*.

This site is now occupied by the National Westminster Bank. The new post office was designed by local architect James Howes, whilst the building contractor was James Wilson. The postal service remained here until it moved to new premises on the corner of Murray Road and Finkle Street. One interesting feature of the early postal service was the introduction of double (or duplex) hand-stamps in the mid 1850s. Now both the date and the place of origin were stamped onto items in one operation. Previously, each was stamped individually onto letters and parcels. All items posted in Workington were stamped with the number "921".

Directly opposite the school at 22-26 John Street, was A. E. Middleton's printing works. They are thought to have moved there from 52 Pow Street in the late 1880s. As well as general printing work, this firm was responsible for publishing both the *Workington News* and *West Cumberland Advertiser*. From June 1888, Middletons also printed and published the *Workington Star*, a weekly newspaper issued every friday. Although in later years it did also appear twice weekly for some period of time. This latter publication would later merge with the Cockermouth based *West Cumberland Times*, to become the *Times and Star* which is still produced today. [01] By 1901 the concern had grown and now traded as *A. E. Middleton & Co. Ltd.* Later the business name was changed to the *Workington Star Limited*, possibility after the death of it's proprietors. In July 1925, the Borough Council approved plans for a new printing works in Oxford Street. The entire business was transferred there upon completion of the building work. In March 1927, they commenced the production of the *Evening Star*, a new evening newspaper covering West Cumberland. This particular daily paper eventually evolved into the present-day *Evening News and Star*. The company are also known to have printed the *Cumberland Evening Mail*. Following the take over of the Workington Star by Cumbrian Newspapers, in 1954 the Oxford Street printing works was rebuilt.

The *Workington and District Industrial and Provident Co-operative Society* (also known as the *Jane Street Co-op)* occupied two large buildings on both sides of Jane Street at it's junction with Central Square. These con-

Middletons in John Street also printed and published the *Workington Star*, a weekly newspaper issued every friday.

[01] In 1967, the Workington Star newspaper was merged with the West Cumberland Times, and became known as the West Cumberland Times and Star, still published today. It is no longer printed in the town, but produced at Carlisle. ■

tained the drapery, millinery, tailors and outfitters, furnishing, and boot and shoe departments. They also had a large cafe, *"commodious"* hall and suite of rooms catering for weddings, dancing and supper parties. This was located above the main block on the south side of Jane Street, and had its entrance in Peter Street. The co-operation movement was initiated in Workington by Rev John E. Carmichael, William Robinson and William Beattie [01] in 1865. They held several meetings in the Wesleyan Chapel in Tiffin Lane. Within two months, thirty people had joined the society, Rev. Carmichael was elected president and shares had been subscribed. Their first shop was in Upper Jane Street (later occupied by Kinnlisides). It was rented for a modest £14.00 per annum, and opened on 6 May 1865. Two of their members were appointed to purchase groceries from a Whitehaven wholesaler and they also ran the shop, on almost a part-time basis. New stock was simply bought out of cash receipts, and no credit was given. The notes of Thomas B. Lindsay tell us that eventually a manager was required to run the shop *"so a local carpenter and his wife were employed, the carpenter agreed to work at his trade until sales developed further"*, the wife was paid 10/- a week".

Sales in the first quarter reached £400, a profit of £15 was made and a first dividend (or "divi") of 1/2d in the pound declared. Gradually sales increased and the carpenter was taken on to help his wife. After three years, a "divi" of 2/8 in the pound was declared. But the society's progress was not without problems, the couple running the shop were found to have given goods away to friends and relations and were dismissed, stocktaking revealed big losses. As dividends fell dramatically, some members were subsequently lost. Strenuous efforts to bring harmony back to the society were made by the original group and new staff were taken on. These employees were only selected if they *"had the co-op spirit and proved to be conscientious and willing workers"*. Eventually prosperity returned and within four years the society had £1,200 in their bank account.

The Upper Jane Street premises were now far too small and the committee gained unanimous approval of its members who bought a plot of land on Central Square. Plans were prepared for a new building on the corner of Jane Street and John Street. It then consisted of a shop with store rooms behind, and a lecture hall, divided by a partition half of which was let to the Caledonian Society. But Bulmer tells us that by the turn of the century *"the commodious block of buildings in Jane Street had been*

The *Workington and District Industrial and Provident Co-operative Society opened their first shop on 6 May 1865.*

[01] John E. Carmichael was a Primitive Methodist minister, who also ran a bookshop in Finkle Street. William Robinson was a foreman of the Paper Mills, on Hall Brow, whilst William Beattie was an engineer. ■

Tarn Street received its name by virtue of the small pond or tarn that existed there until around 1884. It was probably created by the tipping of spoil from the nearby Hope Pit, which once stood close to the junction of Brown Street and Gray Street.

recently enlarged, and was now one of the finest business premises in the town". In February 1901, records of the society show over 1,500 members around this time they appointed Thomas Errington (1868-1934) as their general manager. He was to work for the Jane Street co-operative for over 45 years, having started as a simple shop assistant and later progressed to be the first manager of their Station Road branch.

By 1924, the society had other branches at Marsh side, 106 Corporation Road, Harrington Road, Clifton, Seaton, Branthwaite and Lowca, *"each doing a good and increasing trade"*. And in 1938, a further shop was opened at Salterbeck. During 1932, the Jane Street premises were again altered and a new bakery was built in nearby St. John's Court, off Jane Street. Finally, in November 1949, the former ironmongers shop at 48 Jane Street was converted into a wet fish shop.

As we cross over Central Square and continue down John Street, the large properties to the eastern side of the street were once known as Clifton Terrace. From the late 1930s, at Holmwood (the large house at 55 John Street) was the dental practise of John Graham Fletcher. Whilst next door at Beechwood (57 John Street) was the doctors surgery of Isaac Fletcher (1864-1949) and William Hodgson Fletcher. Like the McKerrow family before them, the Fletcher family cared for the well being of the townspeople for many decades. Dr. Isaac Fletcher travelled on his rounds by bicycle and is fondly remembered by many as the *"cycling medic"*.

The remainder of John Street, Peter Street and the other small cul-de-sacs of Roper Street, Irving Street, Victoria Place and Tarn Street were built during the 1880s and 90s. Like the Milburn Street and Lonsdale Street area, they all started life as virtually similar small two or three bedroomed dwellings, with only the addition of a small scullery or kitchen to the rear. Originally their only toilet facilities were a single *"drafty"* outside lavatory in the rear yard. Today's society insists on the basic facilities such as a bathroom, with hot and cold running water. But again it should be noted that these little Victorian terraced houses when they were first built would have then been considered very adequate. In fact, the ashlar stone properties fronting on to John Street once accommodated some quite respectable middle class families.

Tarn Street received it's name by virtue of the small pond or tarn that existed there until around 1884. It was probably created by the tipping of spoil from the nearby Hope Pit, which once stood close to the junction of Brown Street and Gray Street. The mine closed around 1860, and the new 1864 sewerage system was laid serving the upper part of the town. Drainage water and waste was then allowed to flow down a stone culvert along the line of Nook Street and into the pond. Once the embankment of the C&WJR was built in the late 1870s, this contained the pond and it naturally developed into an *"unhealthy and filthy nuisance"*. The problem was exacerbated by the addition of liquid waste from the Corporation's slaughter house on Harrington Road. A report in the *Maryport and Workington Advertiser* tells us that the tarn was drained and filled, in March 1884. This area was often referred to as the Tarnfield.

Within the cul-de-sac of Irving Street that runs west off John Street. was the premises of Thomas Roseby. He was a carter and removals contractor. In the days before motor transport, a cart was almost the only means of transport for any goods in the town and further a field. In 1901, the business appears to be operated by John Birkett, but continued to trade under the Roseby name. By 1938, James B. Roseby is listed as running the business.

In 1908, the grocery business ran by the Lindsay family opened a warehouse at 129 John Street. Twelve years later they acquired the adjoining premises (131 John Street), so doubling their floor area. This well-established business had been started by John Lindsay, who had opened a little grocers shop in Stanley Street some thirty years earlier. Legend has it that the family still possess the very first shilling (5p) he received when he opened for the first time on the morning of 23 April 1881. This family heirloom is said to carry the date 1871 and *"was received from Nicholas Bird for a tin of salmon"*. The business soon grew and within two years Lindsay had moved to a *"newly built shop"* at 12 Galdstone Street.

He was succeeded by his son Thomas Barnett Lindsay, a founder member of Workington Rotary Club. Both father and son were prominent members of the Workington Grocers' and Provision Dealers Association and the Chamber of Trade. It is said that this firm owned the first *"motor-lorry"* for delivering goods, in the town. By the 1930s, they supplied grocers and hoteliers throughout West Cumberland and a greater part of the Lake District. Thomas' two sons, Frank and Kenneth Lindsay the third generation of the family, eventually took over the business following the retirement of their father.

The premises that Lindsays acquired at 131 John Street, were once occupied by printer, Edward Richardson. Born in 1835, he was the son of Jeremiah Richardson, a blacksmith who had his forge in King

ABOVE - Illustration from a 1902 advertisment for THOMAS ROSEBY of Irving Street. ■

A *"monster piece of ingenious machinery, vulgarly termed an American Devil"* was brought to the town, to cut the long deep cutting.

[01] Today this cutting runs from Harrington Road, under Honister Drive and forms part of the new cycleway, linking the Westfield and Moorclose housing estates to the town centre. Invented in America, the early 1840s, the *'Steam Navvy'* was initially rarely used in Britain, because of the abundance of cheap labour. ■

Street. When in his teens, Edward is known to have served his apprenticeship with one of the printers in the town, but exactly which is unknown. By the start of the 1890s, he had set up his *"Liberty Printing Works"* in John Street. He is thought to have shared the premises with Lancashire born auctioneer Thomas W. Johnson. Certainly, when he printed the *Workington Lantern* newspaper which first appeared in the early months of 1892, Johnson is shown as it's editor and the addresses seem identical. Much of this four-page publication, issued free every Friday, was also devoted to the promotion of his auctioneers business. Exactly how long the newspaper survived is unclear, it is likely to have only survived for a few editions. I have only ever seen one copy dated 18 March 1892.

A little further along John Street from Lindsays grocery warehouse was the joiners and undertakers of Joseph William Douglas (1871-1935). He was the son of Isaac Douglas who had ran a joiners and cartwright business in the town since around 1872. Previously the family had lived for many years in Lorton, near Cockermouth.

The railway line of the Cleator & Workington Junction Railway ran into Central Station between John Street and Gray Street. Construction work on this new railway line began in October 1877. A *"monster piece of ingenious machinery, vulgarly termed an American Devil"* was brought to the town, to cut the long deep cutting above the cemetery. [01] This was an early steam driven, mechanical excavator and had never previously been used in Cumberland. Invented by Dunbar and Ruchton in America (hence it's name) the machine was often also referred to as a *Steam Devil* or *Steam Navvy*. A contemporary description of the earthmover tells us that it resembled the *"appearance and motions of a high crane"*, and was fixed to *"a wrought iron truck, upon which is also placed a 10 hp engine"*. From the jib of the crane was *"suspended a large bucket, having on its front edge a row of steel pointed teeth"*. As it's *"monstrous jaws"* are drawn up the earth to be removed, the bucket is rapidly filled. Then the machine is *"swung round"* and empties it's load into a nearby wagon. Although operated by twelve men, the "navvy" was able to *"scoop out the earth at a rate equal to fifty navvies"*, at a cost of just 1 shilling (5p) per hour.

Many will remember a substantial sandstone railway bridge across Harrington Road, quite close to the junction of Mason Street and John Street. Built in 1877-78, the arched bridge carried the tracks of the Cleator and Workington Junction Railway, towards Central Station.

At it's centre the headroom below the narrow bridge was 14'0" (4.2m), but this reduced dramatically to only around 10'0" (3m) at each side of the road. Essentially, this caused a major headache to taller vehicles like double-decker buses etc. They could only safely negotiate the bridge, whilst in the centre of the road, restricting the carriageway to other users. One veteran bus driver tells how they were *"warned to line the radiator cap of their vehicle up with the white line down the centre of the road"*, to prevent a collision with the bridge. The County Council eventually demolished the bridge and widened the road in 1981.

On the north side of Jane Street was the grocers shop ran by James Smart (1854-1940). Scottish born Smart, a prominent member of the Presbyterian church, began the business in 1877 at the age of just 23. He later told how he would be *"in the shop at eight in the morning and seldom closed the doors until midnight on Saturday and 11 o'clock other nights."* When he first started there was simply no canned or tinned food. *"Sugar was bought in loaves or lumps...we cut it into slices, then strips and finally squares...it was so hard it took a hammer and chisel to make any impression on it."* Shop assistants in those days were also trained to make the sugar and flour bags from sheets of *"stiff blue paper"*. There was then simply no self service supermarkets, everyone was personally served in every shop by the assistant behind the counter.

In 1910, Reginald Henry Skaife opened his ironmongers and cycle shop at 34 Jane Street. His shop was only a few doors away from Smarts grocers, almost opposite Peter Street. Mike Burridge recalls how *"Skaife's was an old traditional ironmonger who would sell you a single nail or nut and bolt, rather than an expensive pre-pack of a dozen or so we are forced to buy today. These were stored in banks of wooden draws and shelves which lined the shop, behind the counter. Whatever you wanted they usually had it. I remember the shop was still there in the 1960s, my father would send me there for paraffin. Our old Esso jerry can was filled from the large tank in the back of the shop"*. A 1935 advert tells us that you could buy a new Standard bicycle from Skaife's for £3.19s 5d. (£3.95).

Much of Washington Street certainly existed on the 1863 OS plan, but in it's early days it was also often referred to as New Street. It is safe to assume that the development of this street must have began around the time St. Johns Church was built in 1823. On the south west corner of the junction of Jane Street and Washington Street, was the Old Crown Inn. It was one of the oldest

"Skaifes was an old traditional ironmonger who would sell you a single nail or nut and bolt, rather than an expensive pre-pack of a dozen or so we are forced to buy today."
Mike Burridge

In August 1937, the Old Crown was sold to the Borough Council for £5,000. The Corporation acquiring the premises in order to *"widen and improve"* the Jane Street and Washington Street junction.

buildings in the street. It existed here in 1834, when Elizabeth Turnbull was listed as the *"innkeeper"*. Although we occasionally then see it referred to as simply the Crown Hotel. The 1881 census tells us that Joseph Yeowart lived at the Inn with his wife Jane and their two sons and six daughters.

During the same year, Joseph Yeowart (1838-1900) added a *"large and handsome new hall"* to the rear of the hotel. This new public hall appears to have first been named the Albert Hall (after Prince Albert, the husband of Queen Victoria). But later renamed the Victoria Hall, perhaps not to clash with the other hall of the same name in Fisher Street. Victoria Hall was regularly used as an auction room, and hosted public meetings, dances etc.

During the 1890s, John L. Yeowart (thought to be the brother of Joseph Yeowart) built the *County Drapery Store* to the south side of the Old Crown. Wallace Ritson revealed that *"Yeowarts fine store"* later became a motor garage. Mike Burridge tells us that the garage had *"petrol pumps virtually on the pavement"*. There was no forecourt, vehicles would then simply stop at the kerbside, in order to fill their tanks. Of course Washington Street was by no means the busy thoroughfare we know today. In later years the garage was occupied by the Gordon family, before they moved to the corner of Guard Street and Harrington Road.

In 1905, the Old Crown was purchased by the Workington Brewery Company. In August 1937, they sold it to the Borough Council for £5,000. The Corporation acquiring the premises in order to *"widen and improve"* the Jane Street and Washington Street junction. It is thought the last licensee of the Old Crown was Joseph Ray. Opposite the Old Crown Inn on the north west corner of the junction was the New Crown Inn (or Hotel). This was the larger of the two premises also appears on the 1863 OS plan, but when exactly it was built is not too clear. It was subsequently demolished in the early 1970s and the Washington Central Hotel was later built on the site.

Jane Young's bakehouse was situated in a yard on the west side of Washington Street. The almost square building was reached through a narrow lane or passage between numbers 22 and 24, and backed on to Thompson Street. Poorer households without a proper oven would prepare their own cakes, bread and buns at home and then bring them to Jane Youngs to be baked. In his youth, Wallace Ritson remembered carrying *"their cakes to Young's on a big tin 30 inches long by 18 inches wide, part of it was rhubarb, and the other end currant"*. In

1881, Jane is listed on the census as living in a small cottage adjoining her bakehouse, sharing the house with her widowed brother Jonathan, a tailor. Earlier trade directories suggest that the bakehouse was probably established by Jane's father, also named Jonathan. The yard in which the bakery was located was also often referred to as Young's Yard.

Almost opposite the end of Edkin Street was Benn's confectioners. From the late1870s, this bakery was ran by Misses Jane Benn (1859-1911) and Sarah Benn (b.1861). Although the business seems to have been originally established by the Osbaldeston family. The two sisters who lived in Dora Crescent, were daughters of Joseph Benn (1831-1906) of Cockermouth. Miss Ethel Anderson later took over the business, although it continued trade as Benns for many years.

From 1860-95, John Millfield Dunn (b.1843) had his drapery business at 2-4 Washington Street. These two shops backed on to the gable end of the Cumberland Union Bank in Pow Street. For many years, the successful draper and his family lived at 16 Nook Street, before moving to Croft House at the top of Elizabeth Street. In 1895, the business was taken over by William Henry Jeffery. Dunn was also a prominent member of the committee responsible for erecting Dr. Peat's memorial, in Portland Square. Between 11-13 May 1935, the family suffered the *"remarkable, but very sad"* loss of all three spinster daughters. The town was stunned to learn that Mary Eleanor (58), Blanche Gertrude (56) and Annie Leah had all died over the *"short space of forty-eight hours"* whilst on holiday at Windsor. A week later, the bodies of the tragic sisters, who were all believed to have contacted septic pneumonia, were buried together in the family plot at Harrington Road cemetery.

Victorian Washington Street like many of the shopping streets in the town then supported numerous little shops and businesses. The majority of which traded side by side from narrow small properties, their proprietors usually living *"above their shops"*. Occasionally this caused problems, in 1895 the Corporation was forced to serve a *"nuisance"* notice on Mrs. Ann Scoon (a butcher and poultry dealer) of 31 Washington Street. She was said to be rearing a large number of hens and chickens *"in her cellar below her house"*.

Up until 1889, Henry Stephenson had a fishmonger and game shop on the east side of Washington Street, next to the Theatre Royal. After which the business was acquired by the Palmer family, who continued the wholesale and retail fish, game, rabbit and poultry shop until

The town was stunned to learn that the three Dunn sisters had all died over the *"short space of forty-eight hours"* whilst on holiday at Windsor.

**THE WORKINGTON
BOOT & SHOE COMPANY**

Had its premises in Washington
Street and was ran by Joseph Wood.

the 1970s. John E. Palmer established the business, after which it was continued by his sons and grandsons. As a child I remember walking past the shop and seeing the rows of rabbits and turkeys hanging from a rail outside the shop.

The 1881 census reveals that Hugh de Bosco Askew (1852-1924) had a chemist and druggist at 5 Washington Street, next to the Ship Inn. Askew was also a trained dentist, who ran his surgery from the same address. He later sold his chemist business and appears to have concentrated on the dentistry side of his business, moving to 11 Curwen Street. Frederick J. Birkett, who is thought to have been an apprentice of Askew ultimately took over the Washington Street chemist's shop. Birkett was the son of master shoemaker William Birkett (1826-1898) who had his cobblers shop around the corner at 36 Wilson Street. Frederick had four sisters and four brothers, one of which was solicitor John E. Birkett who had his offices at 6 Bridge Street.

Another shoemaker Joseph Wood (1850-1901) occupied 8 Washington Street, just across the road from Askew's chemist shop. Lamplugh born Wood, a master boot maker traded as the *Workington Boot and Shoe* company. He claimed that the business had been established in 1826, and above the doorway into his shop hung a *"sign of a big boot"*. It is likely that Wood succeeded Daniel Fisher, another shoemaker who lived in the premises until the 1870s. Wood also successfully traded as an auctioneer and valuer. Holding regular sales at the Albert Hall in Fisher Street, or the sale rooms in Bridge Street. At the time of his death in 1901, he was living in a large house on Charlton Road.

Before 1870, Richard Ellwood (1820-1903) lived and worked at 30 Washington Street, located on the south corner of Edkin Street. Born in Westmorland he had moved to the town around 1850. Richard was the father of James Ellwood who by 1881, lived just around the corner at 1 Edkin Street. Both men were employed as saddlers, James serving his apprenticeship under his father. Around the time of Richard's death, James moved to a new shop at 2 Nook Street. He was later joined in the business by his son, also called James (or Jimmy). He too learnt the craft of cutting, sewing and shaping leather by working alongside his father. By the 1930s, Jimmy had moved to a shop at 22 Wilson Street, where he continued to trade until the 1970s. All three generations of the Ellwood family are famous for making the *Uppies and Downies* balls, used at the town's mass football game played annually each Easter. After his death, Jimmy

Ellwood's tools were acquired by the Helena Thompson museum.

A former resident of Edkin Street was Jimmy Thompson (the son of John and Marie Duff Thompson) who emigrated to Australia in 1892 As the prospector joined many thousands of other miners, living in squalid and fever ridden conditions on the goldfields, he risked his life on the chance of a fortune. But amid the hysterics, where thousands failed, the undaunted West Cumbrian pioneer succeeded. His strike at Carbine in October 1894, around twelve miles north of Dunnsville, near Coolgardie (in Western Australia) was one of the richest ever discovered. The remarkable quality and yield of Thompson's gold, eclipsed even that of the legendary Arthur Bayley, whose finds had triggered the goldrush in September 1892. It was the tales of Bayley's discoveries that had brought Thompson half way round the world to Australia. He too would now be ranked among the heroes of the Western Australian goldrush.

> Some of the gold seams discovered at Thompson's **Carbine** mine were almost *"the size of a man's arm"*.
>
> **Jules Raeside**
> *The Golden Days*
> (published in 1929)

The prospector eventually sold his interest in the Carbine mine, which was successfully worked for a further thirty years. Jimmy Thompson married Emma Agnes Mundweiler in Australia, and the couple had at least four children, all sons. By 1904, he moved with his family to live in North Perth. A quarter of a century later, his exploits were featured in Jules Raeside's 1929 book, *The Golden Days*. Records suggest that Jimmy died on the 5 January 1943 (aged 82) and is buried in the cemetery in North Perth.

Edkin Street was laid out around the start of the 1860s and was originally called Edkins Lane. There seems little doubt that this street is named after Barwise Edkin (1760-1823) who owned the Kings Arms Inn on the corner of Edkin's Lane and Washington Street. After his death the hotel continued to be ran by his wife, Elizabeth. The licensed premises are certainly shown on the 1863 OS plan, although some mystery surrounds the later use of the building.

Perhaps the most important building of an architectural and historic note was the Artillery Drill Hall built in 1900-01. A new battery of artillery volunteers had actually been authorised by the War Office in the 1880s. Its first members were sworn in at the start of April 1883. Very soon afterwards it was proposed to build a new drill hall in the town. A site at the junction of Nook Street and Harrington Road, was first suggested for the 7,500 sq.ft building. However, the new auction mart was eventually built on this vacant land. It was nearly fifteen years later before the town acquired the new military facility in Edkin Street. A key feature of the Drill Hall was its finely detailed red brick front elevation.

To the rear of the Drill Hall was the bank premises of the Workington Savings Bank. After the bank moved to Murray Road in 1935, this building was acquired as office accommodation for the Drill Hall. During WW2, it was used by the 5th battalion of the Border Regiment Home Guard. At this time, a German Messerschmitt 109 aeroplane was also exhibited within the Drill Hall. Thousands of townspeople flocked to see the enemy plane, paying 2/6 (12.5p) entrance money. The event in December 1940 was organised by Workington Bright Sparks Social Club. A group started twelve months earlier to raise funds for the war effort. The Drill Hall was also occasionally used for public dances and meetings, as well as bazaars and sales. In November 1967, the Drill Hall was sold to the Borough Council for £45,000 and later demolished when the town centre was re-developed.

For many years there was a blacksmith shop located

THE DRILL HALL WHICH STOOD ON THE NORTH SIDE OF EDKIN STREET on the northside of St. John's Church. Early records suggest it was established by William Allison, sometime before 1829. Here he is known to have shod horses and crafted farm implements such as ploughs and sickles. Later Allison's blacksmith shop was acquired by Joseph Farish (1833-1881) who was subsequently joined in the business by his son James. Like the Ellwood saddlers, He was the third generation of Farish family to become a blacksmith. Joseph's father was thought to be John Farish who started his own blacksmith shop in Udale Street around 1810. James Farish is known to have altered the single storey Washington Street premises in 1896.

Across the road from the blacksmith shop, on the north corner of Ritson Street and Washington Street was the joiners and cartwright yard of Ralph Ward. Although not entirely clear it is likely that this site was occupied by Joseph Wilkinson's *"motor engineers"*. During the 1920s, he was the *"sole district agent"* for Wolesley, Citroen, Sea Francis and Bean motor cars, as well as B.S.A., Enfield, Rudge and Scott motor cycles. Although he is known to have sold the motor cycles from 43 Washington Street. a little further along the road. By 1938, builders merchants, Leslie's (Workington) Limited had acquired the premises. This company was operated by Robert Leslie, who lived at Aysgarth in High Street, a detached house built within the grounds of Ashfield House. He was responsible for constructing many of the houses to the north end of Newlands Lane.

Almost opposite the Old Crown Inn was Henderson's photographic studio established sometime before 1892. This family business had been started by Robert Henderson in the early 1880s, and was initially located in Finkle Street and then Roper Street. Robert Henderson (b.1924) was the son of James Henderson, a gardener at Workington Hall. And for many years, the family lived at the Park Lodge on Ramsey Brow. Later they moved to 14 Nook Street and built a narrow single-story timber building within the garden, fronting onto Washington Street. This housed their photographic studio and darkroom for over fifty years. After Robert retired, the business was continued by his son James.

In the 1970s, the old photographer's premises was abandoned and in a very dilapidated condition. The felt roofed structure was no longer watertight and in places open to the elements. Scattered throughout the property were wooden trays, containing hundreds of old glass photographic negatives. The majority were once treasured portraits of individuals and their families. A valuable record of real people who lived in and walked the streets

At Allison's blacksmith shop in Washington Street, they not only shod horses, but also crafted farm implements such as ploughs and sickles. ■

Robert Henderson the photographer who had his studio in Washington Street was the son of James Henderson, a gardener at Workington Hall. ■

of the town, upto a century earlier. Sadly, penetrating dampness had caused major damage to virtually all these negatives, others were cracked or smashed beyond repair. There was also no surviving index to identify the sitters. Soon after everything was simply cleared to make way for the Studio Restaurant, built by Ian Lewis Dalby.

The felt roof was no longer watertight and in places open to the elements. Scattered throughout the property were wooden trays, containing hundreds of old glass photographic negatives.

Within the Old Market Place, also sometimes referred to as the High Market Place the weekly markets were once held. Up until 1890, all the markets in the town were controlled by the Curwen family, as Lords of the Manor. Thereafter, *"full regulation"* of all markets and fairs within the Borough passed to the Corporation, who purchased the rights for £600. Wallace Ritson tells us that the Old Market was the location for the weekly *"butter market"*. Women used to walk *"from the outlying villages with their market baskets for butter and eggs on market days"*. Within the museum is also an interesting old oil painting of the Butter Market, by J. Haigh.

Erected around 1865, perhaps the most prominent building in the Old Market Place was the Carlisle, City and District Bank which once projected from the corner of Nook street across the top end of Jane Street.[01] Leav-

ABOVE - Sketch of the BUTTER MARKET which was once located at the intersection of Nook Street and Curwen Street. From an old oil painting by J. Haigh, currently displayed in the Helena Thompson Museum. ■

ing the road here quite narrow and the area of the market place greatly reduced. Joseph Scott (b. 1858) recorded that this bank founded in 1837, first had it's office at the top of Ramsey Brow. Exactly where on Ramsey Brow has yet to be determined. Although we may speculate that the bank was perhaps connected with the Thompson family of Park End (now Helena Thompson Museum).

David Tweddle (1809-75) was appointed manager of the Workington branch of the Carlisle City and District Bank in 1865, he had arrived in Workington in 1840, and up until 1865 had ran a private school at 29 Brow Top. He was eventually succeeded by George Graham (b.1849), who had previously been branch manager of their other premises in Station Road. At one time, Carlisle born George Graham was also the auditor to the Borough Council and the Infirmary.

By 1896, the bank with it's head office in Carlisle had eight branches throughout the county and held deposits of over £740,000. But like many smaller joint stock banks, they had suffered greatly from the 1878 recession in the economy, and never fully recovered. Eventually they were amalgamated into the much larger London and Midland Bank.[02], who paid £290,000 to acquire their assets. In December 1898, following a further merger with the London based City Bank, they subsequently became known as the London, City and Midland Bank. To confuse the historian further in 1918, the name was changed once more to the London Joint City and Midland Bank. Before in 1923, finally becoming known as simply the Midland Bank. [03]

Work to erect the new London, City and Midland Bank in Old Market Place, began in the spring of 1916. It's architects were Woolfall and Eccles, who were responsible for designing numerous new banks for the Midland, particularly in the north of England. The carefully detailed stone facade of the Workington branch with it's tall, semicircular headed windows, pilaster columns and stone balustrades at roof level, is typical of the high-specification adopted by the bank at this time. The building also closely resembled other Midland premises, in particular the Southport branch designed by the same architects in 1921. Following the subsequent merger involving the Cumberland Union Bank in Pow Street, the Market Place branch was closed and the building was eventually sold. In the late 1950s, the building was later used by the Youth Employment Services.

One long established family business in the Old Market Place was Carruthers greengrocers. But before they acquired the shop on the corner of Market Place and

The building also closely resembled other Midland premises, in particular the Southport branch designed by the same architects in 1921.

[01] Today, we know this street as Upper Jane Street, but in the past it was simply referred to as Jane Street. ■

[02] The London and Midland Bank was formed in 1891, by the amalgamation of the Midland Bank with the Central Bank of London. This large banking firm then dominated the UK banking system during the 1890s. Acquiring no less than thirteen smaller provincial banks across the country, up until 1900. These included the Kendal based, Bank of Westmorland in 1893 as well as the Carlisle City and District Bank, three years later. ■

[03] Today the Midland Bank forms part of the HSBC group of companies. ■

WORKINGTON AUCTION MART

On 16 December 1885, Workington's first purpose built Auction Mart was opened at the foot of Guard Street. It was the brainchild of James Duffield, the influential general manager of Charles Cammell and Co. He was very much aware that the town's butchers had to travel to purchase their stock at other marts across West Cumberland. In the process incurring considerable expense bringing the beasts back to the town for slaughter. A new company was formed and the site was chosen very close to where local farmers had traditionally sold their cattle and sheep, each market day for a great many years. Cattle and sheep from Maryport, Aspatria, Cockermouth and also the Cleator, Egremont and Barrow districts were also sold here, brought to the town by rail and herded through the streets to the mart. ■

King Street, it was formerly Fisher's grocers and wine merchants. This business was ran by George (1829-74) and Edward Fisher. They seem to have acquired the *"old established grocers shop"* after the death of David Lowther Hodgson. He had succeeded his father Daniel Lowther Hodgson, who is believed to have established the shop in the 1840s. Following his retirement the business passed to David's son Joseph F. Hodgson (1852-1916). He expanded the business and eventually sold out to the Workington Brewery Company in 1891. Joseph who was living at the Bankfield mansion, accepted a place on the board of directors of the brewery. Workington Brewery then occupied much of the north side of Upper Jane Street with their wines and spirits warehouse. They also had stores within the bonded warehouse upon the South Quay.

At the top of Upper Jane Street on the south corner of Nook Street, was the grocer shop of James McCade (1843-1918). This shop was later acquired by Joseph Parker and was at one time perhaps the oldest surviving grocers shop in the town. One interesting feature of the property is its old original Georgian shop windows, made up of many little panes.

The 1863 OS plan reveals that the south end of Nook Street originally crossed over Guard Street, and included the upper part of what we know today as Harrington Road. Guard Street and the corner of Harrington Road

ABOVE - WORKINGTON AUCTION MART was located on the corner of Guard Street and Harrington Road, next to St. Johns church. Designed by Workington architect James Howes, the large single storey building had an imposing facade of white Yorkshire stone, with hammer-dressed local stone to it's other elevations. The slated roof was supported internally on neat cast iron pillars, and all the floors were paved with Staffordshire blue tiles and bricks. John Milburn's Hawkshead foundry made all the columns, pilasades and gates for the sale ring. ■

was widened and altered in 1930. The police station (or the *"Blue coat barracks"* as it was referred to in one 1879 newspaper) has almost always dominated this narrow street. The 1881 census revealing that William Johnston, the *"inspector of police"* actually lived in the police station building with his wife Janet and their teenaged daughter. There was no real cells, anyone arrested was usually detained in the *"lock-up"* in Ritson Street. It was only after the station was extended in 1883, that a number of new cells were built at the rear of the site backing on to Pinfold Street. A new court room was also added and thereafter the Police court was held there.

To the northside of the police station is a narrow thoroughfare called Rosemary Lane, which runs upto King Street emerging next to the Blue Bell Inn. We can still walk this way, but in Victorian times there was four little cottages in this lane. One was the home of Elizabeth (Bet) Chambers. Tradition tells us some suspected her of being a witch, she certainly told fortunes and was considered a remarkable clairvoyant. Often she would tell of people who had stolen things and how or where to go to retrieve the goods. One wonders if her neighbour Willie Johnston at the police station ever used her services.

On the east side of the street, the Plough Inn was at 5 Nook Street. Exactly when it was opened is unclear, it certainly existed in the late 1820s when Thomas Adams held the licence. In 1885, this small pub was eventually acquired by the Iredale Bros., and subsequently passed to Workington Brewery Company. This two storey pub which opened directly onto the narrow pavement survived until the 1970s.

Opposite the Plough Inn we can still see that the large attractive houses have changed very little in the last two centuries or so. Congregational minister, Rev. James Rennie and his family lived at 14 Nook Street. The same house was later occupied by photographer Robert Henderson and his family. Whilst on the opposite side of the street at 23, was another photographic studio ran by William Sherwood (1820-82). Solicitor J. N. St. George Curwen later had his offices here before he moved to Portland Square.

Around 1904, the *Workington Mail* newspaper had their office at 22 Nook Street. This weekly publication was issued every Wednesday evening and cost ½d. (half an old penny). The proprietor of the *Mail* was Mrs. K. M. Unwin, who was also a dressmaker and milliner. She also published the *West Cumberland Independent*. Very little further is known about either newspaper and how successful they were.

ABOVE - Workington Brewery Company label from the 1950s. ∎

The long serving fire fighter called for a ladder and with *"great courage and coolness"*, climbed into the burning building through the office window.

At the north corner of Nook Street and Ritson Street was the large corn and flour warehouse. Exactly when the property was build is not known, but we certainly know it was occupied over the years by a succession of millers. Suggesting in the past, that it may have served as some kind of corn market or exchange. In the 1840s, Thomas Jackson of Seaton Mill sold much of his produce here, whilst Shepherd Sewell (1824-80) of Workington Hall Mill used the premises up until his death. Furthermore, Robert Walker (1832-82) traded as an auctioneer and corn agent at the same address. But still the actual set up and trading arrangements remain something of a mystery.

By February 1883, we learn for a notice in the local newspaper that a William Irving was now trading as a corn and flour merchant from the property. The business was later acquired by the Sibson Bros., both were thought to be farmers and they were responsible for altering the property. Although much of the rear part of the building was still constructed from timber. The shop was now a large grocers shop, which also sold agricultural seed and feeding stuffs for poultry, pigs, pigeons etc.

In September 1934, the entire property was almost destroyed as fire swept through the building. Captain William Charters of the fire brigade, who lived *"barely twenty yards away"* in Guard Street was quickly summoned and he called out both the town's fire engines. As his men bravely fought the blaze, hundreds gathered in the street to watch the "inferno of flames". When the water pressure was found to be particularly low, a fresh supply was pumped almost 700 yards from the Brewery Beck. But all was in vain, the fire was almost burning out of control, and but for the skill of the brigade *"would have spread to the adjoining homes"*.

When Captain Charters was informed by Harry Sibson, the son of one of the proprietors, that the insurance documents were in a first floor safe. The long serving fire fighter called for a ladder and with *"great courage and coolness"*, climbed into the burning building through the office window. Followed by Harry Sibson, the two men quickly opened the safe and retrieved the papers. As they climbed back out of the smoke filled building, *"flames were licking at the door and within minutes the room was gutted"*. The Sibson brothers would subsequently re-open their shop and warehouse and continued to trade from the same premises until the 1970s. Today, the building is occupied by the Circuit public house.

On the opposite side of the road at 43 Nook Street

lived Sergeant Edward Wilkins Green (1825-83), his wife Elizabeth and their family. Born in Somerset, he is thought to have had a distinguished military career and in 1871 is listed as a *"Chelsea pensioner"*. The family moved to Workington in the early 1860s, although it is not exactly clear why they chose to settle in the town. On 31 August 1864, he was appointed drill instructor to the Workington battalion of the Cumberland Rifle volunteers, a post he held until his retirement in September 1881. For many years he was also parish clerk to St. Michaels and treasurer to the Workington Co-operative Society. When he died in January 1883, he was buried with full military honours in St. Johns Church churchyard.

On the north east corner of Nook Street and Guard Street is the Miners Arms. It certainly existed in 1847 when John Irving was the landlord. Subsequent landladies during Victorian times included Ann Ellor and Ann Allison.

At the foot of Guard Street was the premises of pawnbroker Joseph Sherwood. And in 1871, George J. Smith (proprietor of the Theatre Royal) is known to have lived following his marriage to Sherwoods daughter. The business then briefly passed into the hands of Robert Grisewood of Whitehaven. However in 1883, he was found guilty of forgery and sentenced to "18 months hard labour". Thereafter, it is thought the pawnbrokers was acquired by John Graham. In December 1900, a fire in the three storey building caused extensive damage, estimated at around £3000. Although covered by insurance many of the pawned goods were lost in the blaze. Because of it's location close to St. Johns Church, it was often said that the shop *was "nice and handy for anybody who had been too generous at church".*

Pinfold Street is located off the north side of Guard Street, not far from it's junction with Nook Street. Up until at least the 1870s, there was a compound or enclosure here where cattle and sheep were retained. Then there was only a handful of dwellings in the street. And often in early documents the road is simply known as the Pinfold. It was likely to be the 1890s before the longer name was formally adopted.

On the west corner of the Pinfold at it's junction with Guard Street was the Anchor Inn. It was one of two Anchor Inns in the town the other was located on the quayside. Like the Miners Arms, this Pinfold Street public house certainly existed there in 1847, when William Chadwick was the landlord. Subsequent licensees included Ann Henry and Thomas Broadbent.

In December 1898, the Borough Council completed

It was often said that the pawnbrokers shop *was "nice and handy for anybody who had been too generous at church".*

a new *"mortuary house"* on the east side of Pinfold Street, near the junction with Guard Street. Within this windowless building, post mortems were carried out prior to any inquest. Bill Jackson recently recalled the building was often referred to as the *"Dead House"*, and as a boy he remembers several corpses being brought to the mortuary by handcart. Inside were *"two cold slate slabs, each about six or seven feet long with a drainage channel around the sides"*. During the summer of 1936, after the mortuary was relocated to the infirmary the old building was let by the Borough Council as a store.

During the 1840s, William Holden started a blacksmith shop in Udale Street, moving to 21 Guard Street during the 1860s. The forge of the blacksmiths shop was located almost opposite Guard Street schools on the north side of the street.. During the 1870s, the business was continued by his son Joseph Holden (1839-80) assisted by his wife Mary Ann (1845-1912). During the 1880s, William Holden's grandson Joseph was also taken on as an apprentice blacksmith. But the young Holden later changed career and trained as a gentlemen's hairdresser. By 1892 he had opened a barber's shop at 54 Senhouse Street. Joseph rose to become a very prominent local councillor serving the town for over forty years. It is said that *"many political debates"* took place in Joseph Holden's barbers shop. Holden Road at Salterbeck is named in his honour.

As we approach Cross Hill rising up Guard Street, it is worth noting that the properties on the right hand (or south) side of the street were once also known as St. Johns Place. During the 1920s and 30s, Henry Kitto ran a private school for both boys and girls at 68 Guard Street. He taught classes of mixed classes of upto twenty pupils, and was a typical-looking schoolmaster wearing his black "mortar board" and gown during lessons. Mr Kitto may have lived in the same house as Edward and Betsy Ann Smith, the proprietors of an earlier private school. The 1881 census seems to imply they shared the same address, but over the years the numbering of the houses in this area has changed several times. During the 1880s, the Smiths also ran a private school at the Good Templars Hall in Station Road. Their eldest son was Herbert Smith (1870-1935) who later trained as a pharmacist and for many years ran a chemist shop at 14 Jane Street.

Robert Brown (1826-76), a prominent Workington stone mason built a number of properties on St. Johns Place, the last of which was sold almost two years after his death in 1876. Brown who lived most of his latter years at 14 Finkle Street was also an accomplished sculp-

During the 1880s, William Holden's grandson Joseph was also taken on as an apprentice blacksmith. But the young Holden later changed career and trained as a gentlemen's hairdresser.

tor. Records show he was responsible for numerous head-stones found in the town's graveyards and cemeteries. He traded from a *"stone cutting"* yard in Pow Street, adjoining the old post office on the corner of John street. The property was later purchased by tailor and woollen draper Robert Adair. Today, much of the site is now occupied by the National Westminster Bank (formally the National Provincial Bank).

The Royal George Inn on Cross Hill does not appear on the 1863 OS map of the town, nor does it seem to be recorded on the 1851 census. Although it is listed in 1871, when the landlord was George Carruthers. A decade later it was ran by Robert Thompson and his wife Bessie, although they moved two years later to the Golden Lion in the old Market Place. The "George" later acquired by Workington Brewery Company, was obviously once considerably smaller than today. Adjoining the Inn were several small cottages, which over the years have become part of the pub. In one of these little houses lived William Scott, one of the last coachmen in the town. He was the father of Joseph Scott, the schoolmaster at Victoria School for almost fifty years.

Opposite the Royal George is Stoneleigh, a substantial and elegant large house occupying the east corner of Cross Hill and Park End Road. It was built in 1874 for Henry Fletcher (1821-18850 a wealthy magistrate and major landowner. After Fletcher died on Christmas Day in 1885, the family continued to live at the grand house. After the death of his wife Ann nearly fifteen years later, the property and its contents were sold by auction. Some years later it was acquired by the Borough Council.

During WW2, Stoneleigh was used as the *"Fire Guard"* headquarters. From 1944, the County Probation Officer also occupied some of the offices. Later in July 1946, the first floor offices were also let to the Ministry of Works and the ground floor to the Ministry of Food. In February 1950, after the Ministry of Works vacated their part of the building, the Corporation's Borough Surveyor took over their offices.

At the foot of High Street was the Brown Cow Inn, just above where Ashfield Junior School stands today. William and Matilda Byers took over as licensees of this pub during the 1870s. They were not related to the old sailing family of the town as they had originated in Wetheral, moving to the town around 1875.

The area around the junction of High Street and the north end of Newlands Lane was once quite narrow, with a rows of small terraced houses on either side of High Street. In December 1931, the Borough Council pur-

Robert Brown (1826-76), a prominent Workington stone mason built a number of properties on St. Johns Place,

High Street in the past has also been known as Town Head or Uppergate (Uppygeate).

"This window was fitt up the day before Good Friday 1865 by Quitn Moore, aged 21 years joiner of Maryport. April 13 1865".

chased a terrace of seven small cottages, below the Brown Cow Inn in order to begin widening this street. The dwellings on the opposite side of the street were later demolished when Newlands Secondary school was built in 1931. The Local Council records also indicate that the first houses at the northern end of Newlands Lane were started in the summer of 1929.

Above the Brown Cow we enter what we refer too today as High Street, although in the past it was also known as Town Head or Uppergate. The oldest remaining properties are likely to be Shannon House (formally the home of George Brooker), Elm Bank (residence of ironmaster Joseph Ledger), Grindall Cottage (opposite Elm Bank) and the Travellers Rest pub. Records suggest that the public house was built around 1789, by mason Joseph Ellwood (1768-1809). He leased the site, in an area then known as "near Ennan Close, Uppergate" from John Christian Curwen. Although not mentioned by name we know that by 1837, the property had passed to Joseph Ellwood's son Solomon, who is thought to have remained there till around 1840.

The 1871 census lists Isabella Miller as landlady of the Travellers Rest, and during the following year she was replaced by Mary Freer. A decade or so later, Jane Milller was the licensee. Although it is not known if there is any family link between Isabella and Jane. In 1890, the public house was acquired by the Iredale Bros. (later the Workington Brewery Co.) In June 1937, the Borough Council approved plans for the alterations to the Travellers Rest.

Ashfield House (almost opposite Elm Bank) is believed to have been built for wine and spirit merchant Thomas Crosthwaite (b.1823). He had ran Crosthwaite's Wine Vaults midway up Ramsey Brow, opposite Workington Hall. This large detached house has since been divided into two separate dwellings. In March 2002, the owner of one half of the old house found an inscription under the soffitt of the front bedroom window whilst carrying out some repairs. Written in pencil the note read *"This window was fitt up the day before Good Friday 1865 by Quitn Moore, aged 21 years joiner of Maryport. April 13 1865"*. This suggests Ashfield was built around this time. It certainly does not appear on the first OS map of the town surveyed in the early 1860s, yet there is mention of the house in the 1871 census.

Around the turn of the century we know Ashfield was the residence of ironmaster Joseph Ellis. Previously, it had also been the home of James Duffield of Charles Cammell Ltd. Between 1910-16, it was owned by James

Lawrence Smith, although its unclear if he actually lived there as he then shared Bankfield with his wife's family. Thereafter it passed to John Pearson Bennett, another director of the Workington Brewery Co. Eventually, the large house was bought by Robert Leslie, the builder and developer who built the first houses on Newlands Lane. It was Leslie who converted the property into two houses, and also built the detached house adjacent to Ashfield.

The deeds of Ashfield House reveal that the adjacent property further up High Street was called Grindall Cottage. It was briefly owned by Henry Grayson (1796-1864) a shipowner who lived for some time at Elm Bank. From the early 1880s, William Boadle Burrow, a coach and carriage builder occupied the premises. They then consisted of Grindall Cottage, three dwelling houses, a stable and gig house. Burrow appears to have ran his business from here until at least 1901.

Another significant house on High Street was Highcote, designed by D. Birkett in 1881. It was built for Emily G. and Martha Quirk who had previously lived at 41 Washington Street. It is thought they were the sisters of Peter Gibson Quirk (1849-1893) an ironmaster who invested heavily in the local iron industry and accrued quite a fortune. Peter Gibson Quirk had several sons including Ethelred (1875-1940), Peter Gibson (jnr), George (1877-1939) and James. It was the Quirk family that established the Derwent Engineering Company in Central Square (later Stouts Motor Garage). Peter Gibson (jnr) ran a tobacconist in Pow Street.

After the death of the Quirk sisters, Highcote was eventually purchased by John Andrew Broatch, the Borough Treasurer. His family continued to live in the house until the 1960s. But it later became vacant, run down and neglected and was eventually demolished. Almost opposite the Highcote is Newlands House built in the late 1860s for solicitor William Thompson.

Before 1904, the Row was the former name for Park End Road which connects Ramsey Brow to Cross Hill. This street was named after Park End, the large house at its Ramsey Brow end, now the Helena Thompson Museum. Park End built around 1730, was originally the home of the steward (or agent) to the Curwen estates. Up until 1847, it was occupied by the Thompson family. It was the residence of Benjamin Thompson (1769-1839), the steward to Henry [vi] Curwen (the son of John Christian Curwen). He and his son Charles, were both attorneys and also ran their legal practice from their Park End home. Sometime after his father's death, Charles Thompson (1796-1857) moved to live in Elizabeth Street.

Another significant house on High Street was Highcote, designed by D. Birkett in 1881.

Before 1904, the Row was the former name for Park End Road which connects Ramsey Brow to Cross Hill.

From 1847, the house became the residence of Edward Stanley Curwen, son and heir of Henry [vi] Curwen (then Lord of the Manor of Workington). He probably vacated Park End and moved across the road to Workington Hall shortly after his father's death in 1860. For a couple of years, the property was leased to William Gordon. But around 1869, the Thompson family returned once again to live in the house, when it was leased to William Thompson (1806-73), the son of Benjamin and brother to Charles. After William's death, his widow Mary Thompson (1823-1908) continued to occupy the house. They were the parents of Helena Thompson. She eventually purchased Park End from the Curwen family in 1934.

Miss Helena Thompson was an extremely generous benefactor to the town of Workington. In her will (dated 29 August 1939). She left Park End to the Borough Council, *"primarily as a museum for the town and district"*. In addition she gave £10,000 for it's *"upkeep and repairs"*, together with numerous pictures, books, curios and antiques. With the outbreak of WW2, the Borough Council put all plans for their new museum on hold, and invested Miss Thompsons legacy. The vacant Park End was subsequently requisitioned and used as a temporary *"childrens home"* under the Government's Evacuation scheme.

To the west side of Park End Road, the grand three storey houses (or villas as they were then called) were built around 1881-82. Each had a large rear garden running back on to Carlton Road, and here some had a stable block. These houses were the residences of some wealthy and prominent townspeople, such as brewer Thomas Iredale who lived at Holm Acre.

Thorncroft House, next to the old St. Johns Vicarage on Park End Road, was built by William Dickinson (1799-1882). He was the son of a farmer born in 1799 at Kidburngill Farm, Near Arlecdon. In 1824, he married Jane Norman (of High Dyke) and moved to nearby North Moses. Here he followed in his fathers footsteps and pursued a career in farming. Later, he also held the adjoining Moorside Hall and Moorside Parks farms, farming a total of about 600 acres. Mr. Dickinson progressed to became a land surveyor and valuer, and a leading authority on agriculture in the county. Winning several prizes for his essays on *Agriculture in West and East Cumberland.* He was considered a knowledgable botanist, an expert geologist and also had a keen interest in ornithology, history and local customs. He is credited with the first archaeological excavations at Burrow Walls Roman Camp

Miss Helena Thompson was an extremely generous benefactor to the town of Workington. In her will (dated 29 August 1939). She left Park End to the Borough Council, *"primarily as a museum for the town and district"*.

WILLIAM DICKINSON
(1799-1882)

at Northside and was responsible for producing several books, many in dialect. Dickinson also contributed the botanical notes for Hariet Martineau's 1855 *Guide to the Lakes.*

In his retirement he moved to Workington. Here he further indulged his passion for learning and writing. In recognition of his achievements he was made a Fellow of the Linnaean Society. For many years, he was also a magistrate sitting on the Workington bench. William Dickinson died at Thorncroft on 22 June 1882, aged 83. He is buried in the picturesque little churchyard at Arlecdon, almost within sight of his birthplace. The plot close to the chancel end of the church is marked by an usually large square, red sandstone gravestone. There is also an attractive white marble plaque to his memory within the nave of St. Johns Church at Workington. Unveiled in November 1883, it was designed by Mr. Nelson (of Carlisle).

In 1930, Thorncroft was later converted into a convent for the Poor Clares who assisted the towns Roman Catholic church. Eight years later they applied for a private burial ground at the convent. It is not too clear if the burial ground was ever approved, and if so if any remains were interred here.

Within the Assembly rooms tucked away in the south west corner of Portland Square, [01] many popular artists and performers are known to have appeared. Perhaps one of the most famous was Oscar Wilde, who delivered a lecture on Tuesday 19 February 1884, entitled *"Personal reminiscences of a tour of America"*. At one time, the outside of this public hall was *"illuminated by 250 small fish tail gas burners which kept one of the local characters busy relighting them every time the wind blew them out"*.

Readers should not confuse these original Assembly rooms with the *"Green Dragon Assembly rooms"*. The latter was a large hall at the rear of the Green Dragon Hotel, entered off the narrow Fox Lane. It seems to have been in existence from the 1870s through to its demolition during the 1960s.

We know from the family history notes of Philip Milburn (published in 1937) that the Green Dragon Hotel was erected around 1805, on the site of Salkeld's tannery. This leather dressing business had obviously existed here before 1768, when it was purchased by William Salkeld of Penrith. It is assumed that his grandson Henry Salkeld was responsible for building the Green Dragon. After his death in 1817, the public house was ran by his widow Hannah (nee Steel), and then their

"In Victorian times, fairs were held in Portland Square, and these often overflowed down into Washington Street. Wooden booths sometimes stayed for months in the Square".
Wallace Ritson
1936

[01] See page 125 of History of Workington (from Earliest Times to Ad 1865) for more details of the Assembly rooms. ■

ERECTED
BY PUBLIC SUBSCRIPTION
IN MEMORY OF
ANTHONY PEAT, SURGEON.
WHO
DURING A LIFE SPENT IN
INCESSANT TOIL FOR THE
RELIEF OF HUMAN
SUFFERING WON
THE LOVE AND ESTEEM
OF ALL CLASSES.
DIED
JUNE 4th 1877,
AGED 57 YEARS.

"ITA SPENDEAT LUX VESTRA
CORAM HOMINIBUS, UT VIDEANT
VESTRA BON OPERA,
GLORIFICENTQUE PATREM ILLUM
VESTRUM QUI EST IN COELIS"
MATT. V. 16.

ABOVE - The inscription on the tall grey marble obelisk, erected as a memorial to the memory of Dr. Anthony Peat.

The latin quote from the bible on the above transcription reads - *'Let your light so shine before men, that they may see your good works, and glorify your father which is in heaven'* - Matthew 5.16. ■

[01] A 1877 newspaper report suggests his only surviving relative was John Peat, who was then in Australia. It is believed his aunt Jane Peat married Henry Salkeld, who was for many years the landlord of the Green Dragon. ■

daughter Grace. In 1835, she married Thomas Bowman, a local wine and spirit merchant, who continued as licensee until his retirement in 1865. The property remained in the family until 1899, when it was purchased by the Carlisle Old Brewery Co. Ltd. The new owners later altered and extended the premises several times.

Within this cobbled square there were two other inns, besides the Green Dragon. The Coach and Horses (at 6 Portland Square) which was ran for almost half a century by the McCade family. Their ancestor William McCade is reputed to have driven the stage coach between Workington and Carlisle, and was no doubt responsible for naming the inn. Wallace Ritson remembered the old coachman and vividly described him as *"dapper looking ostler in knickerbockers, tailcoat, legging, and tall hat"*. In June 1925, the Coach and Horses closed and was converted into two cottages. The other pub in Portland Square was the Wheatsheaf Inn (on the corner of Cavandish Street) which certainly existed before 1829. Around sixty years later, it was closed and it's licence transferred to the Wheatsheaf on the Marsh, then ran by William Holliday.

In the centre of Portland Square is a tall grey marble obelisk, erected as a memorial to the memory of Dr. Anthony Peat (1819-77). It is a fitting tribute to an extremely well-loved surgeon, who had diligently cared for the sick of the town for over 32 years. Through several epidemics of cholera, at a time when there was no advanced medicines and surgical techniques, and people often died from the most minor ailments or conditions. Dr. Peat was the eldest son of John Peat of Salmon Hall, and after leaving school was first apprenticed to the long established medical practice of Messrs. W. and J. Dickinson. This partnership (which certainly existed in 1829) was ran by William Lindow Dickinson (1789-1853) and Joseph Stamper Dickinson. Like Dr. Peat, they too had their surgery in Portland Square in what was for many years the commercial centre of old Workington.

Unlike today, it was once very common for a physician or doctor to also be referred to as a surgeon. During his apprenticeship, Anthony Peat went to medical school in London before ultimately returning to the town. He eventually entered into partnership with the son of his former employer, Dr. William Lindow Dickinson (1820-1892). Newspaper reports suggest that it was *"so extensive a medical practice that the time of the partners was largely occupied in attending to it"*. The unmarried doctor [01] was also a long standing member of the Seventh Cumberland Volunteer Rifle Battalion, and he was buried following a sober military style funeral. With upto three thousand mourners, it was said to be the *"largest that had ever been in Workington, since the interment of the late John Christian Curwen, of Workington Hall"*.

His funeral took place on Friday, 8 June 1877, and nearly all the *"principal places of business put up their shutters"*. At around half-past ten, the vast crowd in and around Portland Square was joined by around seventy members of the Rifle Battalion, dressed in their bright scarlet uniforms, and wearing a *"black crepe band"* round their left arm. Whilst a group of soldiers formed the bearing party, the remainder assembled in two lines to accompany the polished oak coffin. As the cortege made its way out of the square, the Workington Amateur Brass Band playing Handel's famous *"Dead March in Saul"*. As well as hundreds of townspeople, upwards of twenty private horse-drawn carriages also joined the procession. Marching in "funeral time", the solemn cortege moved slowly through the streets and out along Bridge Street, commencing it's four mile journey to Camerton Church.

As the coffin reached the village of Seaton many others joined the mourners. Some had even gathered on the Clifton side of the River Derwent, opposite the tiny church, to witness the event and pay their last respects. At the church gate, the funeral was met by Rev. J. J. Thornley (of St. Johns Church) who was to officiate. After the service, the coffin was carried to it's last resting place in the adjoining graveyard. The Volunteer Brigade then formed two lines and fired "three volleys" into the air, over the open grave. By three in the afternoon, the large *"concourse"* had slowly dispersed and the graveyard *"assumed its wonted quiet once more"*.

In the weeks following the death of the beloved doctor, the townspeople were invited to subscribe towards a suitable memorial. Soon around £535 was pledged, and a committee was formed to decide what form the memorial should take. One quite ambitious proposal was to build a new cottage hospital dedicated to his memory. Although it was felt they had raised sufficient to provide the premises, there would really be little remaining to cover the future running costs. This plan was later rejected and it would be another eight years before the town eventually obtained it's first infirmary. A carved statue of the late doctor was then proposed, but there was an *"absence of any suitable photograph or portrait"* for the sculptor to work from. Finally, it was decided to erect the existing obelisk.

As work began on the foundations for the new me-

"The coffin was lifted, and as soon as it was settled on the shoulders of the stalwart volunteers the signal was given for the solemn cortege to move off."
West Cumberland Times
June 1877.

Dr. Peat's memorial was unveiled on 27 June 1881 by William Fletcher. Many thousands once again crammed into the square to witness the event, and pay tribute once again to the memory and work of the beloved physician and surgeon.

morial, a *"rather curious incident"* was said to have occurred. As the *"first stroke of the pick hit the ground"*, a piece of stone rebounded and broke *"the window of the very room, in the house"* where Dr. Peat died. We also know that the foundations were completed on *"the very day four years"* after his death. With the final stone being placed in position, on the *same day four years"* after his burial at Camerton.

Dr. Peat's memorial was unveiled on 27 June 1881 by William Fletcher. Many thousands once again crammed into the square to witness the event, and pay tribute once again to the memory and work of the beloved physician and surgeon. Dr. Peat had lived for many years at 9 Portland Square, only a short distance from his memorial. The pony he rode, and his favourite terrier "Scamp" were almost as well known as the doctor himself.

In 1882, the new County Court building costing £2000 was erected in the north west corner of Portland Square. Previously, all cases had been dealt with at the County Court in Cockermouth. The first cases at the new Workington court were heard in November 1882. Before rooms were set aside at the Town Hall, the court building also accommodated a *"robeing"* room for the Mayor, Aldermen and Councillors to use on civic occasions, such as Mayoral Sunday. At this time processions would be assembled and start from the cobbled square. Until a few years before WW1, there was also a newsroom above the court, which served as a meeting place for the gentry of the town.

At 4 Portland Square, on the corner of Portland street are the offices of solicitors Curwen and Co. This long established business was started by John Neville St. George Curwen in 1902. He was the son of Alfred Curwen (1835-1920) and Laura Naomi Smith, and was born on St. Georges Day in 1879 (hence his unusual christian name). Henry Fraser Curwen (1834-1900) of Workington Hall, was his uncle. He began his legal career, with Brown, Auld and Brown, solicitors of Whitehaven. When he started his own legal practice in the town, it was initially based in the first floor offices at 26 Washington Street. Before moving to 23 Nook Street and eventually its present premises in Portland Square. The practice for many years handled the majority of the Curwen family and estate business.

Christian Street runs off Portland Square at its north west corner. Midway along the east side of this street is the *Discharged Soldiers and Sailors Club*, more commonly known as the *"Vets Club"*. One of its most famous members was Joseph "Joey" Thompson, who achieved remarkable fame winning the English Senior Amateur Billiards Championship in 1936.

Seven years earlier, Joey (the son of Freddie Thompson) was practically unknown, yet he *"blazed a trail across the green cloth"*. In 1931, he won the West Cumberland amateur billiards championship for the first time beating Martin Foley at the Hensingham Liberal Rooms. In January 1934, he was still the West Cumbrian champion when he made a 107 break against Robert Riley (of Carlisle) at the opening of the Station Hotel's new Billiard Room. Two months later he topped this with a remarkable record 365 break against the legendary Joe Davis (of Chesterfield) when they played an exhibition match in the town. He continued to dominate the game winning tournaments across the north of England.

In April 1936, the little billiard player barely five feet tall, won national acclaim winning the English Senior Amateur Billiards Championship at Burroghes Hall in London. Newspaper reports tell us that around 600 people gathered outside Gordons Garage, in Washington Street to follow Joey's progress on the radio. His amazing success was greeted with *"great cheering"*. Lord Lonsdale presenting him with the trophy. When he returned to the town Joey who lived in Dove Lane was afforded a heroes welcome. Later that year he also represented Britain in the Empire Games in South Africa. It was first thought he would be unable to attend the tournament as he had to pay much of the expenses himself. However, a testimonial fund was soon launched in the town to raise his travel and accommodation costs.

After WW2, Joey Thompson won the national title again on two further occasions in 1947 and 48. He is remembered quite simply with a framed photograph hanging on the wall at the Veterans Club. Yet the remarkable achievements of this local sportsman are worthy of some great recognition.

As we leave Christian Street and enter Ramsey Brow once commonly referred to as Turnpike. On the west corner of this junction was a large three storey stone building reputed to have once been a theatre. Unfortunately, no records appear to remain to provide any further information. The property currently accommodates an electrical wholesaler, and its upper floor was removed in the 1960s after a major fire.

Crosthwaites Spirit Vaults was located on the opposite side of the junction. Records suggest this property belonging to the Curwen family had been a wine and spirit merchants since at least the 1870s. The family ran

JOEY THOMPSON

There is a chap in this old town
Who'll rise some day to fame;
he loves to knock the ivories down -
Joey Thompson is his name.

Just watch him when he takes a grip,
of his famous cue;
From the end of its magic tip,
He'll score a hundred or two.

author unknown
1936

"Joey is a frail young man, with a quiet and likeable disposition...It is questionable if the county has ever produced a player to equal Thompson, his play is a delight to watch. A fine potter and all round player with a wonderful accurate eye".
Workington Star

OPPOSITE - A 1929 aerial photograph of the Edkin Street and Washington Street area, showing the Drill Hall to the left, adjacent to the old St. Johns School. Washington Street (from right to left) then ran into the top end of Pow Street. Note the junction of Ramsey Brow, Wilson Street and Bridge Street. ■

business is thought to have been established by Allison Crosthwaite (1772-1832) around 1805, being first located in Brow Top. After his death the business passed to his wife Jane (1785-1834) and thereafter to Thomas Crosthwaite (of Ashfield House).

In April 1903, the council approved plans for the alteration of the Ramsey Brow Spirit Vaults, submitted on behalf of Alan D. Curwen. By 1909, the *"old established wholesale, retail and family wine and spirit merchants"* had been taken over by John Pearson Bennett, who also ran the Station Hotel. An advertisement in the local newspaper records that *"This noted house is the only entirely free house"* in the town, indicating that the outlet had no formal link or association with any brewery and was free to stock and sell any wines and spirits. The Spirit Vaults would then also deliver a gallon stone jar of *Burton & Ulveston* Beer to your door for just 1/8 (8p) - this equates to around 1p a pint. John P. Bennett was succeeded in the business by his sons and the business was later acquired by Workington Brewery during the 1950s.

The Curwen or Curwens Arms was established during the 1820s, when Jonathan Armstrong was the licensee. Although there may well have been a public house here upto forty years earlier. Its name is obviously derived from the Curwen family who were Lords of the manor and lived in the nearby Workington Hall.

The junction of Ramsey Brow, Wilson Street, Bridge Street, Pow Street and Washington Street was once very much different than today. With the increased use of the motor car, traffic moving through these narrow streets and negotiating the tight corners caused major conjestion. Within the timeframe of this book, the junction has been altered twice to *"open up the thoroughfare"*. Wallace Ritson remembered Harry Renwick's drapers shop was one of those removed for *"street widening"*. Originally, Washington Street terminated in a T-junction with Pow Street. Pow Street crossed the end of Washington Street to the foot of Ramsey Brow. Whilst Wilson Street ran directly passed the Curwen Arms into Bridge Street. (See aerial photograph on adjoining page)

Bridge Street which runs through to the top of Hall Brow has now virtually disappeared and was cleared in the 1970s. Many will remember the west side of the street as a long row of about a dozen two-story terrace properties ending with the Grapes Inn on the corner of Udale Street (overlooking the brewery). Almost along the full length of the east side (on the site of the present modern Magistrates Court buildings) was the estate office and stables of Workington Hall. In 1947, after the old his-

toric building and grounds were acquired by the Borough Council, these became the "Corporation Yard", used to store the Councils vehicles and materials.

The only other properties on this side of Bridge Street were the Curwen Arms and Tognarelli's Ice Cream factory, separated by a couple of small terraced cottages, which eventually became part of the Curwen Arms. The Italian Tognarelli family became particularly famous in Workington for their creamy white ice cream. Established by brothers Ferruccio (1875-1915) and Philip (1871-1916) they opened their first confectioners shops in the town around 1902-3. These original shops were situated at 6 Station Road and 8 Bridge Street. It is likely they acquired the latter premises from grocer, Thomas Oliver. Wallace Ritson tells us that it was previously also *"Mr Waugh's old grocers shop"*. It had been established by James Waugh, sometime before 1829. After his death in 1845, his son John is known to have continued the business until at least 1871.

Their classic Italian ice cream is first thought to have been manufactured at the Station Road premises. But in 1945, the Borough Council approved plans for the new ice cream factory at 17 Bridge Street. It was formerly the premises of Poole's dairy and just across the street from their original shop. We know the Council's Public Health Committee visited the premises in 1949, and recorded seeing an *"efficient and clean plant and process"* and complemented the brothers *"on the excellence of their manufacturing business"*.

After the death of the two founding brothers, the business was continued by their respective wives Annunziata and Germana (1879-1934). Before later passing to Harry (1901-1963) and Renzo (1908-1986) who later traded as H. & R. Tognarelli. By the late 1930s, Tognarelli's had three other shops in the town at 18 Senhouse Street, 28 Finkle Street, 46 Pow Street. They later opened a further shop at 2 New Oxford Street (next to the Oxford Cinema).

In 1871, at 2 Bridge Street lived Joseph Walker (1791-1873) whose trade is shown as a mechanical dentist, although there are other references to him being a watchmaker, ironmonger, pawnbroker, straw hat maker. Mr Walker was also an original trustee of *Workington Gas, Coke and Light Company* founded in 1840. He lived in Bridge Street with his son also called Joseph (1831-1886) and who also traded as an ironmonger. By 1881 census we find Joseph junior has retired and Cockermouth born Richard Edward Banks has taken over Walker's ironmongers shop in Bridge Street. He now employed two men

The Tognarelli family became particularly famous in Workington for their classic Italian creamy white ice cream.

OPPOSITE - A 1954 aerial photograph of the Central Square and Oxford Street area. The Ritz cinema on Murray Road can be seen in the centre of the photograph. John Street then ran through to Pow Street and the top of Gray Street was a cul-de-sac. Central Station and the railway line through the town is also still to be seen ∎

FREDDIE CAIRNS
(DUKE OF WORKINGTON)

and two boys. It is believed he was the younger brother of John B. Banks who later established Banks ironmongers in Cockermouth's Market Place, a business that still operates today. By 1902, the Bridge Street business had passed into the hands of J.W. Hodgson (& Co.). It was then one of the first places in the town where you could buy petrol, its licence being issued in 1904.

Udale Street ran from the end of Bridge Street at the top of Ramsey Brow round to the junction of Sanderson Street and Pow Street. Like Derwent Street it consisted of a variety of property, there was the odd very nice Georgian house like that occupied by the surgeon John Guy during the early 1870s. But the majority of homes were cramped and huddled together down narrow little lanes in a poor state of repair. At one time, the homes in Waughs Buildings were "*overcrowded, the tenants, nine in number, huddled together in one sleeping room, with scarcely a particle of furniture, and on the ground floor, in one corner, half a cart-load of ashes: another of the houses in the same place, simply a brothel, with no furniture, and a filthy interior*". In June 1904, the council heard of another case of "*overcrowding*" in Irvings Yard. Here in one small bedroom less than 3.7 metres (12 feet) square lived 6 adults and three children. It was a constant nightmare for the local authority and many times homes here were declared unfit for habitation and owners were forced to bring them up to standard.

One of the most famous residents of Udale Street was Freddy Cairns,[01] a well known character of late Victorian Workington. The self styled "*Duke of Workington*", Freddy earned his living as the local "*rag and bone man*" as well as the "*constructor of paper jumping jacks and windmills*". He features on several early picture postcards displaying these simple handmade toys which were sold to the local children. In January 1895, Freddie (aged about 32) married "*a blooming buxom young lady*" named Mary Moore [02] at Cockermouth Registry Office. The local newspaper recorded in some detail the "*most momentous step of his Bohemian-like life*". The couple "*trained it*" to Cockermouth along with his groomsman or best man Mr. A. Hindle (of Hagg Hill). The ceremony was conducted "*amidst much giggling and jocularity, and with the ingeniousness of expression, for which Freddy is famed*". Speaking in his broad "*Workiton*" accent, he tells how he was that excited "*at ah didn't knaw wedder ah was on me heed or me feet*". When he overheard someone comment that he had turned up in his rather drab working clothes, he replied "*folk can git weddit in ter working cleaz if the like, can't the*".

[01] The 1871 census, reveals Freddy (Frederick) Cairns was born at Harrington in 1863. His parents were Fredrick (1808-80) and Margaret Cairns and at this time they lived at 14 Ramsey Brow. As he told the registrar at his marriage ceremony, his "*fadder*" (father) was a "cwol" (coal) dealer and horse dealer. His conversation also tells us that he died "*fourteen years previous*" to his son's wedding. ■

[02] Although Mary Moore is known to have lived in Workington prior to her wedding. It is thought she was originally from Aspatria, and her father was a "coal hagger". ■

Upon paying the *"six bob"* (six shillings) marriage fee to the registrar, the newly weds had *"a cup of teah to celebrate t'wedding"*. Unfortunately, the couple then had very little *"brass"* (money) left and although Mary caught the train home, her new husband was left to walk. As they parted Mary said *"I'll be yam before ye, and hev yer tea ready"*. Freddy then told how he met a *"trades-man from Workington"* who gave him a ride in his horse drawn cart, as far as Cuckoo Arch. On the way home they stopped at the Lime Kiln Inn at Brigham, and three other pubs at Bridgefoot, Great Clifton and Stainburn for *"two-pennyworth of whiskey apiece"*. On his return to what he described as his *"semi-detached villa"* in Udale Street, he saw his "nice bit of a wife sitting in the chair". And shouted *"Tally-ho! put the kettle on Mrs. Cairns"*, and they celebrated a good day with a *"jolly party"*.

Around the start of the century, another infamous character once often seen in the Workington streets was Bella . She was well-known in every street, as she gathered "old bread, potatoes, cabbages - the leaves of the table" to feed to her pigs. And as Wallace Ritson told us *"she used to have some of the finest in the neighbour-hood"*. The *"tireless little lady"* went from door to door pushing her handcart, almost always wearing *"her soft bonnet"* and *"pattering"* clogs on her feet. She would also clean and boil tripe, which she sold from a bucket in the High Market, every market day.

The even-numbers on the north side of Pow street ran from the corner of Bridge Street. Whilst the odd-numbered properties on the south side commenced at its intersection with Washington Street. Before the building of the Cumberland Union Bank (later acquired by the Midland Bank and today known by the HSBC), there was a small cluster of six or seven properties at this corner, backing on to Sanderson Street. Amongst which were two public houses, Wallace Ritson tells us there was the Pine-apple Inn directly on the corner of Pow Street and Washington Street, with the Cuckoo Inn opposite the chemist shop of Jonathan R. Mason (1850-1908) at 4 Pow Street (later acquired by C. Harrison chemist.). The 1860s OS plan clearly shows these two licenced premises.

Virtually nothing is known about the Cuckoo Inn, other than Ritson tells us this is where Jimmy Dyer[01] is said to have *"sang and fiddled"* as did Matthew *"Doo"* and Seddon and Son. We know a little more about the Pineapple Inn, for in 1829 it was run by Elizabeth Turnbull. By 1834 she had moved to the Old Crown on Washington Street and was replaced by James Donaghy. Three decades later the pub was ran by Samuel Call, who

Unfortunately, the newly married couple then had very little brass left and although Mary caught the train home, Freddie her new husband was left to walk.

[01] Jimmy Dyer was the street musician who travelled from town to town earning his living from busking. He is featured on many old local picture postcards and there is a bronze statue of him in the Lanes shopping centre at Carlisle. ■

by 1871 had taken over the Sailors Return in Church Street. Around this time it is thought that the Pineapple was demolished and replaced by a new shop, its main entrance was located directly on the corner of Pow Street and Washington Street and angled at 45 degrees. One of its first occupants was auctioneer John Jenkinson (1844-1906) where he sold household goods and toys. He had his auctioneers office next door at 3 Pow Street, whilst his auctions were usually held in the Central Hall in Oxford Street.

This shop at 1 Pow Street is another often featured in several old picture postcards from the 1920s onwards. It was then occupied by the boot and shoe shop of John Henry Hattersley (b.1873). And the postcards usually show rows and rows of shoes hanging from hooks outside the shop. He was the son of William Henry Hattersley (b.1846) a clogger from the Glossop area, who married a Workington girl. The family left the area in the early 1870s, moving first to Maryport, then later to Runcorn in Cheshire. Exactly when they returned to the town is unclear but it is likely to have been around the turn of the century. It is thought John's son Albert Henry also ran a boot and shoe repairer in Station Road during the 1930s.

The Cumberland Union Bank was built around 1865, although the bank had actually began business in the town in March 1829. The new Workington premises ultimately became their head office. From 1875, the manager was John Andrew Broatch. He and his wife Jemina and their four boys and two girls actually living in the upstairs rooms above the bank. During the 1880s and 1890s this local bank was under great pressure from its shareholders having advanced no less than 8% of its assets to the *West Cumberland Iron and Steel Company* and another 5% to the *Maryport Haematite Iron Company*. Two companies which would ultimately struggle in the boom and bust years of the iron and steel industry. This made the local bank vulnerable to a takeover from the larger banks.

The *London Joint Stock Bank* which incorporated the *York City and County Banking Company*, and was occasionally later also known as *York City and London Joint Stock Bank* amalgamated with the *Midland Bank* in 1918. The London Joint Stock Bank was run as a highly centralized company under meticulous financial control. The Cumberland Union Bank became one of its 179 branches throughout the country.

William Carruthers (b.1829) had his chemist shop at 16 Pow Street from at least 1870. Two decades later he had been joined in partnership by his son Robert G.(b.1863) By 1902, the chemist shop had been taken

---

During the 1880s and 1890s this local bank was under great pressure from its shareholders having advanced no less than 8% of its assets to the *West Cumberland Iron and Steel Company* and another 5% to the *Maryport Haematite Iron Company*.

over by G. Derwent Paterson. Twenty five years later, the business had been acquired by *Taylors Dispensing Chemists*. More commonly known as Taylor's Drug Store, they were one of the first national companies to appear on Workington's street.

On the corner of Pow Street and Sanderson Street, across the road from the Cumberland Union Bank was another drapers shop ran by brothers Wallace and Eldred Ritson. They were the sons of joiner, Thomas Ritson who lived in nearby Edkin Street. Two other Ritson brothers, Fred and Thomas also ran an ironmongers at 23 Pow Street. Wallace Ritson (1867-1938) was something of an local historian and poet, his work was often published in the local newspapers. We should be quiet indebted to this gentleman whose notes reveal little gems of history, some of which would otherwise be long lost and forgotten forever.

Upon the site of the present Marks and Spencer store [01] was the Griffin Hotel at 38 Pow Street, next door to the District Bank. This building started life as a branch of the Bank of Whitehaven. One of its directors was local building contractor Richard H. Hodgson, who lived at Field House. In the 1880s, the bank agent or branch manager was former shipbuilder and accountant, Joseph Tordiff Fell (1831-1892). In 1916, the Bank of Whitehaven was acquired by the *Manchester and Liverpool District Bank*. Eight years or so later, it's name was shortened and became known as the District Bank.

Almost opposite the Griffin Hotel, set well back from the street was the Workington Savings Bank [02]. The most striking feature of this old building was its portico front entrance, supported on four stone columns. In January 1935, this bank moved into new premises in Murray Road, next to what was then the Liverpool Victoria Insurance company (almost opposite the Bus Station). By 1953, the savings bank had been absorbed into the *Trustees Savings Bank* (now the TSB) moved once again to new premises at 10 Finkle Street (on the corner of Craggs Lane). Thereafter the original Pow Street building became part of the Drill Hall.

Another long standing family business in the town is Haighs pork butchers at 15 Pow Street, almost opposite where the Griffin Hotel stood. It certainly existed in 1892 when it was ran by Jonas H. Haigh. Although his original shop may well have been somewhere on the opposite side of Pow Street. The family also then ran a further butchers shop at 75 Senhouse Street. By the 1950s, the butchers was trading as Frank Haigh & Son. Wallace Ritson tells us that *"where Haighs are today"* was the

[01] In 1974, the old Griffin Hotel, the former District Bank (now amalgamated with the National Westminster) Messengers florists, and the Dewhurst butchers premises were demolished and a new Presto store built on the site. This building was later taken over by Marks and Spencer.■
[02] For more details see *History of Workington* - Vol. 1 (page 206-7)■

home and workshop of woodcarver George Brooker. *"He carved figureheads for windjammers, and it said he was so clever he could have knocked an aphrodite out with a hatchet."* Brooker was *"Liverpudlian"* born in 1824 and later retired to live at Barmon House, in High Street. The exact location of Barmon house is not totally clear, it has been suggested that it was another name for Shannon House.

Just a few doors away from Haighs was the shop of John James Little, another butcher and bacon curer. His business was established in 1867 and traded there until around 1901. Next to the Royal Oak public house was Margaret Marsh's "Taffy" or Toffee shop. In 1935 Wallace Ritson wrote a charming descriptive poem about this little sweet shop, which existed up until around 1890. His poem is reproduced far right and tells us so much about both the building and Pow Street with it's *"odd, old lanes"*.

Lamplugh born, Margaret Marsh (1811-1900) a

RIGHT - The Workington Savings Bank was located almost opposite the Griffin Hotel, set well back from the street. The most striking feature of this old building was its portico front entrance, supported on four stone columns. ∎

"*sturdy little woman*" was also a "*letter carrier or post woman*". After she retired from the "*old whitewashed shop*", she went to live with her daughter Mrs. Mary A. Teasdale at 49 Finkle Street. By 1892, Kit Robinson's cloggers shop now occupied her old Pow Street sweet shop. Margaret died in 1900, aged 89 and is buried in St. Johns Churchyard. But her name lived on for a few more years as her daughters also ran a sweet shop and continued to trade as Margaret Marsh. Bulmers (1901) places her shop close to the Old Appletree Inn, in Finkle Street.

In the 1870s, on the site of the Argentine Meat Company's premises in Pow Street, was once another grocers shop ran by Peter Kelly and Patrick McMullen (father of councillor John McMullen). "Big Pat" McMullen (1821-82) was said to have once been the works manager at the Workington Haematite Ironworks at Oldside, whilst at the time of his death he was the licensee of the Blue Bell Inn in King Street. He is also once believed to have ran a small brewery on Ramsey Brow. The site of this brewery is a little mysterious, how successful the venture was is also not too clear. It is likely that it was located in or close too the former coachbuilders shop at 14 Ramsey Brow. After they closed their grocer's shop, Peter Kelly began building houses. Kelly Street, off Peter Street and John Street is named after the developer.

Set back from the street is the Royal Oak public house at 25 Pow Street. One of at least four pubs in the town to once carry the same name. Others were located in Priestgate (Church Street), Fox Lane and Wilson Street. It is probable that a inn existed on this site well before the 1850s, but its early name(s) remain something of a mystery. There is a suggestion that it may have once been called the Pack Horse Inn or even the Highland Laddie. The Bewley family ran the Royal Oak around the turn of the century.

A large house once stood on the east corner of the junction of John Street and Pow Street. It was occupied by Thomas Iredale [01] (of Iredale Bros.) who ran the High Brewery. Ritson tells us that the house had its kitchens in the cellar, lit by a cavity "*in line with the front of the street*". This was protected by a line of railings to "*guard against anyone coming from the Royal Oak from falling into it.*" The front entrance door of the house was reached by a "*broad flag*" which crossed from the street to the front step. We can compare this arrangement to numbers 33 and 35 Brow Top which still exists today.

When this house was demolished it was replaced by Henry McAleer's extensive boot and shoe emporium. A newspaper advertisement in 1876, boasted the shop had

Margaret Marsh's Taffy Shop

Those odd, old lanes,
　　　those old-time streets,
With little shops where
　　　we bought sweets.
Sweets in bags and paper boxes,
Old Ann Riley's, Granny Fox's.
Else with ha'pence we would dash,
To buy then from old Margaret "Mash".
We called her so, but we had ways,
Of saying names in those old days.
Margaret had the funniest shop,
That ever made the curious stop.
On quainter house sight lit,
Big cobbles formed the base of it.
Its white-washed walls had
　　　lots of stones,
Made round and smooth by Davy Jones.
The chimney, stuck out up the gable,
Gave room inside for bed and table.
Twelve little panes the window made,
In which were shown the things of trade.
Gingerbread horses, blest of nags,
Tins of taffy and lucky bags;
Grand mint marbles and
　　　sticks of spanish,
Lots of things that were
　　　made to vanish;
But we were always short of brass,
And most were nose glued to the glass;
But Oh, to push the quaint half-door,
To spend the little that we bore.
But those times never more can be,
For Margaret is a memory.
And that old curious cobble shop.
A thing that now and then will pop
Up with remembered things we knew,
When we have little else to do.

Wallace Ritson
1935

[01] Thomas Iredale when he was first elected to the Local Board, replace William Birkett. He stood down from the Borough Council in 1901, having served the town for 27 years. Iredale died in September 1913, at Holm Acre on Park End Road, just a fortnight before his 79th birthday.
He was the first deputy Mayor to the first Mayor Henry Frazer Curwen, and Mayor himsef in 1890-1. Having started his working life as a clerk at the Whitehaven branch of the Cumberland Union Bank. After joining the family brewing business, he eventually became a director of the same bank. His brother was Peter Iredale who lived at Bankfield.

In 1876, Henry McAleer who ran his boot and shoe emporium in Pow Street, boasted the shop had in stock over 4000 pairs of boots and shoes. Prices varied from 4/9 to 15/6 a pair (or 24p to 78p).

in stock over 4000 pairs of boots and shoes. Prices varied from 4/9 to 15/6 a pair (or 24p to 78p). In June 1909, a window was erected to the memory of Henry McAleer, at Our Lady and St. Michaels Roman Catholic Church, on Banklands. During the early 1920s, McAleer's shop was replaced by the new premises of the *Bank of Liverpool and Martins Ltd.* This company subsequently became part of the National Provincial Bank, eventually merging with the *Westminster Bank* to become the *National Westminster Bank* we know today.

On the other side of the Royal Oak and next door to Henry McAleer was the clock and watchmaker's shop of John Mandale at 29 Pow Street. At one time above the shopfront was a large circular clock projecting into the street, known affectionately as Mandales clock. Over the years it became a common meeting place for young ladies and men, particularly in the early part of the century. John Mandale (b.1853) and his wife Mary are believed to have opened the shop around 1881. He was born in Harrington and his wife originated in Yorkshire. The watchmaker was later joined in the business by his son and subsequently traded as John Mandale & Son. He also served as a member of the Workington School Board for many years.

On the other side corner, opposite the National Westminster Bank was W. H. Smith & Son, the well-known newsagent and stationer. They moved to this compact two storey shop around 1950, having previously occupied premises at 5 South William Street, opposite the Wesleyan methodist church. Before then the company had a news stand and bookstall at Workington's Low railway station. This national company disappeared from the town when this block of property, which included the Grapes Inn and Goss' grocers shop was demolished to make way for the new shopping precinct in the late 1960s.

The Grapes Inn had been in existence since at least the 1830s, when Elizabeth Kelsick was the licensee. Like the Royal Oak, there were once two other Workington pubs with the same name. These were located in Brow Top and the other in King Street (which still survives today). Up until the 1950s, there was still a number of stables and a hay loft at the rear of the Grapes in Pow Street. A throw back from the days before the motor car, when many people travelled on horseback or in a pony and trap. Just across the road from the Grapes on the corner of Tiffin Lane, was the chemist shop of James Thompson (1845-1906). This site was later occupied by the dry cleaners, Johnston Bros. Who had their head office at the Bootle Dye Works, in Liverpool.

One of the town's first post offices was located at 62 Pow Street where Marks and Spencer later built their first store. (today the site is occupied by the Iceland foodstore). It was ran by Isaac Burnett (b.1838) assisted later by his son George who was the telegraphist, responsible for sending and receiving telegrams. After the post office moved to new premises in John Street, the building was taken over by fishmonger and game dealer Robert Nicholson. He occupied the shop until it was purchased by Marks and Spencers in 1936. Nicholson moved their fishmongers to new premises, almost directly across the road in Pow Street. To the rear of Nicholson's old shop was the joiners shop of Edgar and Henderson. To build their new store Marks & Spencer also demolished a row of small cottages fronting onto Ladies Walk property and others in Tiffin Lane

Marks and Spencer opened their new Workington store on 10 July 1939. Between 1931 and 1939, this fast expanding company rebuilt or completed 162 new stores throughout the country. By 1939 they had a further 72 outlets, all then displaying a range of quality merchandise of which no single item cost more than five shillings. They were growing rapidly to rival the other high street giant F. W Woolworth, who had built their new store in the town almost ten years earlier. Woolworths then boasted that everything in their store was either 3d (1.25p) or 6d (2.5p). Both stores were now located almost next door to each other with only a narrow little shop separating each concern.

The shop at 64 Pow street had previously been a small grocers run by tea dealer John Fletcher. Before being taken over by fruiterer Thomas Jarman (b.1850), who also had a greengrocers in Falcon Place. In 1901, John Smith briefly sold musical instruments from the property. In 1930 it was acquired by Boots the chemist, another national concern and was their first shop in the town. In 1959-60, when Boots relocated to new premises on Murray Road, Marks & Spencer jumped in and bought 64 Pow Street. They demolished the building, extended their store and remodelled the shopfront. Now they did stand side by side with rivals F. W. Woolworths.

The arrival of these major companies such as Woolworths, Boots and M&S really signalled the beginning of the end for the smaller and quite independent local businesses that originally filled both sides of Pow Street. A snapshot of the street in the 1870s, reveals shops ran by Thomas Salkeld - leather seller, William Carruthers - druggist and chemist, Henry McAleer - shoemaker, John P. Waite - hatter, William Barnes - draper, Henry Hall -

Marks and Spencer opened their new Workington store on 10 July 1939. Between 1931 and 1939, this fast expanding company rebuilt or completed 162 new stores throughout the country.

ABOVE - Boots the chemists, first shop in the town at 64 Pow Street, next to Woolworths. ■

watchmaker, John Fletcher - grocer. David Gilson - the tailor. Yet from the 1930s onwards, these larger stores began to appear on the high streets of the country, pushing up rents, property prices and leaving little space for the small local traders. Workington's Pow Street was really no exception.

Immediately beside the large F. W. Woolworth store was the Clydesdale Bank. This quite elaborate three storey building was erected around 1880-1. It extended to the east side of the railway line north out of Central Station, up to Seaton. [01] This double track of the Cleator & Workington Junction Railway ran through a cutting under the bridge at the junction between Pow Street and Finkle Street. This bridge first opened in November 1877, was later widened as the thoroughfare was opened up. Some of the adjoining later properties are actually built over the railway cutting.[02] So much so that when you stand at this point today, it is difficult to imagine the railway passing below your feet. Yet even in the 1950s when this area was still quite open, steam trains regularly passed back and forth along this line, with smoke and steam from their boilers billowing into the street above.

For over twenty years, one of the first managers or agents of the Clydesdale Bank was Workington born Henry Bowes (1844-1908). His father, also Henry Bowes (1798-1859) was an attorney and conveyancer who lived in Christian street. Henry (snr.) was also the first secretary of Workington Savings Bank.

On the other corner of Finkle Street and Speedwell Lane was Wildridges painters and plumber shop. The small shop was *"kept by"* husband and wife, William

[01] Up until 1877, before the C&WJR was built through the town, there were five small cottages on the east side of Speedwell Lane. Together with a much larger house on the corner of Pow Street and Speedwell Lane, for many years occupied by Issac Thompson.■
[02] The underside of the original bridges and these properties can still be clearly seen if you glance upward as you walk down from Central Square down to the Cloffolks along this old line (now a road).■

BELOW - The C&WJR 0-6-0 saddle tank engine BRIGHAM HILL which hauled coal trucks along the railway lines through the town.

(1811-1897) and Jane (1809-1891) Wildridge. Established before 1847, almost four decades later Wildridge employed five men and two boys. The Finkle Street shop is also mentioned in the writings of Wallace Ritson. He well remembered old Mr Wildridge also selling marbles and once he spent *"all his school money there getting a new supply"*. The young Ritson, who then lived in one of the tiny cottages in Tiffin Lane *"got something more when he got home"*.

Opposite the original Marks and Spencer store and next to the Grapes public house was Joseph Goss' grocers shop. Built before WW1, one interesting feature of this single storey corner property was its curved shopfront and slated roof. At one time Goss had three other shops in the town, at 59 Harrington Road, 295 Moss Bay Road and their original store on the corner of Senhouse Street and Station Road. The business was said to have been established in 1848, although the first references to this concern in Workington date from around the turn of the century. Some records suggest Joseph Goss orginated from St. Bees. When the Station Road shop eventually closed in the 1970s, it is believed some of the antiquated old shopfittings were acquired by the Beamish Museum in the north east.

When Pow Street was widened and opened up immediately in front of the Woolworths store a row of new shops were built following the line of the present properties. One of these shop units was the branch shop of Whitehaven based W. H. Moss & Sons. Cockermouth born, William Henry Moss (b.1834) started his printers and stationers business around 1884. When he purchased the Whitehaven printing works of John Welsh, following the death of its proprietor. The Workington branch was opened around WW1, and was thought to have been run by William's son Joseph Mortimer Moss. As the business expanded further it became a limited company, and was eventually acquired by C. N. Print in 1968.

Adjoining Moss' stationery shop was Reas bakers and confectioners. This business was believed to have been established in 1924 by the Rea family from Cockermouth. It is thought to have been initially ran by Florence Mary Rea (1863-1929) the sister of William Wallace Rea (1873-1924) who kept the Globe Hotel in Cockermouth's Main Street. By the late 1930s, the Workington based business passed through the family to Mrs. M. E. Mitchell. Whilst in it's latter years it was ran by Jack Mitchell (1913-88). During the 1950s, their was a *"silver service"* entered through Reas bakers shop. Here was served *"morning coffee, luncheons and afternoon or high*

Mr Wildridge also sold marbles and a young Wallace Ritson once spent *"all his school money there getting a new supply. He got something more when he got home"*.

teas". Whilst a couple of doors along Pow Street, next to Goss grocers shop was Reasbar. Here the confectioners ran a modern 1950s style snack bar, selling *"coffee, light snacks, ice cream and soda fountain drinks"*. In October 1955, the Borough Council approved plans for a new bakery immediately to the rear of Reas shops.

The building that dominates the junction of Pow Street and Finkle Street is the old post office premises on the corner of Murray Road and Finkle Street. Completed in 1904 the towns main post office was located here for over ninety years. It also served as the main postal sorting office, until this was located to James street (within the premises now occupied by G. H. Chambers)

James Howard Messenger's stationers and bookshop at 22 Finkle Street is said to have been founded in 1868. The business was thought to have been first established by Rev. John E. Carmichael (b.1841) Workington born Carmichael was also a Primitive Methodist minister. By the 1930s, the bookshop was then ran by his son-in law

BELOW - The new Appletree Inn in Finkle Street. Built in 1899, by the Borough Council as compensation for an older pub that was demolished so the street could be widened. ■

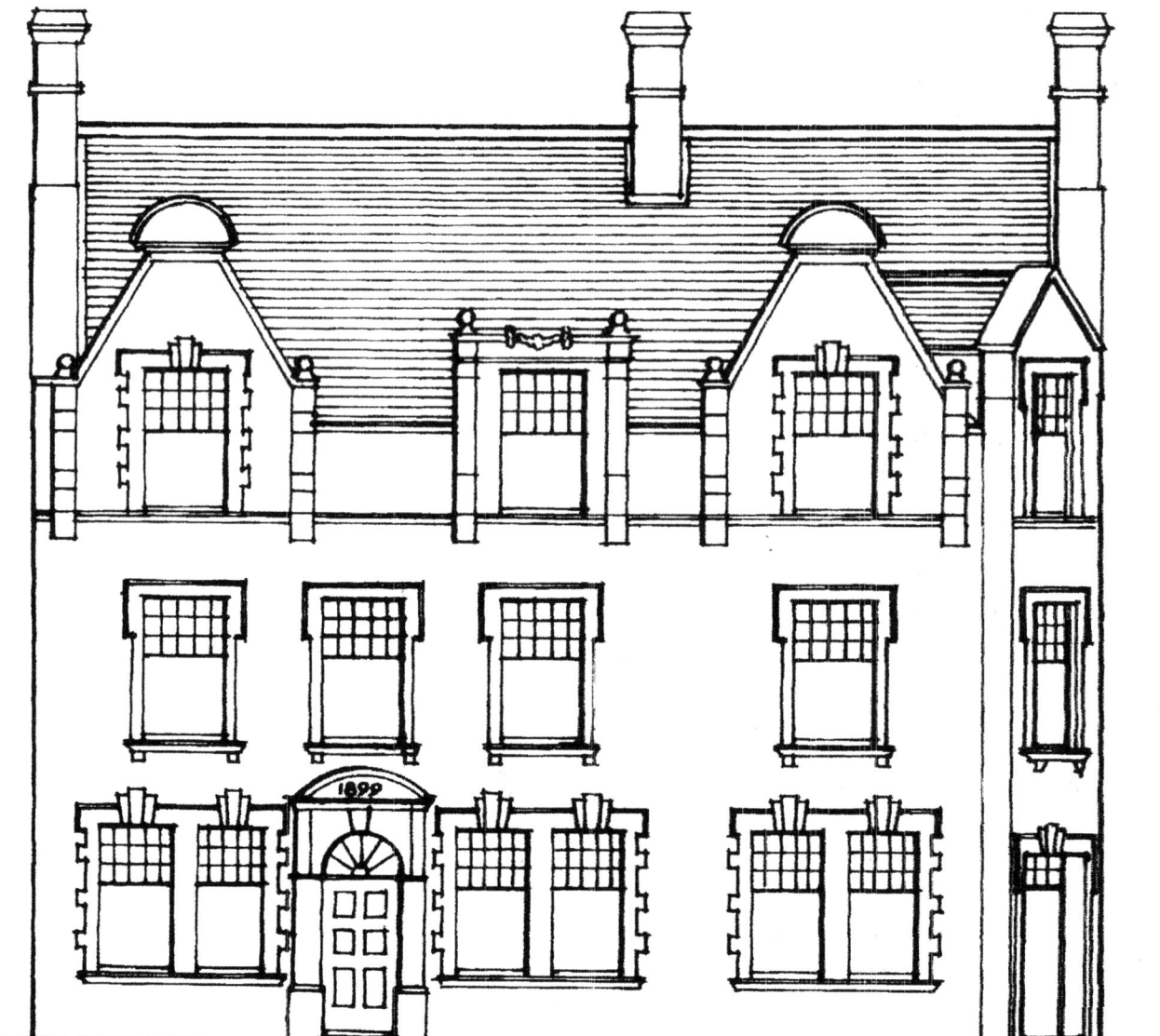

and continued to trade for at least another two decades.

Originally, Finkle Street was once very much narrower than today. The 1936 notes of Joseph Scott (headmaster at Victoria School for fifty years) tell us that he could well remember when *"people could almost shake hands from the opposite windows across the narrow street."* Early photograph tend to suggest that this may be something of an exaggeration. During the late 1890s, in an effort to widen the street, the Borough Council acquired much of the property on its south side.

Amongst these building was the original Appletree Inn owned by Workington Brewery. One condition of its sale to the Corporation was that they replace the public house with a new building, once the street was widened. The new Appletree was built in 1899 by local building contractor, James Irwin Wilson.[01] Upon it's completion it was then exchanged with the older Appletree Inn building. Originally, it was proposed to widen Finkle street by just demolishing the front wall of the old pub and convert the building into a shop and house. But these plans were later abandoned once work had began, and the entire property was cleared.

Some readers will remember that for a great many years the land to the rear of Finkle Street, extending south to Oxford Street and bounded by Vulcans Lane (to the west) and the railway line of the C&WJR (to the east) lay almost undeveloped. It was simply fields, known as the Fairfield, as it was used as a site for visiting fairs and circuses.

Murray Road was first laid out during the early 1900s, and was named after its owner and developer William Murray. The street name was formally adopted by the Borough Council in 1904. He was also responsible for building the majority of houses in Warwick Place and Upton Street.

In 1904, Murray Road, named after the developer William Murray, appears to have been adopted by the Council. He was also responsible for building much of Warwick Place [02] and Upton Street. Plans for the first 13 shops in Murray Road were approved by the Corporation in March 1908. Twenty years later, a further eight shops and dwellings were approved. The street was not fully set out to link Oxford Street and Pow Street until the summer of 1931. One of the longest serving concerns here is John Walker, the watchmakers and jewellers. This business was commenced in the years before 1890 and originally had premises in South William Street, immediately opposite the Wesleyan methodist Church. Although not too clear it is believed that John Walker may

Murray Road was first laid out during the early 1900s, and was named after its owner and developer William Murray.

[01] The 1881 census lists building contractor James Irwin Wilson (1831-1894) living at 5 North Watts Street. He was responsible for building many new properties in the town. His business was also something of a family concern, his sons William and Joseph being stone masons. Whilst John was a joiner and cabinet maker. ■
[02] Up until 1904, Warwick Place was more commonly referred to as Warwick Street. The majority of it's houses were built between 1901 and 1908. ■

well have been related to Joseph Walker, an earlier watchmaker in Bridge Street.

The large three storey department store immediately beside the bus station was built by the Whitehaven Beehive. Opened in November 1936, the branch store trading for many years as Brownes. In 1954, a large illuminated sign bearing the company name in gold lettering was erected at roof level. Another interesting feature of the shop was how Brownes handled the payments for purchases. Each sale was hand written in a receipt book and a copy and the customers money was then deposited in a cylindrical container (about 125mm long and 50mm diameter). This was then placed in a tube and using a blast of compressed air was shot along a network of pipes to the accounts office. Here the receipt was checked and any change was placed back in the container. It was then shot back along the pipe and returned to the shop assistant, who gave the change to the customer. Although more than a little time consuming, we can marvel at this almost magical old check-out system.

The corner of Murray Road, Vulcans Lane and Oxford Street is dominated by the large red brick bus station. Built in 1926 for *Cumberland Motor Services Limited* by Thomas Johnstone. It is said to be the *"first purpose built covered bus station in England"*. Bus services were only introduced in the period following WW1, and by 1924 there was a regular timetable of services to and from the principle towns in West Cumberland. Workington bus station, is enclosed under a trussed roof, and at it's two entrances off Vulcans lane and Murray Road are imposing elevations of red-brick and stone. Originally above each entrance was a large stone mullioned window, but these were later removed and replaced with brick in-fill panels. The offices were once located adjacent to the Murray Road entrance. In the mid 1950s, these were converted into a travel shop. Two smaller windows in the facade were replaced with one large plate glass window, above and below being finished with black ceramic tiles. In September 1939, the Borough Council approved plans to extend the Bus Station along the east side of Vulcans Lane. Here were built a long row of workshops and garages, these were demolished in recent years and the site is presently a car park.

Just across the road from the bus station on the opposite corner of Murray Road was the Westminster Bank. They moved here from 38 South William Street, opposite the Royal Hotel on the corner of William Street. After the merger of the Westminster with the National Provincial Bank (who already had a branch on the corner of

Although more than a little time consuming by todays standards, we can marvel at the almost magical old check-out system in Brownes department store.

Pow Street and John Street) the Murray Road building was acquired by the West Cumbria Building Society (now the Cumberland Building Society).

Like Finkle Street, South William Street was once much narrower than today, particularly opposite the Wesleyan methodist Church. Here there were several small cottages and little shops on the south side of South William Street. One of which was the watchmakers shop of John Walker. In 1899, these were demolished and set back in order "to keep a straight line with" the front railings of the Congregational Church.

Tuscan Villa was the large detached house on the north side of South William Street, set back from the street in its own grounds. The Guy family who built this property lived in the house until the 1880s. In February 1888, Tuscan Villa was put up for sale and it is thought to have been purchased by John Milburn (of the Hawkshead Iron and Brass foundry). He himself lived there until the mid 1890s, when he moved to East Croft, High Harrington. By the turn of the century, Tuscan Villa had passed to John L. Yeowart. Yeowart ran a couple of draper and milliners shops in Wilson street and Washington street. Later, Dr. Fray Ormrod (1843-1903) is noted as living in the property until his death in November 1903. In 1949, Tuscan Villa was converted into a *"Boarding House and Cafe"* by Eric L. Jones and Mrs. Hester (of 45 Elizabeth Street). Demolished in 1979-80, the site is now occupied by Ann Burrows Health Centre.

At the junction of James Street and South William Street, there was once two houses at street level, and two others at first floor level. These were reached from the street by a flight of stone stairs between the houses. On the upper level lived Old Kate Sparks, legend has it she could tell fortunes. Kate (of Irish decent) was the wife of

BELOW - Single deck bus used by Cumberland Motor Services on route in Workington during the mid 1920s. ∎

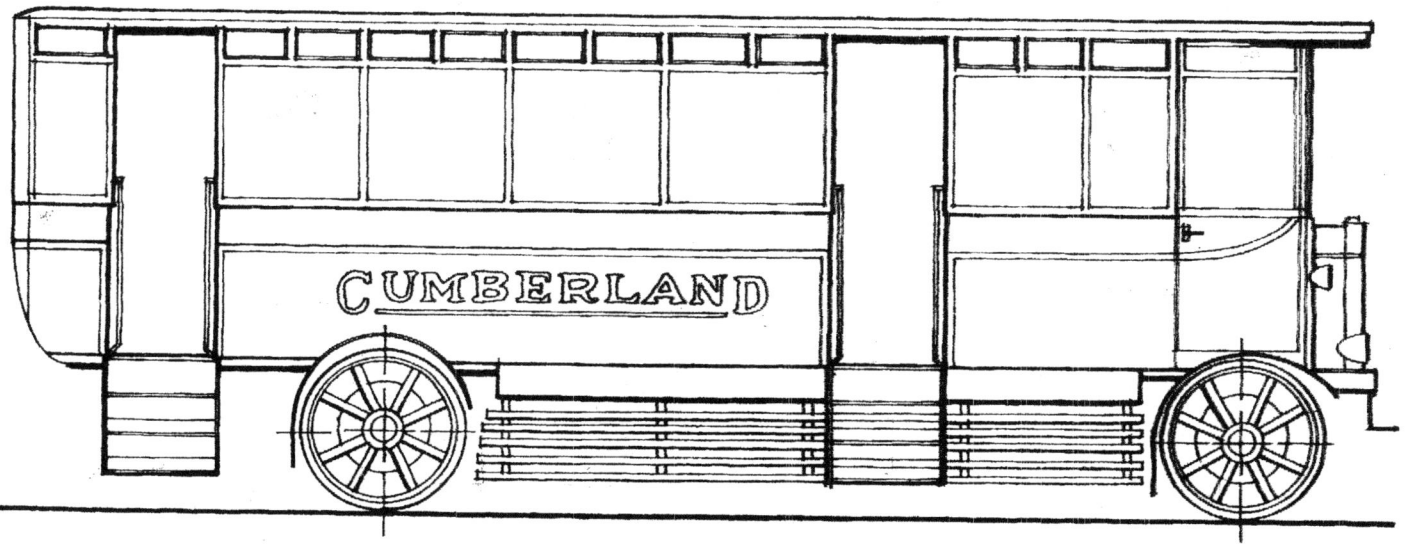

labourer John Sparks

Dr. Charles McKerrow (1855-1940) a physician and surgeon lived at Croft House, in South William Street. He trained at Glasgow, taking up his first appointment in the town around 1880. For a short time he was in partnership with Dr. Alexander Hogg at 9-11 Derwent Street, until his untimely death in 1883. Dr. McKerrow went on to play a major role in the building and running of Workington Infirmary. In 1927, in partnership with his son Mungo and daughter Elizabeth (both qualified doctors) they opened a new surgery in James Street. Mungo McKerrow's son Neil, who himself qualified as a doctor after WW2, later also joined the practice. The majority of the McKerrow family are interred in the graveyard of St. Margaret's church at Wythop. [01]

In March 1935, the Borough Council approved plans for a new joiners workshop, in James Street for G. H. Chambers. This business was formed by George Henry Chambers (1854-1924) when they first moved to the town in 1881. Records certainly suggest that his wife Jessie Amelia Chambers (1856-1936) also played an active part in the family concern. The joinery business was originally based in Dean Street. The couple also ran a glass, china and earthenware shop at 19 Fisher Street for around 30 years. Chambers is credited with building a large part of Station Road, and may at this time have been in partnership with builder Joseph Tolson (of Senhouse Place). After the death of George Chambers in February 1924,

[01] Charles and his wife, Margaret Morison McKerrow are buried at Wythop, alongside their four of their children - Elizabeth (1884-1975), William Alexander Hogg (1885-1972), Charles (1885-1957) and Mungo (d.1966).

BELOW - Tuscan Villa, the large detached house which was built by the Guy family in South William Street. ■

the business was continued by his son Ernest E. Chambers (who lived at Farndale in Vulcans Lane). Today, this long established business is ran by the fourth generation of the Chambers family and is one of the oldest surviving business in the town.

Up until 1877, on the north west corner of Fisher Street and William Street was the Ropemakers Arms. Named by virtue of Fishers ropeworks which was located nearby. This public house was purchased at auction by Iredale Bros. (of the High Brewery). They paid its owner Thomas Sealby, £2,920 for the *"old established inn"*. After extensive alterations the pub re-opened as the Royal Hotel during the summer of 1878. During the 1880's, quoiting was an extremely popular game in the town. Several of the local public houses had their own pits, including the Royal Hotel, Railway Hotel and the Griffin Hotel. In June 1881, the Royal Hotel was the scene of an demonstration by William McGregor, the England's champion quoiter.

In 1883, we know the Albert Hall on Fisher Street (adjoining the Royal Hotel on the corner of William Street) also accommodated the West Cumberland Auction Mart. Auctions in the 600-seater hall, being ran by the partnership of George Kirkwood and John Bland. South Shields born Kirkwood had moved to the town from Middlesborough in 1875. When the Albert Hall was altered in 1935, it's proprietor was Alfred Ernest Goodwin, who ran it as a dance hall with an adjoining billiards saloon.

On the north west corner of Fisher Street and North Watts Street was Dent Hall, another public hall. Here Christopher E. Edmundson (its proprietor) also had one of the earliest dental practices in the town. This dentist is remembered as travelling around the town on a curious 5 hp. motor tricycle, which it is said he built himself. The vehicle had two seats in the front and one in the rear. When it was first registered in March 1904, it carried the number AO 165. A photograph belonging to Joan Crellin exists showing this early motor tricycle. Pictured in the passenger seat beside Christopher Edmundson is Albert Dunn, who ran a motor engineers and vehicle repair shop in Udale Street. The Dudd family also ran a garage in Guard Street. The Edmundson dental business was continued by later generations of the family until the 1980s. Although over the years, the dental surgery moved first to 21 Station Road, and then to premises on the north side of Belverdere Street. By 1938, Dent Hall was occupied by auctioneer James Lancaster.

It was October 1883, when Duke Street was formally

ABOVE - George Kirkwood and George Bland ran regular auction sales at the Albert Hall in Fisher Street. ∎

named by the Borough Council. Situated behind the Royal Hotel, two of the first plots were acquired by the Salvation Army for a new mission hall, and the Plymouth Brethren. The foundation stone for the new Salvation Army Mission was laid on 11 April 1884. The large grocers shop on the corner of Fisher Street and Due Street, next to the Albert Hall was once occupied by the Fox brothers. Charles J. Fox started the business in 1874, and their first shop was on the corner of William Street and Church Street at number 72. Nearly sixty years later the business was still in operation. The Fisher Street shop opened in 1890, and its first manager was James Hesson. He had started with the firm as an errand boy and eventually fulfilled 50 years of service with the long established family grocers.

Brow Top which runs almost parallel with Finkle Street was once the main thoroughfare through the town, and was often referred to as *"Broo'Top"*. Derwent House, almost on the corner of Speedwell Lane was built in the early 1840s by shipbuilder James Alexander (1799-1881) who occupied the property until his death. The *"well-built"* imposing house was then sold at auction by James Jackson (of Duke Street, Whitehaven). The sale particulars reveal the extensive property had its dining room, kitchen and two other *"entertaining"* rooms on the ground floor. Like the majority of larger houses of this period, there was both front and back staircases allowing the servants to easily move around the house. Across the front of the property, on the first floor level was a very large Drawing room *"commanding extensive views of the Solway Firth and the surrounding country"*. Together with two large bedrooms and a bathroom. On the upper floor were four further *"capital"* bedrooms and two dressing rooms.

At the rear of Derwent House, was a large garden which then extended to Finkle Street. The auctioneer naturally pointing out the development potential, where *"premises for trade purposes might be erected"* on this busy *"business thoroughfare"*. Derwent House was purchased for £1,450 by John Jessop. He had a house furnisher's business on the corner of Sanderson Street and Washington Street. By 1892, he had built over the garden at Derwent House and added a further shop fronting onto Finkle Street. What exactly happened to John Jessop has yet to be revealed, but within a decade his business had been acquired by J. T Lister [01] In December 1900, the Borough Council approved plans to alter the premises, providing a new shop and warehouse for Mr Lister. This covered the entire site from Finkle Street through to Brow

Brow Top which runs almost parallel with Finkle Street was once the main thoroughfare through the town, and was often referred to as *"Broo'Top"*.

[01] J. T. Lister lived in Portland Square. It is perhaps likely that Lister was first employed by John Jessop and took over the business, following his death or retirement. The present day Listers, who still trade from 44 Finkle Street, claims to trace it's roots back to 1870

Top, although the facade of Derwent House in Brow Top remained very much intact. The business then trading as the *"Derwent Furnishing House"*, claiming to be the *"complete house furnisher, upholster and ironmonger"*.

By 1924, the company was now trading as Lister and Smallwood. You could purchase a *"strongly made oak 4ft wardrobe and chest of draws, with mirror"* for around £25.00. But this partnership seems to have been dissolved by 1938, as Egbert T. Smallwood (b.1878) then had his own furniture shop at 26-28 Pow Street (next to the District Bank). Listers had also moved to new premises at 44 Finkle Street, still occupied by the firm today. This was formerly occupied by pawnbroker, Caroline Cottier. The furnishers later greatly extended these premises, taking in what was once known as Middletons Yard. This was an area containing around seven small cottages, once located between buildings on Finkle Street and Brow Top. The 1881 census reveals that these little houses reached from Woods Lane, surprisingly accommodated over forty people, mainly ironworkers and their families.

Between 1905-25, part of Derwent House was also occupied by the United Club. This organisation then moved to their present premises in Portland Square, on the corner of Cavendish Street. This large house in the cobbled square was once occupied by Dr. William Lindow Dickinson (1789-1853) the well known physi-

LEFT - Listers furniture store on Finkle Street, which extended into Derwent House on Brow Top. ■

cian and surgeon in the town. After Listers left the Derwent House premises at least part of the building was converted into a billiard hall. In March 1954, Simmons Furniturers received approval to convert the premises back to a furnishers store. This large company had many other stores across the North of England, with branches in Carlisle, Newcastle, Gateshead and Sunderland.. The Finkle Street elevation was somewhat simplified, with the removal of the ornate parapet wall and stonework at roof level.

Almost opposite Derwent House in Brow Top were two small cottages (2 and 4 Brow Top) at a narrow point in the street. These were acquired by the Corporation and demolished in January 1905. For many years, Bridekirk born Robert Moncrieff had his boot and shoe maker at 4 Brow Top. Being assisted in the business by his son David. Osborn House at 31 Brow Top was believed to have been built for ship owner Thomas Osborn. After his death in 1841, it continued to be occupied by his wife Jane and their family. The house then passed to his unmarried daughter Bilhah Osborn (1829-1907). She continued to live in the large house drawing an income from her father's investments.

Derwent Street runs from the west end of Brow Top down to the corner of William Street. There was originally large terraced houses to either side of this cobbled street, many being built in the eighteenth century. Those on the south side were generally much better quality than those opposite and many had large enclosed gardens extending back towards South William Street. Those dwellings on the north side of Derwent Street were built on the top of the steep bank sloping down to what we know today as the Cloffolks and were quite different. Few had anything other than a small back yard and built immediately behind these homes upon this incline were a maze little back to back cottages. This area between Griffin Street and Derwent Street was known as the Brows, and contained a mass of substandard properties. In many cases the floors of some houses were beneath ground level, causing major dampness problems. With the cottages so closely huddled together, there was little natural light or open spaces. Amid the slums and the squalor of the Brows, it was common for three or four adults and several children to live, cook and sleep in a single *"damp and dark"* room. There was often just one water-closet or toilet shared by upto four families. All were virtually low wage earners, often working for less than a £1 a week, *"if they worked at all"*. Of this they paid around 2/6 (12½p) a week rent for their dilapidated homes.

This area between Griffin Street and Derwent Street was known as the Brows, and contained a mass of substandard properties. In many cases the floors of some houses were beneath ground level, causing major dampness problems. With the cottages so closely huddled together, there was little natural light or open spaces.

The hotchpotch of cottages on the Brows were reached from very narrow cobbled passages that fell steeply down to Griffin Street below. As the homes stepped down the slope, these little dark lanes often contained long flights of stone steps with the occasional landing at the entrance to a house. From east to west there were five such passages called Longstairs, Wildridges Row, Robinsons Brow, Stoney Brow and Nags Head Lane.

For decades the overcrowding and condition of the housing in the Brows area was of great concern to first the Local Board and then the Borough Council that succeeded them. Around the turn of the century, Dr. John Highet the towns Medical Officer of Health inspected many of the properties personally and wrote several very descriptive reports. He tells us 28 Derwent Street *"has nine rooms, five of which are bedrooms. In the house there are seven families, consisting of 16 adults and 15 children (aged 1-14). Five families occupy one room for living and sleeping - there is no yard and the water closet is situated so the whole of the inmates must pass through a room occupied by a man, his wife and three children "*.

Dr. Highet also recorded their dilapidated condition and the *"antiquated character"* of the properties. All suffered from severe penetrating dampness, had no real heating and had broken ill-fitting windows for many years. Referring to their *"narrowness, closeness and bad arrangement"*, he added that they *"want for air, light, ventilation and proper conveniences. Some houses are so dark and require lamp light all through the winter months day and night"*. He pointed out that they *"caused a deadly danger to the health of the inhabitants"*, and adding that such an environment can only *"stunt and wither social progress"*. The only real alternative was the *"total extinction of these unfit properties"*.

When many of the worst dwellings were closed by the Council and fell into further disrepair, large blocks of the Brows became unoccupied. By 1902, the Brows contained around 46 *"damp and decrepit"* tenements of which at least 30 were still occupied. The Council had condemned the remainder as being *"unfit for habitation"*. Following the success of its first *"council houses"* in Blackburn Street [01], the local authority came up with an ambitious plan to clear the area, including Griffin Street, and to build 21 new dwellings in five blocks. But the scheme was never implemented.

In April 1909, many of the remaining empty properties in the Brows were considered to be in a "dangerous condition". Apparently, much of the internal timbers had

Dr. Highet pointed out that the condition of the Brows *"caused a deadly danger to the health of the inhabitants"*, and adding that such an environment can only *"stunt and wither social progress"*. The only real alternative was the *"total extinction of these unfit properties"*.

[01] In March 1901, Dr. John Highet (the town's medical officer of health) suggested to the Borough Council that they could use the *Housing Act of Working Classes Act 1890* to provide Workington with new *"housing for the working classes"*. Within weeks, plans had been prepared for the town's first *"council houses"*. These were eventually built on the west side of Blackburn Street. The land was purchased from the town's Roman Catholic church for £640. Each of the eighteen houses, built by contractor R. Bragg cost the equivalent of £189 each. The weekly rents were fixed at 5/6 (27½p), at a time when the average weekly wage of a working man in the town was just 20s (£1) per week. To qualify for one of these new *"corporation"* houses, you had to be *"a bona-fide working man and not earning high wages"*. ∎

been removed and used by adjoining households for firewood. In January 1917, the demolition of much of Longstairs and Wildridge Brow was completed. Although Robinson Brow and Stoney Brow were still standing in July 1920, and described as *"very old and in tumbled down condition"*. Today a walk down Derwent Street reveals nothing remains of the Brows. Semi mature trees now grow on the bank down to the Cloffolks and the only remaining property this side of the street is the old Nags Head Inn.

Below the Brows to the east of the lower end of William Street was Griffin Street, Hayton Square, Bells Lane. Much of the south side of Griffin Street consisted of the lower houses of the Brows. Whilst again the quality and condition of the houses in this area caused great concern to the local authority. Hayton Square off William Street, consisting of around twenty back to back tenements was demolished in 1923. Further clearance of much of the remaining property in Griffin Street took place in 1937-8, when William Street was widened. Originally, the Nags Head was not located directly on the corner of William Street and Derwent Street as it is today. There were once a number of properties immediately to the west of the public house. The last remaining houses on the Cloffolks were Norman Terrace, a block of five terraced houses (below 13 Brow Top) were removed during the late 1960s.

Prior to 1908, Griffin Street at it's narrowest point was only 3.35m (11 feet) wide. The Borough Council then agreed to spent £900 on widening Griffin Street and Skinners Lane. All the property to the east side of Skinners Lane and those houses between Skinners Lane and Longstairs were also demolished. The building known as the Old Barracks in Griffin Street was demolished in July 1909.

At the east end of Griffin Street was the Low Brewery, often also referred to as Kendalls Brewery. Here there was a wooden *"gangway"* or bridge across Griffin Street which linked the buildings on either side of the road. We know that in 1847, Andrew Little was the proprietor of the business. And from 1859-77, the old-established brewery was operated by Lamplugh born, William Kendall. It was advertised for sale in April 1877, when the premises were then described as having *"a twelve-quarter Malt Kiln, a four-quarter Brewing Plant, etc., all in good condition"*. Also included were a "good" family house at 76 Griffin Street and three smaller "tenement" houses. It appears that no purchaser was forthcoming as we know that Kendall's son, also called Wil-

---

"Much of the property is already scheduled as being unfit for human habitation. Large blocks have fallen into such a state of disrepair that they are no longer occupied. The evils complained of and the sanitary defects of the Brows cannot be remedied otherwise unless by total rearrangement and reconstruction."

Dr. John Highet
January 1901

[01] William Kendall (Snr.) was born at Lamplugh in 1825. He died in 1886 and is buried in Harrington Road Cemetery. His son was born at Hensingham in 1855. There is a suggestion that he learnt the trade of brewing at Whitehaven. ■

liam, had taken over the business by 1881. His father, is listed as living at 17 Brow Top and described as a "Retired Brewer" in the census for that year. [01]

Tragedy almost struck the family in April 1874, when the younger William Kendall attempted to commit suicide. Following a failed "betting transaction", he rashly tried to hang himself in the Malting House of his father's brewery. Fortunately, the nineteen year old was discovered and cut down, before "life was extinct". He then obviously recovered to continue the family business. Exactly when beer production ceased here is unclear. Certainly the Council minutes of 1894, indicate the premises were *"mostly unoccupied and in a dilapidated condition"*. However, a couple of years later, there is also a suggestion that some renovation work was carried out on the buildings.

To the north the communities of Griffin Street and Bell Street ended at the mill race or beck, which flows east to west and ultimately discharges into the South gut. Across this beck was the original land making up the Cloffolks. As this mill race curved west past the end of Low William Street, there was a water powered shaft mill at the east end of Bell Street. From around 1854-81, this *"turnery"* which made spade, pick and hammer shafts, was operated by Isaac Fletcher (1818-1881). Shortly before his death, the Hawkshead born tool maker employed three men, including his son also called Isaac. In 1882, the premises were sold at auction by Flectcher's executors. It is not clear who took over the mill, and for how long afterwards it operated. But by 1902, when New Bridge road was built the mill beck was actually moved about 50m northward away from the old water mill..

Low William Street was once often referred to as Dolly or Dollys Brow. It is thought to have received this name by virtue of Dolly Penrice who owned property in the street. Dolly Penrice and later generations of her family also ran a shop at the upper end of Church Street, almost opposite the grocers ran by Henry Jackson (later Armstrong's butchers shop). Wallace Ritson tells us that Dolly Penrices *"shop was where you could buy as many different articles as you can buy in Woolworths"*. He also recalled a *"clever wood carved sign once decorated the shop"*. Also on the western side of Dollys Brow was the Furnace Arms public house, also known as the "La'al Jerry". In the 1950s, one of its most famous regular visitors was Joe Harvey. He was then manager of Workington Reds football club and later guided Newcastle United to European glory.

Church Street ran west from the bottom of Derwent

Dolly Penrice and later generations of her family also ran a shop at the upper end of Church Street, almost opposite the grocers ran by Henry Jackson.

[01] William Kendall (Snr.) was born at Lamplugh in 1825. He died in 1886 and is buried in Harrington Road Cemetery. His son was born at Hensingham in 1855. There is a suggestion that he learnt the trade of brewing at Whitehaven. ∎

One of the few remaining properties in Church Street is the old steam saw mill premises at its west end.

Street after it crossed William Street. This street was once referred to as being *"one of the principal commercial streets in the town"*. Some of remaining properties, particularly in the lower part of Church Street (formerly Priestgate) were generally large Georgian houses, with forecourts surrounded by cast iron railings. Here once lived the sea captains, mariners, solicitors and ironfounders. One such important resident was Joseph Musgrave who ran the Nile Foundry on the Quayside.

From the 1870s, John Fawcett (1832-86) and John Carter (1837-1901) ran a grocer and wine and spirits shop at 24 Church Street. At one time they also held the licence of the adjacent Grapes Inn on the north side of the street. The Fawcett family lived above the Church Street shop, whilst Carter resided nearby in William Street. In June 1881, the Whitehaven Cocoa and Coffee Company took over William Lawrence's former grocers shop at 113 Church Street and converted it into a *"Coffee House"*. It's objectives were not just the sale of drinks, but it also entertained *"charitable and temperance ambitions"*. Elizabeth Symons was the first manager of the coffee house and lived at the premises, along with waiter Hensingham born Walter Harper. William Lawrence is later known to have opened another grocers shop at 20 King Street.

One of the few remaining properties in Church Street is the old steam saw mill premises at its west end. This building with its familiar square tapering brick chimney was built in the eighteenth century. During the active decades of shipbuilding in the town, this saw mill must have handled thousands of tons of timber. In 1899, J. W Jackson and Co. are shown as trading from the saw mill in Church Street.

In 1868, the engineering business of Neil and Turner was established by James Neil [01] and Joseph Turner. [02] This relatively small firm was located to the east of the saw mill yard on the north side of Church Street. In 1913, Joseph Pirt took over the concern which would later become an important ship repairer. During both world wars, the company were awarded several lucrative Admiralty contracts, adding defences to merchant ships. The Church Street premises was also then renamed the Neil Turner works, after their founders.

Around 1901-2, when the new bridge was built over the River Derwent at Northside, part of the Neil and Turner works was given over for a new road through to the bridge. From Church Street the new street looped around the Golden Ball Inn, across the Green and then due north over an undeveloped Cloffolks. The Golden

[01] James Neil (1814-1884) a scotsman, lived at Hag Hill House around 1871. Before moving to 107 Church Street, where he appears on the census a decade later. The engineer was recorded then as employing 5 Men and 2 Boys at his Church Street works.
[02] Joseph Turner was born in 1842 at Moresby and lived at 75 Church Street in 1871. The master engine fitter later boarded with Sarah Lowery at 24 North Watts Street.

Ball certainly existed before 1829, when Anthony Storey is listed as the publican. In December 1880, when the extensive premises were sold at auction on the ground floor was an large *"elegantly fitted bar"*, entered from Church Street. This room was lit by four very large plate glass windows, quite an unusual feature for buildings of the Victorian era. Above the public bar was a large Music Hall, with full stage and scenery, together with dressing rooms and an adjoining bar. This was one of the first buildings to be lit by electric lights, powered by a private generator, years before the town had it's electric mains supply. The Golden Ball was then owned by Mrs. Mary Wilson, although William Carter Brown (1847-93) was the landlord.

It is thought that the Golden Ball was subsequently purchased by Iredale Bros. (of Workington Brewery), and they were responsible for renaming the premises the Bessemer Arms. Certainly the name changed by 1882, and the public house was included in the Workington Brewery Company prospectus of 1891. From 1882 the music hall above the public house was known as the Alexandra Music Hall, and ran by William B. Scraggs (1837-86).

Just beneath St. Michaels Church and to the rear of the south side of Church Street, was Church Lane. Within this very narrow cobbled lane, the remains of which can still be seen today, were upto a dozen very small cottages. One of it's most famous residents was Darkie Joe, who lived there with his wife. He was reputed to be Workington's first negro, having come to the town as *"a stoker on a steamship"*. Apparently, there was an accident onboard his ship, and his feet were badly scalded. Whilst being treated in the infirmary, his ship sailed without him and he was destined to spent the rest of his life in the town. ■

From 1882 the music hall above the public house was known as the Alexandra Music Hall, and ran by William B. Scraggs.

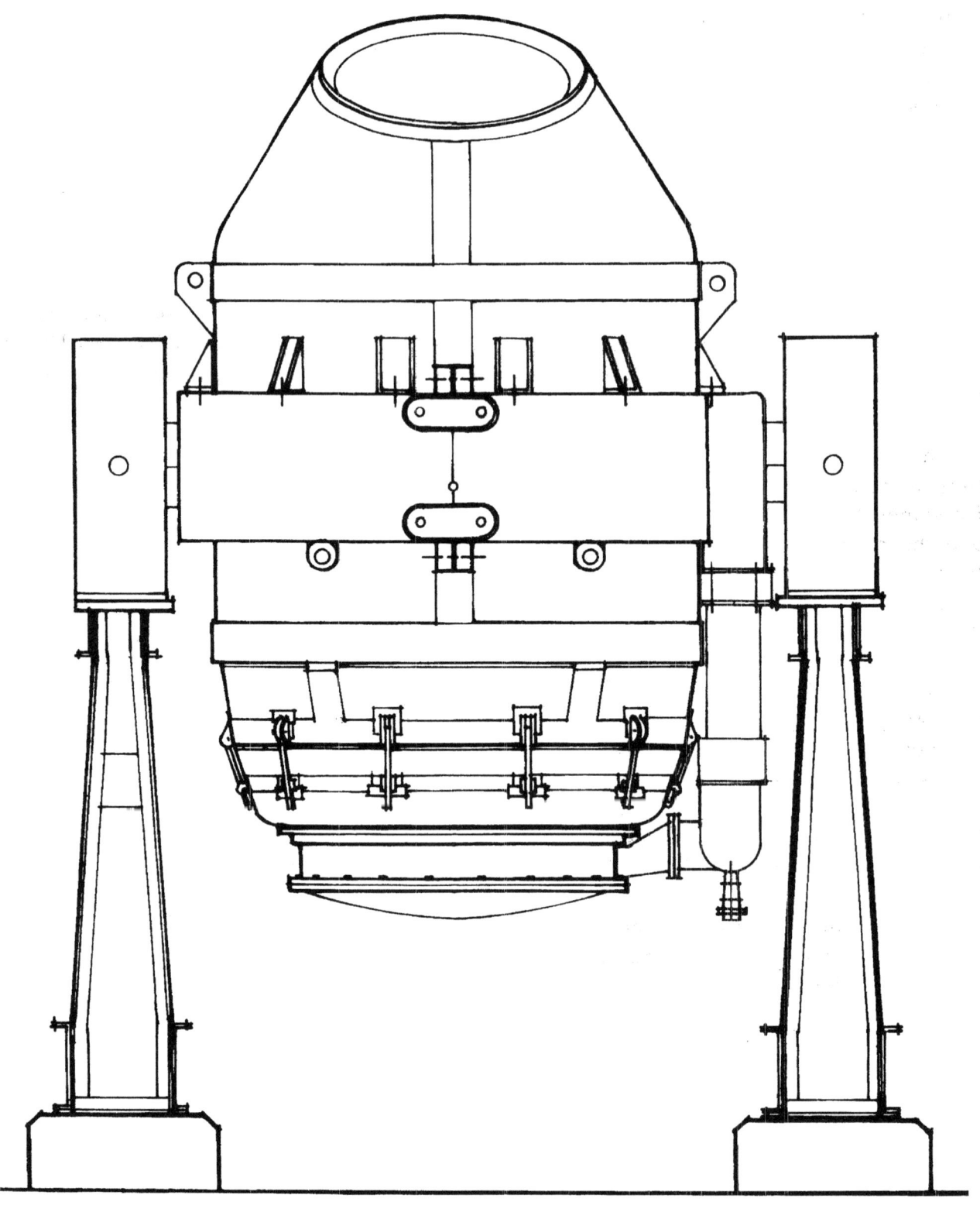

ELEVATION OF THE 25 TON STEWART DEMAG ACID BESSEMER CONVERTER

In 1934, two of these converters were installed at the new Moss Bay steel plant, replacing the 16 ton models erected in 1912. The entire pear shaped Bessemer converter could be rotated on a central axle, in order to be filled and emptied. It closely resembled a builders cement mixer, but was obviously very much larger. Pig iron from the blast furnaces was poured into the converter. By blowing a blast of air through the molten metal the impurities were removed and the iron was converted to steel . ∎

❧ CHAPTER THREE ❧

IRON & STEEL INDUSTRY

IN 1866, the two major ironworks in the town were both located at Oldside, north of the River Derwent. These were the *Workington Haematite Iron Company* (opened in 1858) and the *West Cumberland Haematite Iron Company* (opened in 1860). They were situated on either side of the main railway line north to Maryport. The earlier company occupied the site between the shoreline and the railway, the other was directly opposite to the east. Both plants had direct access to the Whitehaven Junction Railway (opened in 1846) and their establishment stimulated the construction of the new Lonsdale Dock (opened in 1861). Each company had grown rapidly following the discovery of the Bessemer process of steelmaking. For it was in West Cumberland that the process was both developed and refined. The invention also required vast quantities of phosphorous free pig iron, a product that could then only be produced from the iron ore which lay between the Solway Firth and the western fells of the Lake District. The subsequent enoromous world wide demand for steel products brought a boom period to the town and its ironworks. Workington steel attributed to the building of new railway facilities, the construction of iron ships and the trade with America, Germany and Italy. Obviously, it also benefited the town's port, the local iron ore and coal mines and the railway companies.

A long speech made in 1879 by Henry Fraser Curwen provides us with an important insight into the industrial activity of West Cumberland at this time. He tells us that the years of 1868-73, *"brought great unexampled prosperity to the district....All kinds of iron ore and coal were in very great demand and prices rose very high.....The owners of the mines, both coal and iron, benefited most largely....But so did the owners of the furnaces. The traffic of the railway companies had also increased four fold and their dividend rose in proportion. However, by the end of 1874 a change came. Times began to get bad, the demand fell off, prices fell with it, and the transport rates began to be more onerous. Severe competition arose from the North East, where they did not have to import their coke, and their manufacture was so much cheaper."*

Within the timeframe of this book iron and steel was produced on five separate main sites within the town. To assist the reader, below is a list of the companies that operated each works, with their successors listed in italics.

Workington Haematite Iron Co.
Workington Haematite I&S Co.
Oldside Iron and Steel Works

West Cumb. Haematite Iron Co.
West Cumberland Iron and Steel Co.
North Western Iron and Steel Co.

North of England Haematite Ironworks
Lowther Haematite Iron Company.

Moss Bay Haematite Iron Co.
Moss Bay Haematite I&S Company.

Derwent Haematite Ironworks
Charles Cammell & Co Limited
Cammell Laird and Co. Limited.

After 1909, the sites still in operation were amalgamated within:

Workington Iron and Steel Co.
United Steel Companies. ■

"How near may be the day when surrounding the spot upon which I stand may be heard not the din of war, but hammers of hundreds of workmen welding, forwarding, finishing the materials and necessities for the comfort of thousands of homes, not only in England and her colonies, but for every country in Europe".
Issac Scott
on laying the foundation stone at the Workington H. Ironworks (1857)

By 1871, the *Workington Haematite Iron Company* often referred to locally as the *"Old company"*, employed around 300 men. But boom times are inevitably followed by slumps and the town's first major ironworks was forced to cease production around 1874. The company then held *"an enormous stock of pig-iron"*, but were forced to sell at *"much below the cost of manufacture"*. The disheartened directors formally wound-up the affairs of the town's first major ironworks.

Their long-serving manager Joseph Smith, who had run the works for almost fifteen years, was also forced to retire due to his failing eyesight. Six idle years followed, before the works were eventually sold to the *Workington Haematite Iron and Steel Company,* a new joint stock company. Amongst its new directors were Charles James Valentine, Peter Kirk, Joseph Ledger, and Peter G. Quirk. In Victorian times, these men would play a prominent part in the history of iron and steel manufacture in Workington.

By June 1877, all but two of the now obsolete six stone *"skiddies"* (or blast furnaces) had been demolished. Two were later rebuilt on a *"very enlarged scale"*, with about double the capacity of their predecessors. Each was now *"topped off"* in order that the previously lost heat could be recycled.

Pig iron was first smelted again during the first weeks of 1880. The two remaining original blast furnaces, adjacent to the southern engine house, were converted to smelt spiegel. A *"fresh impetus"* in the Bessemer pig iron trade, brought a further period of relative prosperity which lasted three or four years. In September 1882, a further

ABOVE - Sketch of the Workington Haematite Iron Company roundel from the Bessemer Training School plaque at Moss Bay. ■

BELOW - Sketch based on an old print (c.1867) depicting the stone blast furnaces at Workington Haematite Iron Company's Oldside works. For more information see page 189 of the *History of Workington (from Earliest times to 1865).* ■

new blast furnace was brought into service at the Old-side works. By then, the Cumberland furnaces were responsible for smelting 12% of the UK's pig iron.

In 1909, these works were absorbed, along with other local companies, into the newly established *Workington Iron and Steel Company*. The former Workington Haematite works was now more commonly known as the *Oldside Iron and Steel Works*. A 1929 aerial photograph of the Prince of Wales dock exists which clearly shows the works to the north of the harbour.[01] There is no smoke evident from the rows of towering blast furnaces, suggesting production was at a standstill. By the winter of 1933, it is believed there was only one of the remaining three furnaces working at Oldside. This too was abandoned as we learn from local newspaper reports in the spring of 1934, that work had began on demolishing the *"long abandoned blast furnaces at Oldside"*.

In October 1864, work began on further extensions to the *West Cumberland Haematite Ironworks*. A new *"large and extensive"* plate rolling mill was added to the north of their Oldside site. During this work which lasted around eight months, two gigantic steam engine flywheels (each 25 feet in diameter and weighing around 28 tons) were cast on site. The vast steam engines provided the powerful blast of air into each blast furnace. [02] Thought at the time to be *the largest casting ever attempted in Cumberland, the rim of each flywheel was said to have been as fine as if it were turned on a lathe"*. One can easily forget the problems and logistics of building such heavy machinery in Victorian times, work of this kind would still present mammoth problems for today's engineers.

On 23 May, 1865, the extended works was officially opened by Issac Fletcher (of Tarn Bank) when he set in motion the two large steam engines. The plant now covered eight acres and had 32 puddling furnaces (20 of which were then working, with 12 to be commissioned within six weeks). The finishing *"rolling plates"* were 7'0" long and 24" in diameter, and said to be capable of producing 1,400 tons of finished plate a week. In November 1872, soon after the *West Cumberland Haematite Iron Company* was restructured and renamed the *West Cumberland Iron & Steel Company*, [03] steel production began at Oldside. The works had been extended once again, with the addition of four 7½ ton capacity Bessemer converters and a rail mill. George J. Snelus (of the Dowlais Ironworks) was appointed as the first manager of the company's new steelmaking department.

George James Snelus (1837-1906) was a distin-

"The immense works of the West Cumberland Haematite Iron Works and Steel Rail Manufactory give employment to hundreds of workmen, from the most skilled to the humblest labourer".

West Cumberland Times
Dec 1875

[01] This 1929 aerial photograph is on page 42 of *Workington from the Air - Past and Present* by the same author. ■
[02] For a basic description of a blast furnace, and the procedure used to smelt pig iron - please see chapter twelve of *History of Workington (Earliest times to 1865)*. ■
[03] The new company with a share capital of £480,000, are said to have bought the works from the original company for £485,000. Much of which was thought to have been paid "in shares". The board of directors of the West Cumberland Iron and Steel Company included local men, Isaac Fletcher (MP for Cockermouth), Thomas Drane and A. Green-Thompson. ■

guished metallurgist and chemist, who had travelled extensively and closely studied iron and steel production on both sides of the Atlantic. By the time he arrived in Workington, the relatively young man had already achieved significant success. Rev. Edward Haigh Sugden (George Snelus' parish priest at Arlecdon) tells us in his *History of Arlecdon & Frizington*, that he *"laid the foundations of his success by his preliminary study of chemistry and metallurgy, being a student of Professor Roscoe, at Owen's College, Manchester"*. In 1864, he gained the first *Albert Scholarship*, which entitled him to *"£50 per annum and free education for three years at the Royal School of Mines"*. His success here was outstanding, he was the top student for each of his three years, and became an associate in *"mining and metallurgy"*. Upon leaving college, Snelus was appointed the chief chemist at the Glamorgan's Dowlais Iron and Steel Works. The prestigious Iron and Steel Institute later invited him to travel to America as the scientific member of their investigation into Danks mechanical process of puddling. During this visit he also took the opportunity to note any important developments of the American steel industry. Lancaster and Wattleworth in their history of the industry in West Cumbria, commented that this *"was to serve him well in his future appointment"* at Workington.

Perhaps his greatest achievement was the innovative use of dolomitic or magnesitic *"basic"* furnace linings. This invention patented by Snelus in 1872, now allowed quality steel to be made from inferior ore and pig iron, containing a previously unacceptable high phosphorus content. Although initially intended for the Bessemer Converter, his basic linings were more extensively used in the Sydney Thomas' Open Hearth process of steelmaking. For this discovery, Snelus received the *"Bessemer Gold Medal"* from the Iron and Steel Institute in 1883. The medal was inscribed *"for the first to make basic steel in a basic lined converter"*. He was also made a fellow of the Royal Society. Sugden tells us that *"the first piece of steel ever made by this process"* was still preserved by its inventor in 1897. One wonders what happened to the treasured memento of a process, by which many hundred million tons of steel have since been made. He then lived virtually alone at Ennerdale Hall (near Arlecdon), indulging his hobby of growing rare orchids. Seldom was he ever seen in public without one of his floral specimens, proudly displayed in the button hole of his jacket. Within a very short time, George Snelus rose to general manager of the West Cumberland works.

By the end of 1874, when the period of *"unexampled*

ABOVE - George James Snelus (1837-1906), the accomplished metallurgist and chemist, was appointed the first manager of the *West Cumberland Iron & Steel Company* in 1872. Perhaps his greatest achievement was the invention of "basic" furnace linings. This allowed quality steel to be made from inferior ore and pig iron, containing a previously unacceptable high phosphorus content. His innovation is also thought to have greatly contributed to the demise of the West Cumberland Iron ore mines. Home produced haematite could now be replaced with imported cheaper foreign iron ore. ■

prosperity" ended and the industry slid into recession, his experience was to prove vital to the survival of the company. His knowledge and innovation greatly reduced the company's overheads, increased its efficiency and even maintained a modest profit, during these difficult times. A five year period, during which steel prices fell by a massive 65% and both it's close neighbours, the *Workington Haematite Iron Company* and *Lowther Works* were forced to close. Rather than rebuild three of the six furnaces at the WCI&SCo., they were extensively repaired and remodelled. In 1875-6, each was raised by 15 feet (4.6m), and now measured around 70 feet (21.3m) in height. The company who already owned their own limestone quarry at Brigham, also acquired the colliery (and brickworks) at Clifton, to guarantee supplies of coal for coking.

Their representatives also exhibited at the Paris Exhibition of 1878. Achieving remarkable success by winning gold medals for their exhibits of *"Haematite pig iron, Bessemer steel ingots, castings, rails and plates".*[01] Shortly afterwards Henry Bessemer adopted the Snelus linings for his own converters.

We know from the writings of Henry Fraser Curwen that *"by the end of 1879"* the heavy industries of West Cumberland were beginning to recover. *"Iron prices were very high again and the iron ore mines and coal pits were again scenes of activity"*. Within a few months, all six blast furnaces at the West Cumberland works, were again "in blast" as production of pig iron rose. The rail mills were remodelled to allow the manufacture of steel and boiler plate. In September 1882, *"the works had never been so busily employed"*. In the year following the appointment of Rowland Hill (1817-1883) as rail mill manager, the WCI&SCo. produced between 3000-4000 tons of rails each week. In June 1883, a new *"iron cast"* blast furnace was blown-in at the works. Built on eight massive columns, the 70ft high structure was heated by four of *"Mr. Snelus' patent stoves"* and was capable of producing 1000 tons of pig iron each week. Just five months later (December 1883) the No. 5 blast furnace was recommissioned after being totally rebuilt. The West Cumberland works were described as *"by far the largest concern in the town"*.

Yet the industry was still riding a roller coaster of boom and bust and by 1888, a serious slump occurred once more. The company were subsequently forced into liquidation in December 1888. It was not until October 1889, that they began trading once more. The West Cumberland works struggled on for a couple of years, parts

[01] Promoting their products at such international exhibitions, brought vital export orders to the Workington works. In July 1881, we known they also exhibited at the Adelaide International Exhibition, in Southern Australia. ■

of the plant were closed and workers were laid off during several periods of inactivity. Finally in May 1892, the directors agreed to finally wind up the company and attempt to dispose of the works. Although they saw little prospect of a sale during a recession described as *"the very worst in the history of iron and steel in West Cumberland"*.

Nearly seven years after it's closure, the now dilapidated Oldside works was eventually sold to the *North Western Iron and Steel Company* (formed in 1898). By February 1899, this new company had *"overhauled and modernised"* much of the old West Cumberland works, and anticipated production would soon recommence. Initially, just two of the five remaining blast furnaces were restarted, with the remaining three put in blast during the following year or so. The furnace plant was also *"entirely overhauled, and more modern stoves erected"*. However, this enterprise was very short lived as by July 1902, the entire works was closed and advertised for sale. No purchaser was forthcoming and the once thriving works was dismantled soon after.

On 1 May 1872, Andrew Barclay (of Kilmarnock) and David George Hoey (of Lanark) were granted a 99 year lease of land on the north bank of the River Derwent, mid way between the Lonsdale Dock and the Whitehaven Junction Railway bridge over the river. Here they built the *North of England Haematite Iron Works*, more generally referred to as the *Lowther Ironworks*. The Lowther was ideally situated close to the dock and railways. It was also granted powers to tip its slag waste into the sea, at the high water mark. The local newspaper tells us that work on building the new ironworks began in August 1872. Within ten months, the first blast furnace was completed and *"blown-in"*. During its first year the company are recorded as making a respectable £17,000 profit. On paper the Scotsmen made a perfect team, Barclay provided the technical knowledge, while accountant Hoey handled the financial management. But unfortunately, they too were seriously affected by the recession of 1874. The *North of England Haematite Iron Company* was subsequently forced into liquidation.

For six months, the creditors allowed production to continue at the Lowther works, whilst a new company was sort to take over control. During this time they lost the services of the works manager, Hugh Jamieson (1839-75) who died suddenly in March 1875. By June, they accepted that the workers must be laid off and its two furnaces dampened down. As the bankrupt ironworks lay

Nearly seven years after it's closure, the now dilapidated Oldside works was eventually sold to the *North Western Iron and Steel Company.*

idle, talks and negotiations continued for several months. Finally in October, it was purchased by the *Lowther Haematite Iron Company,* new joint stock company with a capital of £250,000. After negotiations with his creditors, David George Hoey made a surprise return as a director of the new business. Almost immediately, both the blast furnaces were restarted. But during 1879, the recession in the iron trade resulted in the works *"standing idle for a considerable time"*. It appears that during this stoppage at least some of the blast furnaces were heightened and remodelled. In January 1880, William Wilson, the former secretary of the West Cumberland I&SCo. joined the board of the Lowther Haematite Iron Co. One of his first tasks was to *"blow-in"* their blast furnaces, signalling the reopening of the works.

A decade later the works were seriously hit by the 1892 Durham miners strike. This lasted several months and the shortage of coke virtually brought the plant to a standstill. It subsequently closed in February 1893. Three years later, it was reported in the local press that *"not a single blast furnace was in-blast at any of the works north of the River Derwent"*. Oldside which had once been the hub of the town's iron and steel industry stood *"desolate and almost deserted"*. Production at the Lowther works did recommence and by the turn of the century Bulmer tells us there were *"three large modern blast furnaces"*. But the minutes of the C&WJR reveal that it was *"at a standstill once more"* by August 1901. Four years later, Cammell Laird and Co., acquired the Lowther Ironworks. It's furnace being relighted on 7 September 1905. But following the 1909 amalgamation of the town's iron and steelworks, the plant at the Lowther works was now considered *"outdated and obsolete"*.

To the south of the River Derwent, the *Moss Bay Haematite Iron Company* was established in the early years of the 1870's. From the Curwen archives, we learn that Henry Fraser Curwen leased the land at Salterbeck to Peter Kirk, Charles James Valentine, Henry Kenyon and Mary Gibson, on 24 July 1872. Charles J. Valentine (1837-1900) was the brother in law of Peter Kirk (1840-1916) having married his sister Annie Kirk. Both men were already quite successful running the Quayside Forge or Ironworks in Stanley Street. Here production was limited to the manufacture of wrought iron in the puddling furnaces. Douglas R. Wattleworth writing in 1965, believed that *"it was from the Quay Forge that the origins of the Moss Bay works can be traced"*.

The Moss Bay works was originally erected entirely

A decade later the works were seriously hit by the 1892 Durham miners strike. This lasted several months and the shortage of coke virtually brought the plant to a standstill.

for the production of Bessemer pig iron, the basic raw material of steelmaking. The company then simply cast and sold the *"pigs"* or blocks of iron to steel plants up and down the country and abroad. But by January 1876, they announced that they too were to *"add the manufacture of steel to their already extensive business"*. Moss Bay then intended to adopt the relatively new process patented by William Deighton. Pig iron from the blast furnace *"was kept in a fluid state"* and transferred immediately to the converter. They installed three Bessemer converters and constructed a new rail rolling plant. This rolling mill was driven by another enormous steam engine, built by Miller and Anderson (of Coatbridge). It's massive flywheel measured 25 feet in diameter and was said to weigh around 50 tons. In June 1877, the steel plant was completed and undergoing trials, two months later the first steel rail order was produced. In December 1879, the company were performing around 18-20 Bessemer blows per day.

In order to fund this growth and re-finance the works, Moss Bay was converted into a new limited company in March or September 1881. With both Peter Kirk and Charles J. Valentine [01] being appointed joint managing directors. It had a share capital of £350,000 and now trading as the *Moss Bay Haematite Iron and Steel Company*. From 1882-8, the chairman at Moss Bay works was Joseph Ledger, formerly of the West Cumberland Haematite Iron Company. Among it's other first directors was local businessman Peter Gibson Quirk (1849-93).

In November 1884, Peter Kirk patented his design for the first steel railway sleeper and production was commenced at Moss Bay. The Cleator and Workington Junction Railway were amongst the first to use these innovative sleepers, intended to replace the conventional creosoted timber sleeper. In October 1885, they ordered 9000 steel sleepers, paying 7/6 (or 37½p) each. These were required for their northern extension, being built to link Central Station to Linefoot. [02] It is very likely that the order was greatly influenced by Charles J. Valentine who was then a director of both Moss Bay and the railway company. Other larger orders are known to have been completed, including 160,000 steel sleepers, shipped from Workington to Bombay in India. There is a Moss Bay steel railway sleeper (dated 1899) currently displayed at the town's Helena Thompson Museum.

During the next decade, Moss Bay expanded to employ over 2000 local men, although they were often trading at a loss or made only minimal profit. The company also had to deal with a degree of industrial unrest, with

[01] Charles James Valentine (1837-1900) was born in Mossley, Lancashire. He was the brother in law of Peter and Henry Kirk and a co-founder of the Moss Bay Haematite Iron Co. Becoming a director of the reconstructed Moss Bay Company in 1890.
On 5 December 1885, Charles Valentine (Conservative) was returned as the MP for the Parliamentary constituancy of Cockermouth, which then included Workington. Beating Liberal Sir Wilfred Lawson by only ten votes. Parliament was dissolved on 15 June 1886, and although Sir Wilfred Lawson opened his campaign at Workington. Charles Valentine declined to stand for re-election. Henry Curwen stood instead and lost to Sir Wilfred.
Valentine was also one of the initial promoters of the Cleator and Workington Junction Railway, and served as a director of this railway company from 1876-87. He resigned due to pressure of work at Moss Bay Ironworks, after Peter Kirk emigrated to America. Valentine himself is known to have visited America, during the summer of 1887. ■
[02] These Moss Bay steel railway sleepers remained in use on the Northern extension of the C&WJR until 1899. After less than fourteen years, many were found to be defective and were subsequently replaced with timber. Interestingly, the railway company then paid just 3/ 8½ (or 18.5p) each for the conventional creosoted timber sleeper - under half the original cost of the steel sleepers. ■

several drawn out strikes affecting production. Workers organised themselves into trade unions, in defence of their poor pay and harsh working conditions. In difficult times, when iron and steel prices were falling, the company often insisted their employees take a wage reduction. Naturally, a dispute between the ironmasters and their workmen was almost inevitable. The Moss Bay's workers had at their helm the socialist and union leader, Patrick Walls (1847-1932). A founder member of the Labour Party, he would also pioneer many improvements in working conditions. These ultimately benefited, not just those at Moss Bay, but almost every worker at every ironworks throughout the country. Perhaps the major achievement of the tall Irishman, affectionately known as Paddy, was the establishment of a shorter working week. Previously his blast furnacemen, had been forced to work an exhausting eighty four hours a week. In 1890, Walls secured a new *"eight-hour"* daily shift system. He was also a founder member and the first president of the blast furnacemens union. Douglas R. Wattleworth writing in 1965 told how *"he secured improved conditions through militant action, whilst steering his often unruly members along the path to peaceful negotiation and conciliation."*

In recognition of his service to the Trade Union movement, Patrick Walls later received an OBE. Between 1893-1931, he also served as a Borough Councillor, and became the town's first Labour Mayor in 1915-16. He was eighty four years old when he retired from public life in November 1931. Less than a year later, this remarkable man died at his home in St. Michaels Road. Patrick Walls is buried alongside his wife Catherine, in Harrington Road Cemetery.

In 1886, a disillusioned Peter Kirk had left Workington and emigrated to America, seeking out *"new and hopefully more prosperous opportunities"*. Upon hearing that iron deposits had been discovered in the Cascade mountains of Washington State, he saw an ideal opportunity to build a modern iron and steel works, on the shores of Lake Washington. This exciting venture was welcome relief for Kirk, away from the burden of running the troubled Moss Bay company. Interestingly, the Lake Washington area of America was so similar to West Cumbria, with coal and limestone resources (the essential elements of steel production) readily available in surrounding districts. He modelled much of his new plant on that at Workington, and even named it the *"Moss Bay Iron and Steel Works"*. The town around the proposed plant would also become known as Kirkland, named after it's founder. Alan J. Stein in his *History of Kirkland,*

"From early morn until dewy eve was the labourers day of not less than 12 long hours."
West Cumberland Times
Dec 1875

believed Peter Kirk envisaged developing the area into the *"Pittsburgh of the West - a bustling new town whose economy would be focused around steel production"*.

In reality, the success of his plans relied heavily on the building of a new ship canal through Seattle to the Puget Sound and a connection to the existing railroad system. But the Tacoma based *Northern Pacific Company* had control of this rail network and refused to allow a spur line to be built into Kirk's new works. Tacoma was in direct competition with Seattle, bidding to become the predominant seaport of Lake Washington. Consequently, they were reluctant to give Kirkland, and therefore Seattle, any great help or assistance. Surprisingly, Kirk seemed even more determined to see his dream project attain fruition. Along with prominent Seattle businessmen, he bought up thousands of acres of vacant land. Streets were laid out, and new houses were erected for the workers. Kirk also built Fir Grove, a new mansion for his large family. Today it is described as *"one of the finest homes in Kirkland"*. His wife Mary Ann and their children left Bankfield to join him in July 1887.

The fatal blow to his dreams was the American stock market crash of 1893. Without a booming economy, no rail line would be built, no canal dredged, and no steel plant could survive. The works never opened and no iron and steel was ever smelted at Kirkland. It's founder, Peter Kirk later retired to the Island of San Juan, [01] where he died in 1916. Today, Kirkland is a thriving city with a population of around 44,000 people. Peter Kirk's vision of a vibrant community on the eastern shore of Lake Washington has been fulfilled, although not exactly as he imagined it.

It is believed a number of the towns workers actually followed Kirk to seek employment in his new works. Certainly, his travels brought rail orders to Workington from that area of the United States. In 1886, three hundred tons of T-section railway line were shipped out of Workington for the Puget Sound Construction Co. then constructing the new Seattle, Lake Shore and Eastern Railway. John Boykin of Seattle revealed recently that he possesses samples of these original *"56 lb. per yard"* rails, rescued from a scrap yard and bearing the old Moss Bay mill marks. Records confirm that there was also other batches of rails, sent out to Seattle and Vancouver in British Columbia. We certainly know Charles Valentine visited Kirk in the United States in the summer of 1887, and for many years, Kirk is thought to have still retained some shares and an interest in the Workington works.

Once again a new company was formed to take over

It is believed a number of the towns workers actually followed Kirk to America seeking employment in his new works.

[01] The idyllic San Juan Islands are located on the west coast of America, in the northern reaches of the Puget Sound, around 80 miles north of Seattle. Peter Kirk is said to have discovered "their peace and solitude" whilst seeking out a limestone supply for his new ironworks. He first built a 500 acre hunting estate at Deer Harbour, to the north of the island. Where he spent much of his latter years, surrounded by his family. Following the tragic death of his daughter and his beloved wife Mary Ann, he moved to a new smaller residence on the outskirts of Friday Harbour. In 1916, at this elegant little house (built in 1907) he died peacefully in his sleep. Today, it has been sympathetically renovated and converted into a luxury guest house. It remained in the family for decades, with several of Peter Kirk's children marrying islanders. ■

the bankrupt works and to continue production at Workington. Also named the *Moss Bay Haematite Iron and Steel Company*, it was incorporated in March 1891, with a share capital of nearly £310,000. Among it's first directors were Charles James Valentine, John Scurrah Randles (1857-1945) and Robert Ernest Highton (1858-1931). Prior to his arrival in Workington, Highton had been employed as the London representative for the old Moss Bay I&SCo. Highton was the son of Keswick schoolmaster, the late Edward Highton. He had joined the Moss Bay works in 1881, after four years employment as a clerk with the CK&PR. Within a decade, Highton had risen to become the secretary and commercial manager of the new company. During their first year, several further improvements were undertaken at the Moss Bay works. Lancaster and Wattleworth tells that *"both the Bessemer department and the rail mill were able to report record outputs"*. But the Durham miners dispute, which also seriously affected output at the Lowther works also brought production at Moss Bay to a halt. The Cumberland Union Bank withdrew it's support and forced the Moss Bay company into liquidation. But the company appears to have successfully negotiated with its creditors and traded through the problems.

In the first decade of the new century, Moss Bay struggled once more to make respectable profits, as it found it's worldwide markets very much in decline. Like the other local iron and steel producers, Moss Bay was eventually amalgamated into the Workington Iron and Steel Company in 1909.

As the first iron was smelted at the Moss Bay plant, construction had began on another new ironworks. The *Derwent Haematite Ironworks* was built on the vacant land immediately to the north of Moss Bay, across the fields from New Yard. Construction work started on it's first blast furnace in November 1873. Each of the town's iron manufacturers traded quite independently of each other and were established to meet the extraordinary demand for Bessemer pig iron. The majority of the investors in the new Derwent works appear to have been from the Kilmarnock area of Scotland. The Derwent's first blast furnace was *"blown-in"* during June of 1875. However, production was delayed for several months due to an unfortunate series of *"mechanical breakdowns"*. Despite the apparent recession elsewhere in the iron trade, the company began building a second blast furnace in March 1876, and added a third by 1880.

In July 1879, the directors of the Derwent Haema-

Prior to his arrival in Workington, Robert Ernest Highton had been employed as the London representative for the old Moss Bay I&SCo.

The *Derwent Haematite Ironworks* was built on the vacant land immediately to the north of Moss Bay, across the fields from New Yard.

tite Ironworks, now managed by manager Thomas Barbour (1827-96) are known to have approached the Wilson Cammell and Co.(of Dronfield) [01] *"with a proposal that the two companies merge"*. Austin & Ford in their 1983 book *Steel Town,* tell us that *"the Dronfield works was, in terms of output and productivity, one of the foremost rail producing plants in Britain, if not the world"*. It appears that the Derwent works had regularly supplied Bessemer pig-iron to the Sheffield company, for conversion and rolling into rails. By September 1881, the local press in Yorkshire now confirmed that *"an arrangement had been made for the Dronfield steel works to be removed to Workington, where it will be placed beside the Derwent furnaces"*.

Throughout the 1870s, many technological advances had occurred in Bessemer steelmaking. Primarily, it was now accepted that *"iron be now transferred from the blast furnace direct to the converter in molten state"*. Dronfield had no blast furnaces, and it was over 120 miles from Cumberland's haematite iron ore reserves, then essential for the Bessemer steelmaking. The company also suffered geographically in other ways, all export orders had first to be sent by rail, long distances to the nearest port. The economic advantages of combining both plants at Workington were obvious. But this situation was not unique to Wilson Cammell, other Sheffield rail producers faced just the same problems. One such company was Charles Cammell and Co. who then ran the nearby Cylops and Penistone works. Despite trading independently, these two companies essentially belonged to the Cammell and Wilson families, as their respective names would suggest. They also shared several directors, many of whom were *"old and trusted friends"*. The two Sheffield companies then struck a happy compromise. Charles Cammell and Co. would now purchase both Wilson Cammell's Dronfield works and Workington's Derwent works. Dronfield would still close and transfer as planned, to the site adjacent to the Derwent blast furnaces. The combined Workington plants would now be operated by Charles Cammell and Company, and would concentrate principally on export orders for steel rails.

Cammell's purchased the Derwent Ironworks for £105,000, the whole amount was paid by the creation of £300,000 worth of additional share capital. They also acquired two adjacent fields belonging to Joseph Thompson. They now had a large site covering between 80-90 acres. By the summer of 1882, the £50,000 contract for the new steel plant at Workington, had been let to local contractor Richard H. Hodgson. William Tomlinson (of

ABOVE - James Duffield (1835-1914) of Charles Cammell and Co., responsible for moving the entire Dronfield steelworks to Workington in 1882. Later became a prominent member of Workington Borough Council, the town mayor and an Alderman. ■

[01] In 1875, Wilson Cammell and Co. was re-structured from the Wilson Cammell Patent Wheel Co. Ltd. In 1872, the latter company had been created to built and operate, a new specialised Bessemer steel rail plant at Dronfield.■

Dronfield) was appointed as clerk of works for the scheme. Production ceased at the "doomed" Dronfield works on Saturday 1 March 1883. Amidst a sombre *"good natured"* ceremony, more reminiscent of a *"wake"*, James Duffield (then manager of the Dronfield works) thanked the Dronfield workforce. As a genuine gesture of atonement, he said he would gladly offer jobs *"to any old hands"* who planned to move north to Workington. The closure spelt the phenomenal decline of the Derbyshire town By 1886, more than a third of the 934 houses in Dronfield were unoccupied, as upwards of 2000 people left the town. Shop after shop in the main street was vacated and their windows boarded up. Dronfield, the once thriving industrial town, *"became known throughout the district as the deserted village"*.

Almost immediately a considerable number of Dronfield's workmen *"were engaged"* to assist in the dismantling of their former workplace. Most of it's machinery and plant was then brought by rail to Workington, and re-erected at the Derwent Ironworks site. One newspaper report tells us that Cammell's even brought the *"tin sheeting roofs from Dronfield"* to re-erect at Workington. Trusted Cammell engineer Josiah Purser (1848-1928) oversaw this process and subsequently settled in the town.[01] In the weeks and months following the Dronfield closure, many hundreds of his former workforce joined him. Their arrival triggering the development of the Moss Bay area (formerly referred to simply as Westfield). The majority of it's houses were built to accommodate the incoming steelworkers. Whilst the steelwork move had turned Dronfield into something of a ghost town, Workington became a boon town.

The *'Dronnies'* as they became known, were initially greeted with some hostility, by the local people. They were *"more skilled and often better paid"*, and their arrival *"on mass"* resulted in higher rents and rising prices. It took some time for the two communities to become fully integrated. Whilst it is not easy to calculate the actual number of 'Dronnies' who migrated to the town. It is suggested that in excess of 1400 men, women and children made the journey north. It should be noted that less than 45% of these were actually born in that area of Derbyshire (or neighbouring Sheffield). A significant number had simply migrated to the Dronfield works, when it first opened in 1873. Now they in turn, moved once more to Workington, in search of employment..

The local newspapers tell us that production at the new Derwent steel plant commenced in the autumn of 1883. There were then six 12 ton capacity Bessemer con-

"Dronfield, a once thriving industrial town, has become known throughout the district as the deserted village"
Yorkshire Post
1883

[01] Josiah Purser (1848-1928) was born in Bedfordshire. He lived at Moss Bay and was employed by Charles Cammell Co. until his retirement in 1905. In 1896, he was first elected to the Borough Council, representing the South Ward. In 1914, Purser was elected an Alderman, following the death of another former Dronfield resident, James Duffield. ■

"Since the turn of the century, the diameter of new blast furnaces had been increased from around 8ft to 17ft, with double the blast."

Mike Burridge

OPPOSITE - The blast furnaces of the United Steel Companies at Moss Bay. Within these tall blast furnaces pig iron was produced, used mainly for conversion into steel. In the square building to the right of the page, at the end of the row of blast furnaces, was a large steam engine, used to generate the powerful blast of air to the foot of each furnace.

Wilkinsons wagon works on Moss Bay Road can be seen in the distance. Here railway trucks and wagons were manufactured and repaired. ∎

verters arranged in three casting areas or pits. The first steel rails were rolled on Thursday, 18 October, just six months had elapsed since the machinery *"was last in motion at Dronfield"*. Under the watchful gaze of Messrs. Wilson, Duffield, Bradbury and Oates, the process went *"without a hitch"*. Records point to these first rails being supplied to the North Eastern Railway Co. Around this time, they also supplied 72,000 tons of steel rails to be shipped to New South Wales; and a further 2000 tons to the Belgian Railway in Brussels, further orders soon followed from Argentina, Japan and India. The output from its three original Derwent blast furnaces was often inadequate to meet the demands of the new rail mill. Each was raised in height, to increase their capacity by about 30%. Lancaster and Wattleworth reveal that it was still necessary for Cammell's to *"buy in"* pig iron from elsewhere. This was converted to steel and rolled into more rails, in order to fulfil their backlog of orders. To remedy this shortfall two additional blast furnaces were added by the winter of 1898.

In October 1903, Cammells merged with *Laird Brothers Limited* and afterwards traded as *Cammell Laird and Co.* A year later, they purchased Lonsdale Dock. This was an obvious move for in the 1880s, vast iron ore deposits had been discovered in Spain and North Africa. Large quantities of this cheaper and far-richer foreign ore was now shipped to the UK, and Cammells felt gaining control of Workington port was both essential and cost effective. Douglas R. Wattleworth writing in 1965, commented "the British steel industry was no longer dependent on Cumberland ores and iron.".

From the writings of Patrick *"Paddy"* Walls, we learn that during the first decade of the new century it was feared that iron and steelmaking in Workington *"would be crushed out as a result of the severe competition exerted by the large steel combinations of the United States, and the powerfully organised and state-aided works in Germany"*. To alleviate these problems, the *Workington Iron and Steel Company Ltd.* was created in August 1909. It was formed by a fusion of the Moss Bay Haematite Iron and Steel Company, the Workington Iron and Steel Company Limited, Cammell Lairds Cumberland properties and the Harrington Iron and Steel Company. There is some dispute as to who initiated the proposal to amalgamate, some imply it was Sir. John Scurrah Randles (of the Moss Bay works), others suggest the board of Cammell Laird. Despite this confusion, it is clear that all the local companies eventually saw the real logic and mutual advantages of combining all their activities. The new

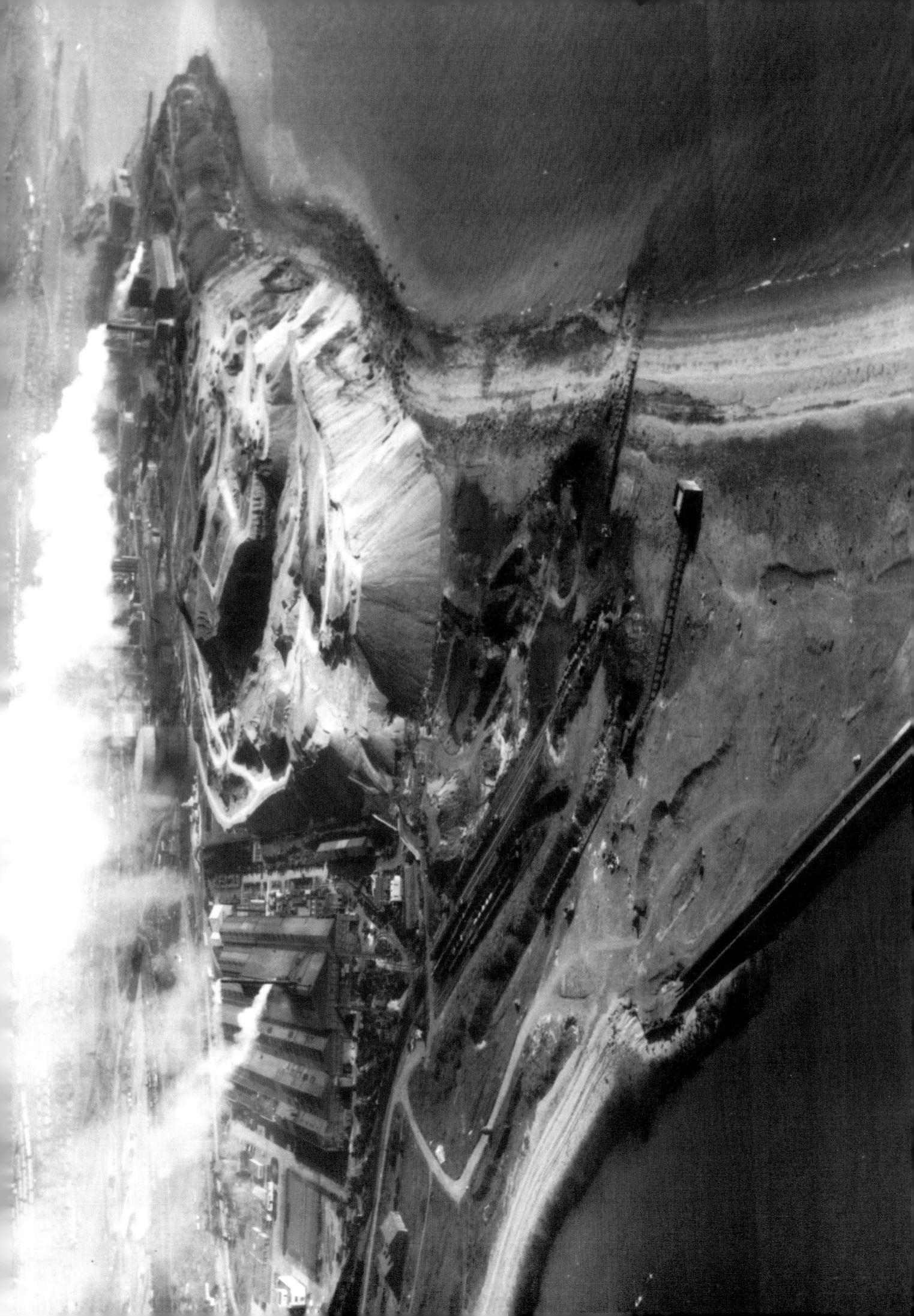

company often referred to as the *"combine"*, now boasted 22 blast furnaces, 11 Bessemer converters, two open hearth furnaces, six iron ore mines, a number of collieries and even a *"valuable manganese mine"* in Mysore, India. They also effectively controlled both Workington and Harrington harbours. Sir John was appointed the first chairman of the WI&SCo. It's board of directors also included Joseph Ellis, Herbert Valentine, W Burnyeat, R. E. Highton and H. E. Wilson. Joseph Ellis and Herbert Valentine were the brother-in-law and son of the late ironmaster, Charles James Valentine.

One of their first decisions was to cease rail and steel sleeper production at the former Cammell Laird Derwent plant. This would now be concentrated only at the Moss Bay part of the new *"combind"* works. A new tyre and steel mill was then established at the old Derwent rail mill. Although the early years of the new WI&SCo. were still not very productive. They did achieve a *"more efficient"* output of 13,000 tons of pig iron per week. In September 1911, the company also suffered paralysing stoppages due to the *"general strike"*, and all the furnaces at Moss Bay were damped down. But this did not affect the profits of the iron companies, life among the working class families in the town, was then said to be one of *"poverty and little hope of improvement"*.

By 1913, Cumberland's blast furnaces were producing less than 7% of the UK's pig iron. Thirty years earlier, they had manufactured almost twice this figure. Then of course they held the geographic advantage, of being located so close to the iron ore resources of Cleator and Frizington. This reduction could be attributed to wide spread use of the innovative *"Basic"* process of steelmaking. Now previously inferior iron ores could easily be smelted into the Bessemer quality pig iron, required for steelmaking. No longer was it essential to use the low phosphorus haematite mined only in Cumberland. Millions of tons of cheap foreign iron ore was now imported into Britain, and used extensively by all the countries iron companies. The introduction of the *"Basic"* method, also signalled the demise and ultimate closure of the West Cumberland iron ore mines. George J. Snelus (of the West Cumberland I&SCo.) was responsible for developing much of this process. Ironically, in later life he would move to live at Ennerdale Hall, near Arlecdon, amidst one of the very iron-ore communities, his invention had condemned to a bleak future.

In the early years of WW1, Workington (and the nation generally) were slow to adapt iron and steel production for the war effort. It was not until after Lloyd George

One of their first decisions was to cease rail and steel sleeper production at the former Cammell Laird Derwent plant. This would now be concentrated only at the Moss Bay part of the new *"combind"* works.

OPPOSITE - The coastline to the south of the Derwent estuary in 1969. The Distington Engineering Company works are to the left of the aerial photograph, the massive slag banks to the centre. ∎

[01] In October 1915, a fine brass and copper panel listing these 800 WW1 volunteers was unveiled by Sir. John S. Randles, the chairman of the WI&SCo. Over 150 of which were killed in action and destined never to return. Exactly, how many male workers remained at the works during WW1 is difficult to determine. In May 1915, we know there was still 250 men employed in the Derwent mills, between 350-400 at the Derwent blast furnaces and 700-800 at the Moss Bay steelworks.■

BELOW - Scale drawing of a 15 ton Steel Type Hopper Wagon, belonging to the Workington I&SCo. (date approx 1920) Each wagon was fitted with brakes at both sides. Livery - body, solebars amd ironwork were painted black, with white lettering. The wheel rims were also painted white. ■

established the *Ministry of Munitions* in May 1915, that the industry was truly mobilised. All production (and prices) at the WI&SCo. were then controlled by the Government. No iron or steel could be bought or sold without a *"priority"* certificate, issued by the Board of Trade's *Iron and Steel Department*. During the war there was an *"unprecedented and almost unlimited call"* on nearly every manufacturing resource in the country. Despite these restrictions and the loss of those workers who enlisted, production (and profits) at Workington became exceptionally high.

Throughout the autumn and winter of 1914, a serious shortage of artillery ammunition developed. To simply defend our troops in front line trenches, it was estimated that the 18-pounder field guns alone, required a minimum of 30,000 rounds per day. The war archives reveal that the government really struggled to supply this ammunition. The consequences of the deficiency were tragic and heavy casualties resulted. Workington I&SCo. were not an established munition works, but by the summer of 1915, they were manufacturing large quantities of shell steel. As more than 800 Workington steelworkers had volunteered for military service, [01] women were trained and replaced their *"menfolk"* at the iron and steel works. The news of horrific losses due to the shell shortages, had only recently been made public. The outcry brought an immense increase in women volunteers, and bolstered their commitment to the cause. In order to accommodate women in this previously *"male preserve"*, essential work had to be swiftly carried out at the plant, Conditions left very much to be desired, particularly the *"very primitive"* toilet facilities which were to-

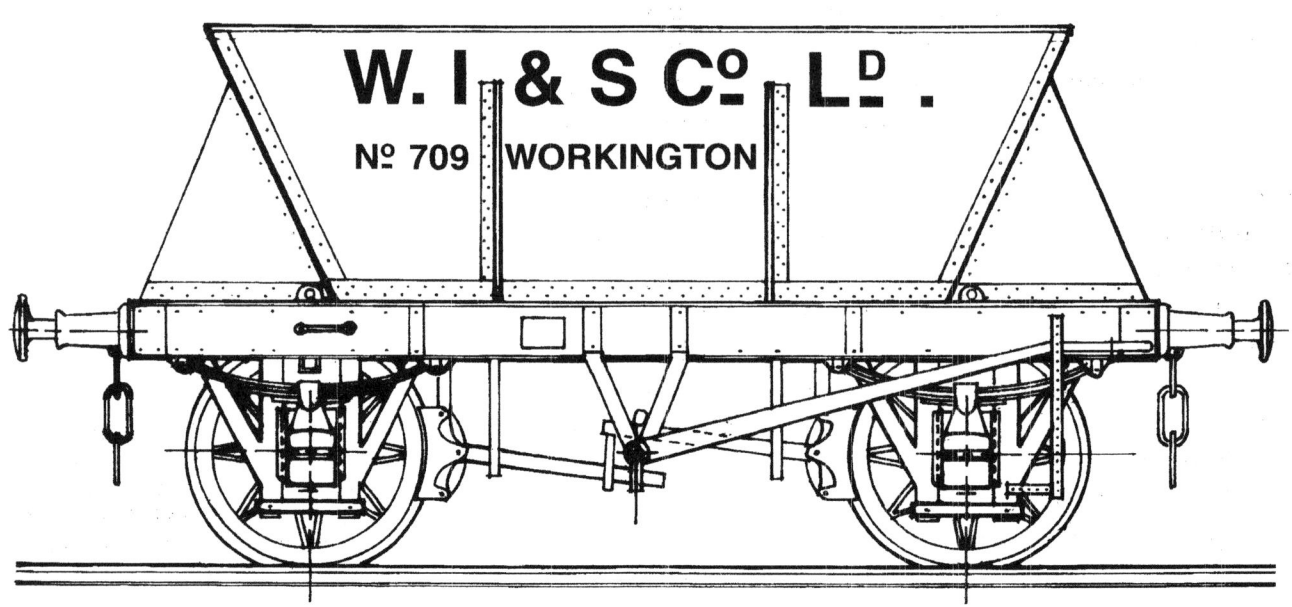

tally inappropriate. H. B. Williams, the Borough Engineer, inspected the steelworks around this time and wrote *"at one toilet near the shore, was a simple low beam on which the men would roost, there was no divisions to form separate compartments, hence no privacy. The excrement was simply carried out to sea by the action of the waves"*.

On 17 May 1917, King George V and Queen Mary paid a visit to Workington's iron and steel plant, in order to *"see the actual work being carried out during this state of war"*. During these war years, George V was seen as very much a *"people's' king"*. His frequent and often "dangerous" trips to the battlefields of France and the Grand Fleet, earned him the greatest respect of the country. At home, his morale-boosting visits to important "munition works" like Moss Bay, further encouraged the *"hearts and hands of the workers playing a different, but equally vital part"* in the bitter conflict. On such occasions, the Royal family always requested a very simple, low-key reception, with no pomp or ceremony. The Mayor and Councillors were not to wear their robes, and there was to be no addresses or salutes. After spending the morning in Barrow, the Royal Train arrived at Workington's Low Station at 3.15pm. It was met by Lord Lonsdale, then Lord Lieutenant of Cumberland and Sir John Scurrah Randles MP. They travelled by royal car to the works, via Station Road, Oxford Street, down John Street and along Harrington Road.

ABOVE - King George V who visited Workington's iron and steelworks in May 1917. ■

The King wearing his khaki military uniform, was then escorted around the plant by Thomas W. Graham (works manager) and Joseph Valentine Ellis. Whilst Sir John Randles also accompanied Queen Mary during the tour. They were shown a blast furnace being *"tapped"* and watched the molten iron flowing into the pig beds. They witnessed a Bessemer *"blow"*, the King commenting that the magnificent spectacle was *"one of the best things he had seen that day"*. From there they moved to the cogging and finishing mills, the acid open hearth furnaces, fish mill and power house. During their visit, the Royal Party were also introduced to Patrick Walls (of the Blastfurnacemens Union), Thomas Cape (Cumberland Coal Miners Assoc.), T. Gavin Duffy (Cumberland Iron-Ore Miners Assoc.), William Cowan (Cumberland Quarrymens Assoc.). The King and Queen spent the night aboard the Royal Train at Brayton Junction, before concluding their tour of the area, with a visit to Carlisle the following day. A few days later, a letter sent from the Royal Train to the town's Mayor, read *"the King and Queen were very pleased with the warm reception ac-*

corded them at Workington".

In March 1918, the Workington I&SCo. was taken over by the rapidly expanding United Steel Group. This Sheffield based company, had it's origins in the nucleus of *Steel, Peech and Tozer* (of Rotherham) and *Samuel Fox* (of Stocksbridge) in 1917. Further acquisitions in Scunthorpe and Appleby (Lincolnshire) followed in 1918. Thereafter it was re-structured into a limited company, and traded as United Steel Company Limited. The purchase of the Workington plant essentially guaranteed supplies of haematite pig iron to the Sheffield works. Initially, there was considerable overlap of production, as the various parts of United Steel had previously traded independently. It was not until the 1930s, that any major rationalisation of production took place, and this was not fully implemented until after WW2. The manufacture of railway lines and associated products within the group was concentrated at Workington, together with the haematite and blast furnace ferro-alloys trades.

The end of the Great War (WW1) was greeted by everyone, with enormous relief and expectancy. But after a very brief and hectic boom, a catastrophic slump followed lasting many years. Between 1920-21, UK steel production fell by over 55%. This reduction was attributed to the major coal strike, and seriously affected the town's iron and steel works. Almost six months production was lost, when the workers were laid off and the plant stood idle. Many iron and steel workers were once again jobless, their families hungry and destitute. This serious recession now eclipsed the acute depression of the mid 1890s. As unemployment in the town rose to record levels, the Borough Council attempted to ease the hardship and poverty. They set up an unemployment register, and rented an office at 31 Station Road, where the jobless could seek out part-time work.[01] A Local Employment Commitee was established with the primary aim of *"getting men to work on local projects"*. Municipal improvement schemes being created to make use of this *"idle and needy"* workforce. Much like today, it was a requirement that those out of work registered each week.

Although they could not always offer anything like full-time employment. Many were taken on, making up Oxford Street (the new road between Central Square and Station Road), covering the Cloffolks with top soil or widening Salterbeck Road. Others laid stones to protect the riverbank of the Derwent, repaired roads or dug new sewers and gas mains within the town. By the winter of 1922, many began work on constructing the new Prince of Wales Dock. Later schemes involved the laying out of

---

"The great depression of the country has borne very hard upon Workington on account of the fact that its staple industries, namely the manufacture of Iron and Steel have been most affected"

Thomas Cape
(MP for Workington) Jan 1923

"The local iron and steel industry might well have foundered in the 1920s, if United Steel Companies had not only had faith in the possibilities of West Cumberland, but also a strong sense of responsibility towards the local community".

Douglas R. Wattleworth
1965

[01] The Borough Council records reveal there were 900 men unemployed in the town in December 1919, many of which were ex.servicemen. In March 1921, the Council moved its *"labour exchange"* onto Finkle Street, and there was still 304 men out of work. Generally each week, work was now being found for only around 10% of the unemployed.■

Central Park [01] and the creation of Salterbeck Cemetery. This system of unemployment relief under the management of the Borough Council continued into the 1930s. Then of course, this type of work was principally labour intensive. There were no suitable mechanical diggers or earthmovers, digging trenches was hard back breaking work, done entirely by hand.

The period 1930-39 saw *"physical re-equipment, ordered price structures and technical progress in the steel industry"* which led to something of a revival. By 1932, United Steel replaced one of Moss Bay's older blast furnaces with a modern unit, complete with skip loading equipment. The remaining two blast furnaces were also later rebuilt, and provided with bucket type chargers. Two years later, a new Bessemer steel plant comprising of two 25 ton converters, with a 400 ton hot metal mixer was commissioned. This replaced the three 16 ton converters which had been installed in 1912. A new steel ingot casting shop, with a capacity of sixty-four 3 ton ingots and two new soaking pits were also erected. In addition, a double stand pig iron casting machine was brought into use in 1936, and thereafter all sand casting ceased.

That same year, a new coke oven plant was also erected. Built by the Woodhall-Duckham Company, it had 53 individual ovens. By 1940, a further eleven were added bringing the companies weekly blast furnace coke production to 7,000 tons. That same year, eleven new coke ovens come into operation. Mike Burridge in his 1963 notes on steelmaking later wrote *"Workington now possessed one of the most modern steel-making plants in Europe, if not the world"*. As production almost trebled during this decade, the recovery stood the Workington works in good stead for the difficult war years that followed.

Much of this work had been carried out under the guidance of Workington's general manager Thomas Whitley Graham. He had spent a lifetime in the iron and steel industry, gaining a vast experience. At 15, the youthful Graham had started his working life at the Derwent blast furnaces, working under Mr. Paterson. In 1907, Graham took over as manager of the Moss Bay furnaces, before becoming the manager of that works two years later. After the merger of the Workington iron and steel plants he subsequently became manager of the *"combine"*. A decade later he was appointed general manager of the Workington branch of the United Steel Companies. In 1938, the *Workington Iron and Steel Company* name was again revived when United Steel converted it's Cumberland branch into a new subsidiary company.

"Workington now possessed one of the best Bessemer plants in England"

T. W Graham
General manager
United Steel Companies
(Workington branch)
1936

[01] Central park was later re-named Vulcans Park. This scheme would employ around 60 men, who were paid just 8 shillings (40p) a day. A greater proportion of these workers were ex-servicemen, all were selected by the local employment commitee. Records show that there were 264 ex.servicemen on the town's unemployment register in June 1924. ■

Although now administered by a local board based in Workington, the parent company retained the assets and general control.

Despite all the lessons learnt from the Great War, with the outbreak of WW2 the country was again relatively slow to increase its munitions manufacture. It was the shock of Dunkirk in May 1940, that awakened the nation and prompted Winston Churchill to swiftly address the situation. Very similar wartime controls and restrictions were once again imposed, essentially *"almost nationalizing"* the industry. Several changes and developments in armaments, now posed a major problem. During the first war, munitions were manufactured from *"cast iron and mild steel"*, but special heat-treated steels were now required. Although traditionally only made in and around Sheffield, a new electric alloy steelmaking plant was installed at Moss Bay. The plant funded by the government, was capable of producing all qualities of steel, including the alloy steels used for armour and bullet-proof plate, used to build tanks and armoured cars. A new shell machining department was also installed at the plant..

Workington was chosen for this additional war production, because of it's location well away from the risk of major bombing attacks. Although the town eventually came through the air raids untouched, it was always a constant preoccupation and a *"great hindrance to getting on with the job"*. An old picture postcard depicts a night scene at the Moss Bay works, it's furnaces and chimneys brightly lighting up the sky. If the German Luftwaffe had ever managed to reach West Cumberland, they would have had no problem identifying their target. Quite late in the conflicts, a number of Hispano anti-air craft guns were installed to defend the works, manned by the Home Guard. Aeroplanes were sent over twice a week, in order that the civilian volunteers could practise their drill.

Again thousands of Workington's working men left the town to enlist in the armed forces, and fight for their country. As during the Great War, women were once again called upon to work in the town's iron and steelworks. In 1942, the Borough Council aided the war effort by opening two nurseries to assist with child care, and leave mothers free also to work. One of these single storey temporary wooden buildings was sited at the junction of Cross Street and Casson Road. The other nursery was in Gray Street, on land to the rear of the Oxford Picture House (today occupied by the telephone exchange).

As the town's population well exceeded "the minimum 10,000 inhabitants", the Borough Council was also required to set up *"efficient salvage schemes"*, to aid the

"A major step in the final concentration of iron and steel manufacture at Workington was the building of the coke ovens"

Douglas R. Wattleworth.

"Previously the bulk of the coke used at Workington had been processed in the coke ovens at Risehow, St. Helens and Moresby collieries. Now coal could simply be brought in by rail or from the nearby Solway pit and then processed on site in the companies own coke ovens."

Mike Burridge

war effort. And in September 1941, the Ministry of Supply informed the town that they must *"requisition all unnecessary iron and steel railings and gates for scrap"*. The country was then so desperately short of basic raw materials, [01] it was intended that this scrap would be melted down and recast. By 1942, the Borough Surveyor had prepared a full schedule of all the *"unnecessary"* ironwork to be removed and salvaged. Adverts were then placed in the local papers, informing the townspeople of their imminent requisition. The towns streets were relentlessly stripped of their iron railings, gates and many other (now priceless) ornamental features. Today, anyone walking through the town can still clearly see where railings were removed from the many low forecourt walls, infront of our older houses. Even the ancient cannon which once stood outside the Town Hall in Oxford Street was sold for scrap, during the early years of the war.

By 1942, the home production of iron ore had increased by 25%. But due to mining difficulties, this barely exceeded 1 million tons a year. The far-richer foreign ore was essential for *"oxidizing the charge in the steel furnaces"*. Britain turned to Brazil for supplies, but this meant a round trip of 16,000 miles through U-boat infested water. 224 ore-ships were sunk or lost, restricting further urgent supplies to the nations steel works.

Early in WW2 when the German army invaded Norway, they essentially cut off the UK's supply of essential *"special steels"*, such as alloy and stainless steel. Although for a short time some supplies were shipped across the Atlantic from America, it was soon clear that further electric-arc furnace steel plants [02] had to be built in this country. Workington was chosen as one location for such a new plant, because of it's isolated location away from the enemy. By February 1942, a new 20 ton furnace had been installed at Moss Bay whilst an additional one was commissioned at the new Chapel Bank works by the summer of 1943. Four others were later installed, although the last one was thought to have never been commissioned during the war years.

Work began on the construction of the Chapel Bank works in February 1941. Also known then as the *'Workington Shore works'* it was formally opened by W. T. V. Harmer (of the *Ministry of Supply*) in October 1941. The plant being entirely funded by this government agency. Located on a 43-acre site below the shore hills, between the south bank of the River Derwent estuary and the blast furnaces of the Derwent works, it is still in production today. Although presently part of *Corus Engineering*,

[01] Before WW2 Britain depended on nearly a third of it's consumption of iron ore being imported (about 7 million tons). The pre-war primary sources were France, North Africa, Sweden, Norway and Northern Spain. At the outbreak of war, supplies were almost immediately restricted by shipping difficulties, as the majority of ore was brought to the UK in foreign vessels. By May 1940, Germany had advanced through Europe and cut the sources of foreign ore by almost 80%. After December 1941 and the Japanese attack on Pearl Harbour, matters got very much worse.■

[02] An Electric-Arc furnace is quite different from a Bessemer converter. Because very precise control of the composition of the final product is possible, such furnaces are used for the more expensive, quality steels. Cold scrap is also generally used in an electric-arc furnace, unlike the Bessemer which is charged with hot metal. ■

over the years it has been known by a succession of different names. It started life during those early war years as the *Distington Haematite Iron Company* given this name to confuse the enemy as to it's location and true purpose. This company name did still exist, but was inactive and had previously been associated with the blast furnaces at Distington on the outskirts of the town. As well as baffling the wartime German intelligence, in more recent years, it has also confused several local historians who still believe the new electric-arc furnace was actually built at Distington, not at Chapel Bank. Lancaster and Wattleworth confirm this by telling us that *"the only connection with Distington were the ornamental and imposing gates at the entrance to the works"*. Which were said to have once *"graced the entrance to Distington Hall"*.

The Chapel Bank works, named after it's close proximity to remains of the ancient chapel on the shoreline, was said to be the largest electric steel plant in the country. But after the war the works were suddenly closed in December 1944. Newspaper reports tell us that the redundant plant was subsequently purchased from the government and operated thereafter by the newly formed *Distington Engineering Company*, a division of the *United Steel Company*. The plant was now a modern foundry, largely specialising in the manufacture of haematite iron castings. The old furnaces were stripped out and *"the latest"* new machinery was installed, with an engineering works, machine shops, press shop, and fabrication shop for platework and larger heavy items. Much of its foundry work was the manufacture of ingot moulds and converter bottom plates used in steelmaking. The works also produced specialist mining equipment for Goodmans of Chicago, most of it being shipped out of Workington harbour. The company also became the sole manufacturer of tunnellers, duckbill loaders, ropebelt conveyors and shaker conveyors. By the 1960s, Chapel Bank housed the largest iron foundry in Europe, employing around 300 men and was capable of producing about 2,000 tons of finished castings each week.

After the end of WW2, the British Government implemented controls to restrict the expansion of the steel Industry. There was still difficulties in obtaining supplies, and shortage of particular steel products persisted long into the post war period. Despite this the British steel industry emerged as a very *"strong going concern"*. As David Murray commented it was *"lean, battle scarred, but fighting fit"*. The 1946 White paper on the Iron and Steel Industry, proposed Workington should principally

"Geographically, United Steel Company was a multi-works concern with widely dispersed interests. Workington Iron and Steel Company was their most isolated plant being 72 straight line miles from Consett Iron, and 132 from United Steel Companies' main plant at Sheffield (to whom Workington supplied spiegeleisen and haematite pig iron) and 122 miles from their Rotherham plant."

Mike Burridge

concentrate their efforts on heavy steel rail production. An extremely logical suggestion in view of the modernisation work carried out at the plant during the previous decade or so. The Moss Bay works now covered 500-1000 acres and was the sixth largest in the country by area. By 1949, a new rail finishing mill was installed at Workington, and the old cogging mill was replaced by a new 36 inch cogging mill. This rolled its first ingots in August of that year. Around six months later, a new turbo-blower with a capacity of 30,000 cubic feet per minute was installed to provide a more efficient blow to the two 25 ton Bessemer converters.

By the 1950s, Workington was the only surviving bulk production acid Bessemer steel plant in Britain. Moss Bay now possessed three mechanically charged blast furnaces, having a gross output of 8,600 tons per week. The present blast furnace plant, located on the site of the old Derwent Ironworks, having been completely rebuilt and modernised. A second new cogging or rolling mill with electric drive and a capacity of around 8000 tons per week was installed. The majority of the old mill buildings were replaced, the remainder modernised.

Although a degree of government control was maintained, the industry itself already had *"a voluntary, central organisation in the British Iron and Steel Federation"*. In February 1951, the ninety four main companies that made up the UK's iron and steel Industry were nationalized. But after the general election in October 1952 returned the Conservatives, the industry was quickly returned to private ownership. The United Steel Company, still one of the largest companies, reappeared in much the same form as their pre-nationalised counterparts. Many believe an *"opportunity to reconstruct the industry was lost with this denationalization"*. It would be a further fifteen years before the Labour government got the opportunity to nationalize the industry once more.

In addition to the production of pig iron and steel-making that brought vast employment and prosperity to the town, there were also several smaller independent foundries that used the puddling process to manufacture bar or wrought iron. With the exception of the New Yard works that was a little further to the south. These works were all located quite close to Stanley Street which runs parallel to the South Quay. The Kirk family had an active interest in the New Yard works and two other such concerns, the Marshside Ironworks and the Quayside Forge.

Before being taken over by the Kirk Bros. around

By the 1950s, Workington was the only surviving bulk production acid Bessemer steel plant in Britain.

At the beginning of 1880, Kirk Bros. began the construction of a blast furnace at the New Yard works.

1861, New Yard had existed for many years as an iron foundry. However, like several of the other similar small concerns in the town, it's very early history is something of a mystery. What we do know is New Yard certainly existed in the 1840's as it appears on the plans of the proposed Whitehaven Junction Railway, prepared by the eminent engineer George Stephenson. There are also several records that suggest this small foundry was once operated by the Curwen family, perhaps in connection with their mining activities. Plans also show that around the works were built a number of small cottages which generally housed the employees. In fact New yard in those early days, seems to have existed as a small community, somewhat isolated from the remainder of the town. Because of it's close proximity to the ancient chapel of How Michael, it also seems to have been occasionally called Chapel town.

At the beginning of 1880, Kirk Bros. began the construction of a blast furnace at the New Yard works. It was sited at the rear of the *"moulding sheds"*. A powerful new steam engine was also installed to provide the powerful *"blast of air"*, needed to smelt the pig iron. This was located in a new brick built engine house, located beneath the tall chimney which can clearly be seen on the several old photographs of the works that exist today. Douglas R. Wattleworth who started work in the town's iron and steel industry in 1907, vividly remembered the New Yard works around that time, and later recorded that *"the blast furnace was on the sea side of the public footpath that ran through the works, with the puddling furnaces, etc. on the other. Hot metal was taken by ladle to the pre-treatment furnace, before charging to the puddling furnaces."*

In February 1881, when the new blast furnace at Kirk's New Yard works was *"first charged"*, there was a massive explosion which totally *"wrecked"* the top of the new structure. One newspaper report tells how the "enormous boom" could be heard over the town. Thankfully no one was killed or injured in the explosion, and the blast furnace was rapidly repaired. It was finally commissioned and cast its first pig iron two weeks later. Despite having what was described as a *"plethora of orders"*, Kirk Bros. found themselves on the brink of bankrupcy within just a few months. Perhaps due to their huge expenditure at New Yard and their recent purchase of Ellen Rolling Mills at Maryport. But after continuing to trade during these difficult times, they eventually reached an agreement with their creditors and the *"liquidation was closed"*.

New Yard must have enjoyed some years of relative prosperity, Bulmer tells us their output in 1901 was about 25,000 tons of pig iron. But they must have found it difficult to compete alongside the other much larger iron producers in the town. Kirk Bros. remained in control until well past the turn of the century, employing *"about 350 men and boys"*. Then as we know from Joseph Huntrods' biography, the works passed to *"Mr. Morrison, one of the richest men in the country"*. And it was he who first brought Huntrods to the town in an attempt to *"restore it's fortunes"*. But it was also described as *"an impossible task"*. The New Yard works were eventually acquired by the *Workington Iron and Steel Company*. Lancaster and Wattleworth telling us that much of their new coke oven plant erected in 1936, occupied the site. However, the enterprising Huntrods did remain in the town and went on to establish the successful *Workington Bridge and Boiler Company*.

The Kirk family eventually also acquired the Marsh Side puddling furnaces and rolling mill, established by Dixon and Bayliss in 1869. The OS plan tells us that the *Marshside Ironworks* were located between the rear of the houses on Stanley Street and at the back of the houses on Marshside, close to the south end of Marsh Street. Lancaster and Wattleworth tell us that in 1872, *"after a period of idleness"* Marsh Side began trading as Price and Dixon. They also suggest that the works were presently undergoing some *"alterations and extensions"*. Exactly when it was acquired by the Kirks is not clear. Although when Henry Kirk read a paper entitled *"puddling in the single hand furnaces"*, to the *Iron and Steel Institute* in September 1876, he is listed as being of *"New Yard and Marsh Side works"*.

In June 1881 around the time of the Kirk Bros. financial difficulties, Marshside is known to have been idle. But production was recommenced soon afterwards. By 1901, Bulmer tells us it employed around 150 men and had one forge and a single rolling mill. He added that the combined annual output at this time (from both the New Yard and Marshside works) was 25,000 tons of bars and rivet iron; and from 650 to 1,000 tons of iron and brass castings. The Marsh Side works was still operating in 1907, as a factory inspectors report exists in the Borough Council files.

The Quayside Forge or Ironworks on the south side of Stanley Street immediately west of the gasworks, began life as the Derwent Ironworks. The early history of this foundry was included in the first volume of Workington's history [01]. Readers should not confuse this

The Kirk family eventually also acquired the Marsh Side puddling furnaces and rolling mill, established by Dixon and Bayliss in 1869.

[01] Please see chapter twelve of the History of Workington (From Earliest Times to 1865). ■

smaller concern with the very much larger Derwent Haematite Ironworks, later established at Moss Bay. Several local newspaper reports confirm that the Derwent Forge lay idle for around six or seven years during the 1860s. Lancaster and Wattleworth suggesting that it was purchased by Henry Kirk and Charles Valentine in 1869. But thereafter almost all reference to the forge, appear to suggest that it was operated by Kirk Bros. Eitherway, this is likely to have been when the works were renamed the Quayside forge. The works continued to be operated by the Kirk family until 1885, when they were sold to the Moss Bay HI&SCo. The Quayside premises closed in the early 1900s and were acquired by the Workington Corporation, sometime before 1907. After the buildings were demolished, the town's gasworks was extended over the site. ■

RIGHT - Sketch of a coal truck with the livery of the Cleator & Workington Junction Railway. In wagons such as these the company transported many thousands of tons of coal and coke to the towns iron and steeloworks. ■

✃ CHAPTER FOUR ✄

COAL INDUSTRY

IF WE TAKE a snapshot of coal mining in the town around 1856, we find just Jane Pit in production, with both Buddle and Jackson pits lying idle. Jane Pit was located between what we now know as the Ellis sports ground and Moss Bay Road. The site is easily identified by the familiar remains of the old *"castellated oval engine house and two tall chimneys"*. As detailed in the earlier volume of the town's history, it was sunk in 1843 by the Curwen family. In its early years it reached the Hamilton seam, [01] at a depth of about 120 metres. With some of its workings extending as far south as Harrington. Buddle Pit was located around 500 feet (154 metres) southwest of Jane Pit. Whilst Jackson was situated almost midway between Westfield and Moorclose farms.

In its early years Jane Pit appears to have been very productive, with much of the coal being shipped out of the town's harbour to Ireland. [02] But following the death of Henry [vi] Curwen in the autumn of 1860, the situation changed. The Workington estates had been inherited by Henry's second son Edward Stanley Curwen. Henry had over thirty years experience in coal mining, whilst Edward was predominately a military man. There is a suggestion that he struggled to manage his father's colliery, and production at Jane Pit proved barely adequate. In 1864, he leased off the colliery to William Irving (1815-1872). The 1871 census shows Irving and his wife Janet (1811-1891) living at 14 William Street. Few records appear to have survived to give us a clear picture of production thereafter, but we do know William Irving later sank a new shaft about 500 feet (154 metres) north east of Jane Pit. This site today is occupied by the T.A. Centre. Here he established Annie Pit, which ultimately gave its name to the lane leading down to Clay Flatts.

At Annie Pit, much of the production was from the Yard and Hamilton seams which were found to rise to the north east at a slope (or angle) of 1 in 47. After William Irving's death in December 1872, the lease of both Jane and Annie Pits was acquired by H. K. Spark of Darlington (later Penrith). Exactly when production ceased at Jane pit is not clear. It appears much of the coal was subsequently raised from Annie Pit, whilst pumping was continued at Jane until at least 1875. The workings of both pits were

The remains of Jane Pit were immortalised in a drawing by the famous *"matchstick man"* artist L. S. Lowry. In 2001, the picture was sold at Christie's auction house in London for nearly £13,000.

William Gibson
Manager at Jane Pit
died 23th January 1867
aged 27
fell down the pit shaft

[01] See page 154 of *History of Workington (Earliest times to 1865)* for description of coal seams under the town. ■

[02] This coal was transported from the pit head down to the harbour along a wagonway or tramway. This followed the line of Annie Pit Lane, passed New Yard, before curving north towards the South Quay, passed Chapel Bank Farm. The tracks then passed very close to the south end of Henry Street, before entering Harbour Place. ■

ST HELENS COLLIERY
Management 1882-1950
1882 J. H. Johnson (Manager)
1888 J. H. Johnson (Manager)
1888 John Davidson
            (Under Manager)
1890 James Gilchrist
            (Manager)
1896 Geo. Scoular (Manager)
1896 Joseph Morrison
            (Assistant. Manager)
1902 Joseph Morrison
            (Manager)
1902 John Underwood
            (Manager)
1914 A. C. Scoular
1914 John Coates (Manager)
1914 John Underwood
            (Under Manager)
1921 T. Banks (Agent)
1921 C. D. James (Manager)
1921 John Spence
            (Under Manager)
1930 T. Banks (Agent)
1930 C. D. James (Manager)
1930 James Johnson
            (Under Manager)
1940 T. J. Hughes (Manager)
1945 J. H. Lloyd (Manager)
1945 R. Easton
            (Under Manager)
1947 J. H. Lloyd (Manager)
1950 J. H. Lloyd (Manager)
1950 T. Crellin
            (Under Manager) ■

[01] The *Workington Colliery Company* was formed in 1875, for the *"purpose of acquiring the collieries of H. K. Spark"*. None of it's initial subscribers were locally based although Thomas Pattinson Martin, a mining engineer from Airdrie, is thought to have taken up residence in the town. ■

thought to have been connected underground.

By then, the demand for West Cumberland coal again slumped, with the cost of extraction being simply far too high. The rapidly growing railway system now brought supplies of cheaper Scottish coal, into the area. The mineowners in an effort to remain more competitive, attempted to reduce the miners wages by around 15%. A fourteen week strike ensued, with the men reluctantly returning with a 10% wage cut. Workington's coal industry was permanently and seriously affected, and never really recovered from this crisis. During the strike, Scottish coal proprietors had stepped in and grabbed an increased market share. In the winter of 1875, Annie Pit was closed and coal mining ceased in the town once more.

For many years, Spark obviously still retained the lease and made several attempts to reopen Annie Pit. But the abandoned workings had become flooded, and months of pumping was necessary before coal could be extracted once again. By May 1882, a newspaper report disappointingly suggests that Spark had *"got no further than clearing the pits of water"*. It was also reported that the newly formed *Workington Colliery Company* [01] was planning to take over the lease of these royalties, with the intention of reopening the Jane and Annie pits. But the company would collapse soon after and no further coal was raised at this colliery.

In the meantime, Mulcaster and Bell are known to have acquired the lease of St. Helens colliery, from Sir James Lowther in 1870. This covered a total area of 7,000 acres of *"land and sea coal royalties"*, from the River Derwent north almost to Maryport. A decade earlier, Mulcaster and Bell had been part of a group which had reopened and extended the two original St. Helens pits at Flimby. Now they planned to sink a new shaft at Siddick, just north of Oldside. In 1878, work began on this third pit, north of the West Cumberland I&SCo works. This pit eventually became known as *"St. Helens No. 3"*. Although some early records are quite confusing and occasionally also refer to it as *"William Pit No 3"*.

On the 6 November 1876, the *St. Helens Colliery and Brick works Company Limited* were first registered and they would run these pits thereafter. The new company paid £35,100 to acquire the *"colliery and brickworks"*, including *"all plant, inclines and railways"*, nearly all of which was paid in shares. The lease of the colliery would still remain in the name of William Mulcaster. On the 1 July 1885, we know this was renewed once again by Lord Lonsdale, but in the names of William Mulcaster and Richard Senhouse.

By 1880. the new No. 3 pit at Siddick reached the Ten Quarters seam, at around 50 fathoms (90m). Two years later, it is thought they were working the Cannel and Metal Band seams. Certainly it is also quite probable that the workings on these levels extended westward, out under the sea. As production continued the pit was ultimately sunk deeper to the Lickbank seam by 1889. The relativity narrow Lickbank band of coal lay at a depth of around 170 fathoms (306m).

Tragedy struck St. Helens on Thursday 20 April 1888, twenty eight miners lost their lives in a huge underground gas explosion. The huge blast described as *"of an overwhelming character"* and the ensuing horrific fire ripped through the mineworkings, around 300 yards from the pit shaft. Many of the colliers suffered horrendous injuries. These were graphically described in the local newspaper reports of the accident.

In 1899, at least 100,000 tons of coal from St. Helens was exported out of Lonsdale Dock to Belfast, Dublin, Cork and the Isle of Man. In 1900, they were said to employ over 771 men at Siddick. During this period the village of Siddick was also laid out by the colliery company, built to accommodate its employees and their families. A decade or so later, St. Helens No 3 was raising coal from around 225 fathoms, much of it's working extending well out into the Solway Firth. John Coates was now the colliery manager and the pit employed 741 men and boys below ground and a further 286 at ground level.

In 1919, the colliery was thought to have been taken over by A. E. Barton. But a strike in February 1920 is thought to have caused major hardship and problems, not just for the striking workers, but also for much of the town. St. Helens then supplied *"nine-tenths of the inhabitants of the town"* with coal used for heating and cooking. By 1921, Sir Samuel Kelly (of Belfast) had taken over the St. Helen's company. Certainly he is listed as the chairman in 1924, along with directors J. K. Harper, Lady Mary Kelly and Samuel Moss. [01] Around this time the St. Helens No. 2 shaft at Flimby was abandoned, leaving just the pithead at Siddick. There appears to have been few redundancies as the workforce here was almost doubled to over 1,500.

On 27 November 1922, a further six men lost their lives in another explosion at St. Helens No. 3. The inquest put the cause of this disaster down to the *"opening of a flame safety lamp"*. Among the dead were three members of the Davison family, who lived at 102 Main Street, Ellenborough. The casualties were George Davison (Snr.), George Davison (Jnr.) and John Davison.

Bodies recovered from the mine were frightfully mutilated. One poor fellow dismembered, others disembowelled and the horror of the situation reached a climax as the burly form of one miner was picked up with the whole of the top of his skull blown off, his head being emptied of brains and looking like the half of an emptied coconut".

Dr Fray Ormrod
April 1888

St. Helens Disaster
20 April 1888
The dead were listed as John Nicholson 34, James Moffatt 53, James P. Smith 35, John Martin 58, George Wright 42, Wiggan Beaty 24, John Ballentine 54, Joseph Stephenson 42, Richard Jackson 27, William Gavan 28, Joseph Iredale 44, John Davidson 53, Robert Labourn 22, John Williams 31, James Hogg 31, Robert Townsley 39, Robert Hodgson 39, William Banton 37, William John Beattie 37, William Peel 47, William Tunstall 41, John Johnston 26, Isaac Gaskin 42, William Holstead 45, Thomas Marrs 32, Thomas Hannah 25, Thompson Moore 25, Henry Nicholson 22. ■

[01] Details published in *Mining Manual and Mining Yearbook*, published in 1924. ■

"Unlike the town's earlier collieries where the distinctive pit heads were built from massive timbers or ironwork. The pit head supporting the winding gear at Solway Colliery was constructed almost entirely of reinforced concrete, a relatively new material in the 1930s."

Mike Burridge
1964

SOLWAY COLLIERY
Management 1940-1950
1940 R. Neill (Manager)
1945 T. H. Dobson (Manager)
1945 J. A. Allen
         (Under Manager)
1947 T. H. Dobson (Manager)
1950 A. Machin (Manager) ■

By 1930, C. D. James was the manager of St. Helens and the company still employed over 1,500 men. But by 1934, the workforce had been cut by half. Six years later, annual production reached 350,000 tons. Once again they employed a *"healthy"* workforce of over 1,500 men, each day around 1,320 of which would go below ground to work the coal. Following the death of her husband, Lady Kelly had now taken over as chairman. The colliery manager was now T. J. Hughes, who was also a director. He is listed as living at Morven, the large detached house on the west side of the main road north to Maryport.

In 1943, St. Helens Colliery and Brickworks was purchased by the United Steel Companies Limited, who also ran the steelworks at Moss Bay. In 1947 when the countries pits were nationalised, the Siddick pit was handed over to the newly formed *National Coal Board*. The workforce at this time was now around 470, of which 350 miners. Production continued until July 1966, when St. Helens was closed, leaving the Solway Colliery as the only remaining working pit in the town.

Solway Colliery was situated to the south west of the Ellis Sports Ground (off Moss Bay Road) and very close to the abandoned shaft of Buddle Pit. It was sunk by the *United Steel Companies*, who owned the iron and steelworks on the opposite side of the main Whitehaven to Workington railway line. Although the work on the new pit began in 1937, it did not come into production until the end of WW2, which had almost halted its construction. Costing in the region of £486,000 the colliery was planned as an integral part of the steelworks. The United Steel was undergoing a major modernisation of the works (see previous chapter) and had recently opened a new modern coke oven plant. An overhead conveyor was constructed over the railway line to link the two sites. Coal could now be raised from the pit and easily transported only a short distance to the nearby coke ovens, without incurring any railway charges.

In 1947, ownership of the Solway Colliery also passed to the newly formed *National Coal Board*. Production at the pit continued for another twenty six years before Solway closed in 1973. This was the last working coal mine in the town, and the site has now been completely cleared. After many centuries, coal production in Workington looked to have ceased forever. A stones throw from Solway are the two chimneys and castellated oval engine house of Jane Pit. This is virtually all that remains in the town to remind us of our once rich coal trade. Without which the iron and steel industry, our harbour and the town itself may never have developed.■

CHAPTER FIVE

SHIPBUILDING

FROM THE 1850s, we know that more and more new ships were built of iron, rather than timber, and steam power was gradually replacing sail. This brought about a rapid decline of Workington's once proud and renowned shipbuilding industry. It's relatively small shipyards, which traditionally built only timber vessels became uneconomical and were forced to cease trading. The last entirely timber sailing ship built at Workington was the *Omega*, launched in 1869. It was built at the Low Shipyard located to the west of the Dock Quay, on the south bank of the Derwent estuary. [01]

With the decline of timber shipbuilding and the shortage of similar work in West Cumberland, a significant number of the skilled shipwrights, ship carpenters, shipsmiths, sail makers, riggers etc., migrated from the town seeking out new employment. They settled with their families throughout the length and breath of the country close to the major dockyards. Places where their traditional skills were still in demand, despite the new trend of building ships in iron and steel. Mike Burridge in his unpublished notes on *Shipbuilding in West Cumberland*, carefully studied these migration patterns through detailed analysis of census records. He pinpoints the bulk of Workington's redundant shipbuilders moving to Merseyside. Although others are certainly also known to have relocated to Barrow-in-Furness, Tyne and Wear, Woolwich, Devonport and Glasgow.

The busy shipyards of Liverpool, centred around the second largest port in Britain, were perhaps the obvious first choice for the unemployed workers. Passage to Liverpool could be easily obtained aboard the many cargo ships that regularly sailed out of Workington harbour. Passenger steamers also made the trip twice a week, between the two ports. Burridge revealed that well over fifty shipyard workers who learnt their skills building timber ships at Workington, eventually settled in Liverpool.[02] Several generations of the same family uprooted and made the permanent move to Merseyside. For example, the familiar family names of Gallantry, Hellon, Fraser, Carr, Tomlinson, Doharty, Andrews and Gambles, regularly appear in the 1881 census for the Liverpool dock-

ABOVE - Sketch of a typical carved figurehead which once adorned the bow of nearly every new sailing ship. The figurehead of the *Omega* was believed to have been carved by Workington's George Brooker (1824-1912). He is known to have carved many other figureheads for several new vessels launched from West Cumbrian shipyards. ■

[01] See Chapter Eleven of *History of Workington* (Earliest Times to AD 1865) for more information. ■

[02] From the 1881 census, Mike Burridge identified just over ninety shipyard workers who he believed had moved from Workington after the ceasation of timber shipbuilding in the town. Of these 61% had eventually settled in Liverpool, 16% in the Barrow-in-Furness area, with 23% elsewhere (Devonport, Tyne and Wear, Glasgow etc.). ■

land areas. The majority were shipyard workers who were born in Workington. Other family details point to them settling on Merseyside around 1860-70. This period clearly coincides with the closure of shipyards in Workington.

Low yard once described as *"one of the finest on the Cumbrian coast"* and responsible for building many elegant and graceful sailing ships now lay virtually idle. We know from the 1871 census that shipbuilder, Anthony Peile employed just six men, probably carrying out basic repair and maintenance work. By May 1874, the *"inner and outer sheds"* at the shipyard were sold off by the local auctioneer J. R. Wallace. Who actually then acquired the yard is not clear, but it is believed Messrs. Ritson and Potter occupied the premises in 1876. But no new ships would be built here for another seven years.

Bulmers 1901 *Directory of Cumberland* tells us *"Williamson & Son, who for many years carried on the business of shipbuilding at Harrington, formerly building wooden vessels, but latterly iron ones, removed to Workington and began iron and steel shipbuilding here in 1881"*. At Harrington, Richard Williamson and Son had built and launched seventy three sailing ships between 1839-79.

Moving their shipyard from Harrington to Workington had very obvious advantages. The Workington yard

"I vivdly remember as a child seeing the harbourside and merchants quay strewn with large blocks of Canadian timber used to build graceful ships in the shipyards. When these were launched the whole town seemed to turn out to witness the event."

Joseph Scott (1936)

BELOW - Sketch of the inner sheds at the Low shipyard, occupied by Williamson and Sons from 1881. Ships had previously been built in this area of the Derwent estuary for over 130 years. Generally, Williamsons built small steamers in this part of the shipyard. ∎

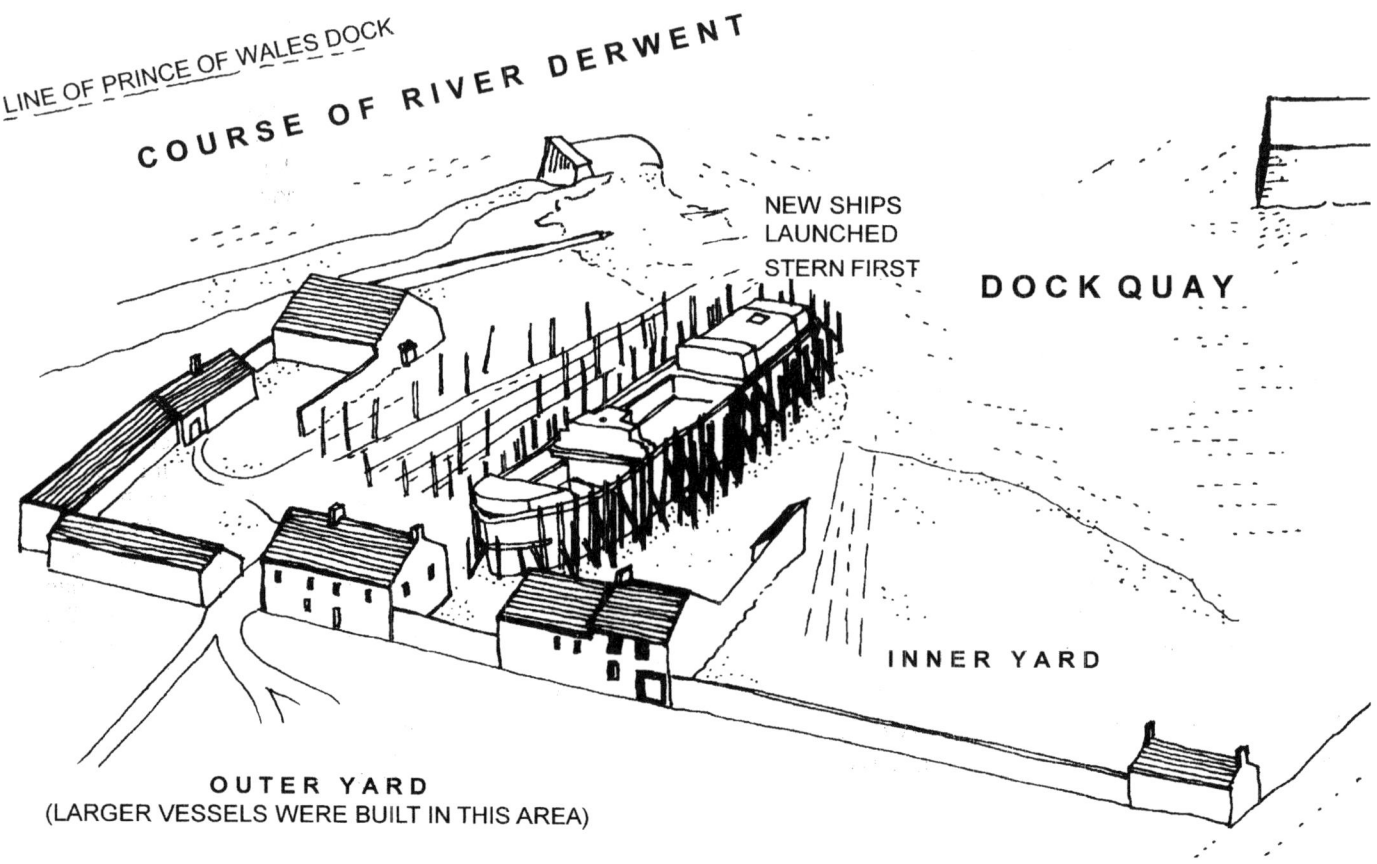

LINE OF PRINCE OF WALES DOCK

COURSE OF RIVER DERWENT

NEW SHIPS LAUNCHED STERN FIRST

DOCK QUAY

INNER YARD

OUTER YARD
(LARGER VESSELS WERE BUILT IN THIS AREA)

was much larger and would allow them to build the longer and bigger iron ships, now so much in demand. It was also located within the heart of the town's iron and steel producers, where the raw materials were readily available. It was November 1879, when the Williamsons first prepared to sell their Harrington shipyard. By February 1880, their obsolete plant and machinery was sold at an "extensive" auction, lasting three days.

It was January 1881, when Williamsons relocated to Workington. Their new shipyard was located adjacent to the old Dock Quay, often also referred to as the *Low Yard*. On the same site, Messrs. Falcon and Alexander, as well as the *Harrington and Workington Shipbuilding Co.* [01] had built ships up to 1869. This site was possibly first sold by auction in May 1874, but its purchaser is unclear.

Williamson's first ship to be built at Workington was the 1842 ton *Grassendale*. She was a three masted (full-rigged) iron ship, built for R.W. Leyland & Co. (of Liverpool) at a cost of £22,400. This vessel was launched *"amid much ceremony"* on Thursday 19 January 1882. Unfortunately the *Grassendale* was mysteriously lost in May 1884, on route from New York to Shanghai. She was last sighted at the end of August that year, off Rio de Janeiro, but never seen again.

In 1885, Williamsons would built a second *Grassendale* for Leyland & Co. She was almost identical to the

[01] See chapter eleven of *History of Workington (Earliest times to 1865)* for more details. ■

BELOW - Sketch of part of the outer area of the Low shipyard (looking east), also occupied by William-son and Sons from 1881. This was located to the west of the inner sheds shown on the previous page. Larger vessels were constructed here and launched stern first into the River Derwent.

We can easily locate this site today, as the small circular stone tidewatchers post can still be seen on the south bank of the estuary. There was also a collection of larger buildings in this area. ■

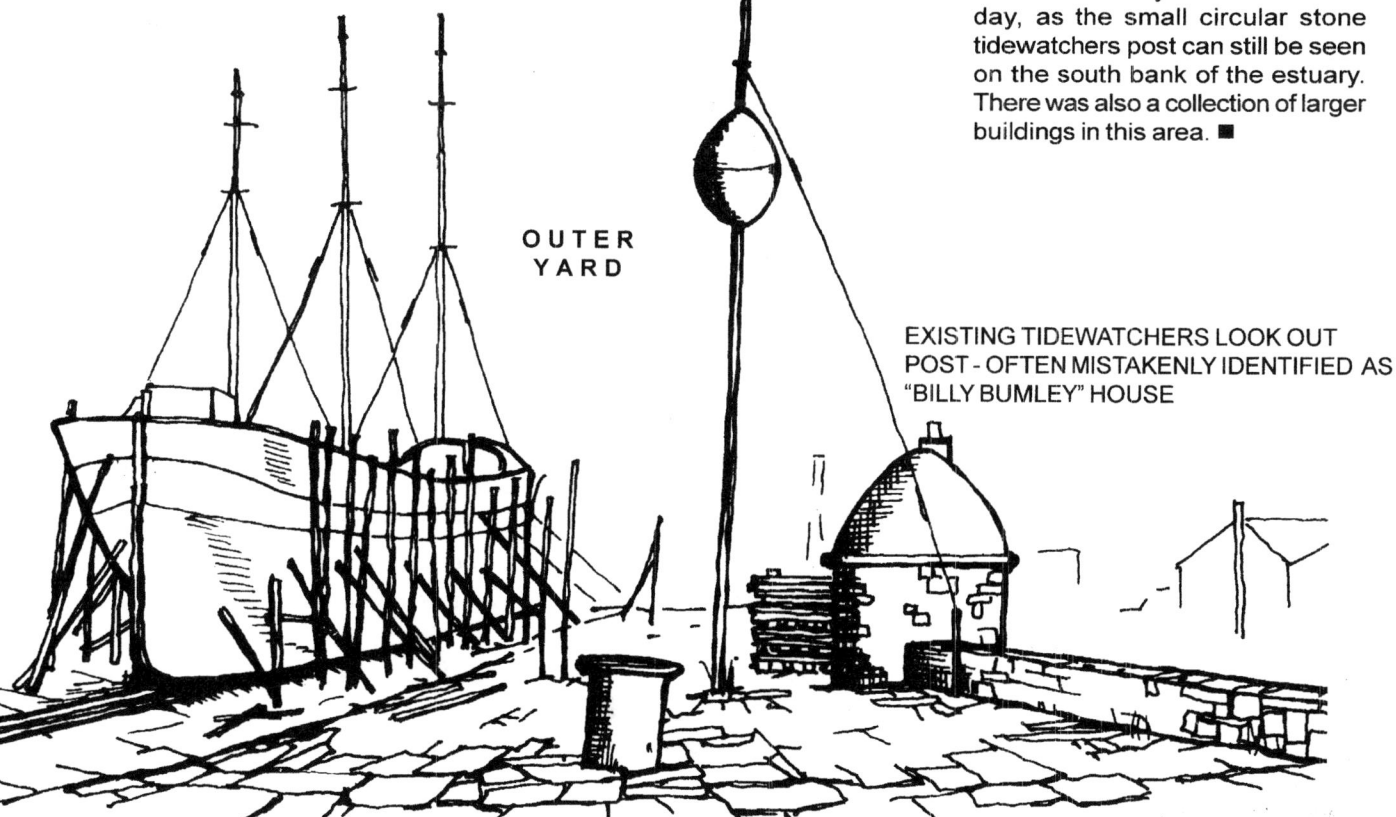

OUTER YARD

EXISTING TIDEWATCHERS LOOK OUT POST - OFTEN MISTAKENLY IDENTIFIED AS "BILLY BUMLEY" HOUSE

In April 1920, the old Workington ship was sunk by a mine in Hertha Flak, off the Danish coast.

[01] The Grassendale was 267ft (82m) in length, 39.1ft (12m) breath, with a depth of 23.6ft (7.26m). There are a number of photographs of the vessel in the State Library of Victoria, and a half model in Finland's Rauma Maritime Museum. ∎

earlier ship. [01] In 1906, this vessel was sold to a company in Finland and renamed *Imperator Aleksander II*, after the Russian Tsar. Subsequently in the next decade or so, it changed ownership many times. Eventually in 1918, it was acquired by Svenska Handelsoch Sjfarts-kompaniet (of Stockholm), and renamed the *Ernst*. In April 1920, the old Workington ship was sunk by a mine in Hertha Flak, off the Danish coast.

Williamson's busy shipyard built a further two ships for Leyland and Co. These were the *Aigbirth* (launched in August 1882) and the *Garston* (completed in September 1883). Each was 267 ft (82m) in length and 39 ft (11.9m) wide and was virtually identical once again to both the *Grassendale* ships. Suarts Almanac for 1883 tells us that the *Garston* was the first steel ship built at the yard. By a strange coincidence, as the *Garston* set off from Workington on her maiden voyage, it was reported in the local press that her sister ship *Aigbirth* was on fire in London. The *Aigbirth* was obviously later repaired and served the company till it was wrecked off New Guinea, in 1904. In less than four years, the Merseyside company spent almost £100,000 with the Workington shipbuilders and kept around 150 workers at the shipyard gainfully employed.

In February 1883, the yard had also built the 1800 ton *Crown of England* for Roberton and Cruikshank (of Liverpool) this was the third iron sailing ship built since the Williamson's had relocated to Workington. Contemporary newspaper reports tell how the vessel "glided majestically into the water". At this time they also completed their first steam ship, the 229 ton *Scale Force*, built for William Kennaugh & Co (of Whitehaven) later to be known as the *West Coast Shipping Company*. This was the first of eight vessels built by Williamsons for this local shipping company all believed to be named after Lake District waterfalls. They included *Holme Force, Stanley Force, Stock Force, Colwith Force, Skelwith Force, Aysgarth Force, and Colwith Force*.

Launched in March 1884, the 1798 ton *Cumberland* was also built at the Workington yard. This three masted (full-rigged) iron ship was first registered on the 30 November 1884. She is believed to have been built for Thomas Williamson himself, as his name appears in the register. Two years later, the 1877 ton *Silverdale* was launched. She was eventually sold in 1889 to R. Thomas and Co. (of Liverpool) and soon renamed *Criccieth Castle*. These two vessels were also very similar to the earlier iron sailing ships built for Leyland and Co. Although records show very minor differences in length, they were all 39ft in breath and 23.6 in depth, suggesting Williamson's were producing a somewhat standard ship at this time.

With this experience the Workington company embarked on building much larger vessels. Subsequently they produced six further four-masted steel barques, each around 2500 tons, measuring just over 303 ft (92.4m) length, 42.2 ft (12.9m) breath and 24.5ft (7.46m) depth. These much larger ships became known as the *"Six Workington Sisters"* and were named *Andelena, Eusemere, Pendragon Castle, Vortigern, Caradoc* and *Conishead*.

In October 1889, Williamson's launched the 2512 ton *Andelena*, the first of the *"six sisters"*. She was built for E. F. & W. Roberts (of Liverpool) and sailed predominately between North America, India and Japan. On the 14th January 1899, the Andelena capsized and sunk at Tacoma, Puget Sound (on the west coast of the USA) with the loss of all nineteen crew. When I first uncovered details of the loss of the *Andelena*, I wonder what Peter Kirk (the founder of the Moss Bay Ironworks) would have thought when he heard the sad news. For by then Kirk and his family had settled at Kirkland, quite close to Tacoma and the Puget Sound. [01] Was he aware the *Andelena* had been built at Workington perhaps with steel made at his Moss Bay works?

The second of the *"six sisters"* was the 2512 ton *Eusemere* launched in June 1890. She was purchased by Fisher and Sprott (of Liverpool) and in her early years sailed between the British Isles, North America and India. In the autumn of 1896, she was sold to Wencke and Söhne (of Hamburg) and renamed the *Pindos*. In February 1912, she was wrecked on Guthen rocks off the Cornish coast. There exists an old picture postcard of the wreck of the Pindos, and interestingly it's figurehead is also preserved at Hamburg's Altonaer Museum.

In January 1891, Williamson's launched the 2510 ton *Pendragon Castle*, another of the *"six sisters"*. She was built for James Chambers and Co. (also of Liverpool) and sailed predominately between the British Isles, North America and Australia. During WW1, the *Pendragon Castle* was confined to port at Iquique, in Chile. Rumour has it that part of her cargo of welsh coal had been supplied to the German Navy, at a time when there was an obvious embargo on such a deal. In 1920, the vessel past to the French government as *"war damage"* compensation and was eventually acquired by a Hamburg shipping company. In 1927, she ended her days at Port Glasgow where she was broken up. Some records point to her figurehead being displayed in the gardens of Rockferry Hotel

These much larger ships became known as the *"Six Workington Sisters"* and were named *Andelena, Eusemere, Pendragon Castle, Vortigern, Caradoc* and *Conishead*.

[01] See page 105 for more details of Peter Kirk and his move to the USA. ■

in Cheshire, during the 1930s.

The fourth of the *"six sisters"* was the 2529 ton *Vortigern* launched in August 1891. Williamson's built her for Brown, Jenkinson and Co. (of London), agents for the Vortigern Ship Company Limited. In May 1900, the *Vortigern* was also acquired by Wencke and Söhne (of Hamburg), who by now already owned the *Eusemere* and *Conishead,* two more of Williamson's "six sisters". The German shipping company renamed her the *Hebe.* As a German registered vessel, she was seized by the Allies during WW1 and transferred into the ownership of the Peruvian government. The South Americans re-named her the *Contramaestre Duenas,* and she is known to have been used as a school ship at Callao, before being broken up in 1929.

In April 1892, Williamson's launched the 2531 ton *Caradoc,* the fifth of the *"six sisters".* She was built for Caradoc Ship Co. (of London). Very little is known of her history, some suggest she was lost at sea having left Kobe for Port Angeles in either 1898 or 1900. In October 1892, they completed the last of the "six sisters", the 2526 ton *Conishead,* built for the Workington based partnership of Bourke and Huntrods. We appear to know little of the Bourke side of this partnership. Certainly an 1883 trade directory, lists a Bourke and Co., as iron merchants of Belle Isle Place. Whilst it is safe to assume that the other partner was very likely to be Joseph Huntrods. He was the chairman of the Workington Bridge and Boiler Company, a director of Whitehaven Iron and Steel Co., and at one time in charge at the New Yard Ironworks. In August 1898, as previously mentioned the *Conishead* was to be acquired by Wencke and Söhne (of Hamburg), and renamed the *Athene*.

During WW1, yet another one of Workington's *"six sisters"* found herself under the German flag and was seized by the Allies. On this occasion the Australian government captured the *Athene,* and escorted her to Kerosene Bay. As hostilities continued, the vessel was chartered to Scott, Fell and Co. (of London) and renamed the *Cooroy.* By a strange twist of fate, the *Cooroy* was sunk by a torpedo fired by the German submarine UC-75 on the 29 August 1917.

Soon after completing the *Conishead,* the Williamson yard started work on the *"last of the large sailing vessels"* to be built at Workington. These were the 2949 ton *Centesima,* (launched in September 1893) and its sister ship the 2958 ton *Iranian* (completed in March 1895). In their early years both these four-masted steel barques were thought to have been operated by the Williamson

"During 1898 Williamsons shipyard employed over 150 hands"
Bulmers Directory (1901)

family themselves. By 1901, the *Centesima* was sold to Visurgis AG (of Bremen). But eight years later, she was destroyed by fire while in the Chilean port of Antofagasta. In April 1900, the *Iranian* capsized and sank at Inzu, in Japanese waters, whilst on-route to Yokohama from New York.

Low Yard only completed one further sailing ship the smaller 1867 ton *Carmanian*, launched in April 1897. During the 1890s, Low yard went into something of a decline and the yard survived by simply building much smaller vessels. Many of these were barges used to transport coal or carry refuse out to be dumped at sea. Workington Borough Council employed this method of waste disposal before the land on the Cloffolks was reclaimed and used for tipping. Several photographs still exist of the town's 60 ton refuse barges moored alongside the Dock quay.

Around the turn of the century, the company were also employed in building smaller steam ships mainly used to transport grain. These dozen or so vessels averaged around 300 tons and were supplied to companies such as Carr & Co, Liverpool Grain Storage & Transport Co., and the Grain Elevating & Automatic Weighing Co (also of Liverpool). Thereafter there followed a decade or so of relative prosperity upto WW1. Williamsons completed over forty further steam ships ranging in size from around 250 to over 800 tons. These were supplied to a variety of customers, many based in Liverpool. But records also reveal the locally based companies such as Kennaughs and the Stainburn Steamship Co (Murphy & Sandwith) also ordered new vessels. In January 1915, Borough Council records show us that upto 94 people were still employed at Williamson's shipyard.

In the years that followed the war, production at Williamsons declined once more. There was a fresh flurry of activity between 1918-20 when the Admiralty ordered six 200 ton vessels, but thereafter only seven further ships were launched in the town during the next twelve years, and three of these were built for the Northwest Shipping Company Ltd., owned by the Williamson family. In 1923, the shipbuilding yard was incorporated and thereafter traded as Richard Williamson & Son Limited. Work on the final ship to be built at Workington began in 1932, but the 829 ton vessel was never completed. The partially built vessel was finally purchased by Goole Shipbuilding & Engineering Co Ltd., and launched on 2 April 1938. She was towed to Goole and completed for F. T. Everard & Co. (of London) being named the *Sodality*. Shipbuilding had ceased forever in Workington. In the half a cen-

Around the turn of the century, the company were also employed in building smaller steam ships mainly used to transport grain.

tury or so that the Williamson shipbuilders had been at Low Yard they had built around 23 new sailing ships, 75 steamships and over 50 other steel barges or smaller vessels of various designs and tonnage. ■

LIST OF SOME OF THE EARLIER SHIPS BUILT BY WILLIAMSONS AT WORKINGTON

Ship	Year	Ship	Year	Ship	Year
Aigbirth	1882	Pendragon Castle	1891	Baltic	1897
Crown of England	1883	Vortigern	1891	Braeside	1900
Amy	1883	Black Rock	1891	Point Lynaz	1900
Scale Force	1883	Bell Rock	1893	Hamm	1900
Derwent	1883	Jersey	1893	Shad Thames	1902
Wray Castle	1889	Guernsey	1893	S. S. Seagull	1902
Andelana	1889	Brest Rock	1896	Stock Force	1905
Rock Channel	1889	S. S. Eden	1896	Skelwith Force	1908
Queens Channel	1894	Carmanian	1897	Thomas Dear	1918

⪧ CHAPTER SIX ⪦

THE CURWEN FAMILY

THE CURWEN family who can trace their roots back to Orm (son of Ketel), have dominated the town's history for almost a thousand years. During this period, the ancient title of Lord of the Manor of Workington has been past down through more than twenty six generations. This chapter contains a biographical account of each Lord of the Manor, within the time frame of this book (ie. 1866-1955). Readers are referred to my first volume of Workington's history for information on the earlier members of this influential family.

Edward Stanley Curwen (1810-1875) The second son of Henry [vi] Curwen and Jane Stanley, born on 10 July 1810. He married Frances, daughter of Edward Jesse of Hampton Court, on 22 January 1833. They had at least eight children, five sons and three daughters. These included Henry Fraser (1834-1900), Alfred Francis (1835-1920) who was Rector of Harrington for 38 years and Edward Hassell.

Edward began his career as a lieutenant in the 14th Light Dragoons. He succeeded to the Workington estates following the death of his father in 1860. His eldest unmarried brother John Christian Curwen (1808-1842) having died some eighteen years earlier.

He is thought to have taken an active interest in the family's coal mining activities. His initials can still be seen today, on the date stone of the western chimney at Jane Pit. [01] Although there is a suggestion that he spent a great deal of his later life away from the town, perhaps leaving the Workington estates in the capable hands of his son Henry Fraser.

On Thursday 1 April 1875, Edward Stanley died after a short illness at his residence near Cowes, on the Isle of Wight.

Henry Fraser Curwen (1834-1900) The eldest son of Edward Stanley Curwen and Frances Jesse. Born on 18 April 1834 at Hampton Court, his mother's family home. In April 1863, he married Mary Anne Susan (Susie) Johnson, daughter of Col. Charles Christopher Johnson (Seigneur of Argentenil, Canada). They had two sons

ABOVE - The Curwen family coat of arms. Note the unicorn in the centre, this became an accepted symbol for the family. Large timber carved unicorns were fixed to the gateposts at the entrance to the grounds of Workington Hall. It was also used on the arms of the old Borough Council, depicting the link between the family and the town.

BELOW - A chronological list of the Lords of the Manor of Workington since 1860. ■

Edward Stanley Curwen (1810-75)
Henry Fraser Curwen (1834-1900)
Alan De Lancy Curwen (1869-1930)
Isabel Mary Chance (1897-1967)
Edward Stanley
    Chance Curwen (1924-1983)

[01] Edward Stanley Curwen's initials ESC also appear on the central tower of St. John's Church. It is said a *"sharp eye can view them from an elevated position, about half way up Guard Street"*. ■

Edward Darcy (1864-1891) and Alan De Lancy, and four daughters Lucy Mabel, Ethel Maria, Henrietta Frances and Mary Susan Geraldine. Edward Darcy became the Honorary attache to the British Embassy in Constantinople.

Educated at Sandhurst's Royal Military College, Henry Fraser later joined the 55th Regiment of Foot (Pampadours). He served in the Crimean War (1854-6) when Sebastopol was taken, and at the Indian Mutiny (1857-8) when the British were called upon to repel a rebellion in the Bengal Army. After leaving military service, he trained in law at the Inner Temple, becoming a barrister in 1865.

He succeeded to the Workington estates following the death of his father in April 1875. Henry Fraser gave *"considerable attention"* to the local administration of Workington, serving as chairman of the Local Board for many years. On 9 November 1888, he was also unanimously elected as the first mayor of the newly created Borough of Workington. Later to commemorate the event, he presented the town with a new mayoral chain of office. This was worn with pride by the town's successive mayors, for over sixty five years.

Henry Fraser was appointed High Sheriff of Cumberland in 1888 and also later served as Deputy Lieutenant. He served as president of the West Cumberland Liberal Association, and supported Sir Wilfred Lawson in his parliamentary campaigns. After he opposed Lawson's pacifistic views on war, he stood against him at the July 1886 General Election. Contesting the seat for the Parliamentary division of Cockermouth (which then included Workington). Following a well publicised contest, the *"Workington Squire"* lost by just over 1000 votes. Interestingly in 1895, Sir Wilfred Lawson's second daughter married Henry Fraser's second son and heir, Alan De Lancy Curwen.

Like his father, Henry Fraser also had a particular love of sailing. In 1879, he purchased the *Ladye*, a *"handsome"* new trim-built racing yacht. In June of that year with his crew of four, he proudly sailed it from Devon to Workington. When it was moored at the Dock Quay, it was said to have attracted *"great attention from the townspeople"*.

During his later life, Henry Fraser made several trips to Europe, *"travelling abroad because of ill health"*. It was on one such trip that he died on Wednesday 6 March 1900, at Pau in the South of France. In August 1907, his son Alan De Lancy Curwen presented a portrait of his father to the Borough Council, *"to be placed in the Town Hall"*.

Henry Fraser later joined the 55th Regiment of Foot (Pampadours). He served in the Crimean War (1854-6) when Sebastopol was taken, and at the Indian Mutiny (1857-8)

Like his father, Henry Fraser also had a particular love of sailing.

Today, this painting still hangs in the mayor's parlour alongside those mayors who succeeded him.

Alan De Lancy Curwen (1869-1930) The second son of Henry Fraser Curwen and Mary Anne Susan Johnson, born on 21 July 1869. He married Mabel (d.1918) the second daughter of Sir Wilfred Lawson on 5 November 1895. They had at least two sons Alan Henry (1899-1920) and Eldred Arthur. Their daughter Isabel Mary (1897-1967) married Frederick Selby Chance of Carlisle.

Educated at Oxfords Charterhouse and Corpus Christi colleges. Becoming an accomplished linguist, speaking Latin, French, Italian and German. Also a notable all-round sportsman, especially in archery and gun shooting. Prior to WW1, he established the finest pack of foxhounds in the north. After university, he trained as an engineer, working for Armstrong Whitworths in Newcastle. His career ended when his brother Edward Darcy Curwen died in 1891. Afterwards, he was required to return home to help run the family estate. Following his father's death, he himself became Lord of the Manor.

Unlike his father, Alan De Lancy had something of a quiet retiring nature, and took little interest in the public or social life of Workington. He spent most of his married life living at the Curwen family's Belle Isle home upon Windermere. On the few occasions he did return to Workington Hall, he seldom stayed more than a couple of nights. It is known he had an interest in sculpture and examples of his stone carvings once existed at Workington Hall. Records from 1925, state a coat of arms, a boar's head and a bull-dog's head *"carved by the present squire"* were then displayed in the courtyard. He also had an interest in archeology, and in the 1920s opened up and renovated the Curwen burial vault beneath St. Michaels Church. There he discovered several lead lined coffins containing *"the remains of Curwens of old"*. During the excavation work, assisted by J. R. Mason and H. Valentine, significant pre-norman carved stones were also unearthed. These suggested the existence of a church upon the site dating from Anglo-Saxon times. [01]

On 7 January 1930, Alan De Lancy died of a heart attack at the Carlisle Nursing home. He had recently undergone surgery, but failed to recover. Following his funeral at St. Michaels Church, conducted by Canon. Stanley Patricius Lamplugh Curwen (his cousin) and Rev. J. R. Croft, his remains were also laid to rest within the family vault. Records suggest he was the last Curwen family member to be interred below the ancient parish church.

Alan De Lancy had something of a quiet retiring nature, and took little interest in the public or social life of Workington.

[01] For information on this excavation and the carved stones discovered - please see Chapter 3 of the *History of Workington (Earliest times to 1865)*. ■

BELLE ISLE, WINDERMERE

See page 54 of *History of Work-ington* (Earliest times to 1865) for more information. ■

[01] John Neville St. George Curwen (1879-1967) was the son of Alfred Curwen (1835-1920) and Laura Naomi Smith. He was born on St. George's Day in 1879, hence his unusual christian name. Henry Fraser Curwen (1834-1900) was his uncle.

He persued a career in law, first being articled to Brown, Auld and Brown, solicitors of Whitehaven. In 1902, he started his own practice in Workington, initially at offices in Washington Street. Later he moved to 23 Nook Street, and finally to 4 Portland Square.

Over a century later, his long established practice is still in existance trading as *Curwen & Co,* occupying these same premises.

Isabel Mary Chance (1897-1967) The only daughter of Alan De Lancy Curwen and Mabel Lawson, born on 17 July 1897. She married Frederick Selby Chance (1886-1946) on 4 December 1923. He was the son of Sir Fredrick William Chance of Carlisle. The couple's main residence was not Workington Hall, but at Homeacres, Carlisle. They had two sons Edward Stanley (1924-1983) and John Frederick (1928-1970).

Isabel succeeded to the Workington estates following the death of her father in 1930. During much of her time as Lady of the Manor of Workington, she appears to have relied on her solicitor cousin John Neville St.George Curwen (of Curwen & Co.) to handle much of the estate affairs. [01]

In October 1944, she gifted Low Park (also known as Hall Park and later renamed Curwen Park) to the people of Workington. (see chapter seven). Following the death of her husband on 27 May 1946, she also gave the run-down Workington Hall to the town. It was her particular wish that her ancestral family home be converted into Workington's town hall and this was initially made a condition of the transfer to the Borough Council. Her gift of the now somewhat dilapidated property was likely to have become a necessity in view of the enormous cost of renovation and the pending death duties on her late husbands estate.

Edward Stanley Chance Curwen (1924-1983) The eldest son of Frederick Selby Chance and Isabel Mary Curwen, born on 20 November 1924 at Homeacres, Carlisle. He received his education at Aysgarth School in North Yorkshire, before moving to the Royal Naval college at Dartmouth. He later rose to the rank of Lieutenant Commander, serving on submarines and the battleship King George V.

When he was 21, he was said to have inherited upwards of £80,000. This was squandered in little less than three years. He lived the *"high life"* in London, Paris and the Riviera, *"went round the clubs"* and bought a yacht.

In 1948 after leaving the Royal Navy, he moved to the Curwen family's Belle Isle home upon Windermere. A year later, he married his first wife Caryl Catcheside (daughter of Col. H. O. Catchside). She later divorced him in 1952, citing cruelty. In later life, he told how he was *"not proud of many things in his past"*, referring to the loss of his fortune and the events of the break-up of his first marriage.

In 1956, he assumed by Royal Licence the surname and Arms of Curwen, in addition to his own. This fulfilled the legal requirements allowing him to eventually inherit the

Curwen family estates at Workington and Windermere. Furthermore, it then allowed him to draw an annual income of around £3000.

On 29 September 1962, he married Elizabeth Honor Susan Calcotte (daughter of George Calcotte) They had two sons, Eldred Christian (b.1967) and John Henry (b. 1971).

The couple opened the grounds of Belle Isle to the public in 1972, and the house itself in 1975. Visitors were transported from the main land in a 12-seater boat, driven by Edward Curwen himself. On display at this time, within the Curwen's *"roundhouse"* was a copy of George Romney's famous portrait of Isabella Curwen.[01] and the Viking sword found at Northside. Along with the small agate cup (traditionally called the Luck of Workington), the portrait of Mary Queen of Scots and the sixteenth century clock, all of which were claimed to have been gifts from the Scottish queen. [02]

On 22 October 1983, Edward Stanley died at Belle Isle. His body was later cremated and his ashes were scattered by his wife over the waters of Lake Windermere. The simple ceremony performed from the western or *"back jetty"* of his peaceful island home was attended by the Bishop of Carlisle. The title of Lord of the Manor (of Workington) then passed to his wife. ■

[01] See page 145 of *History of Workington* (Earliest times to 1865) for more information. ■
[02] See page 225 of *History of Workington* (Earliest times to 1865) for more information. ■

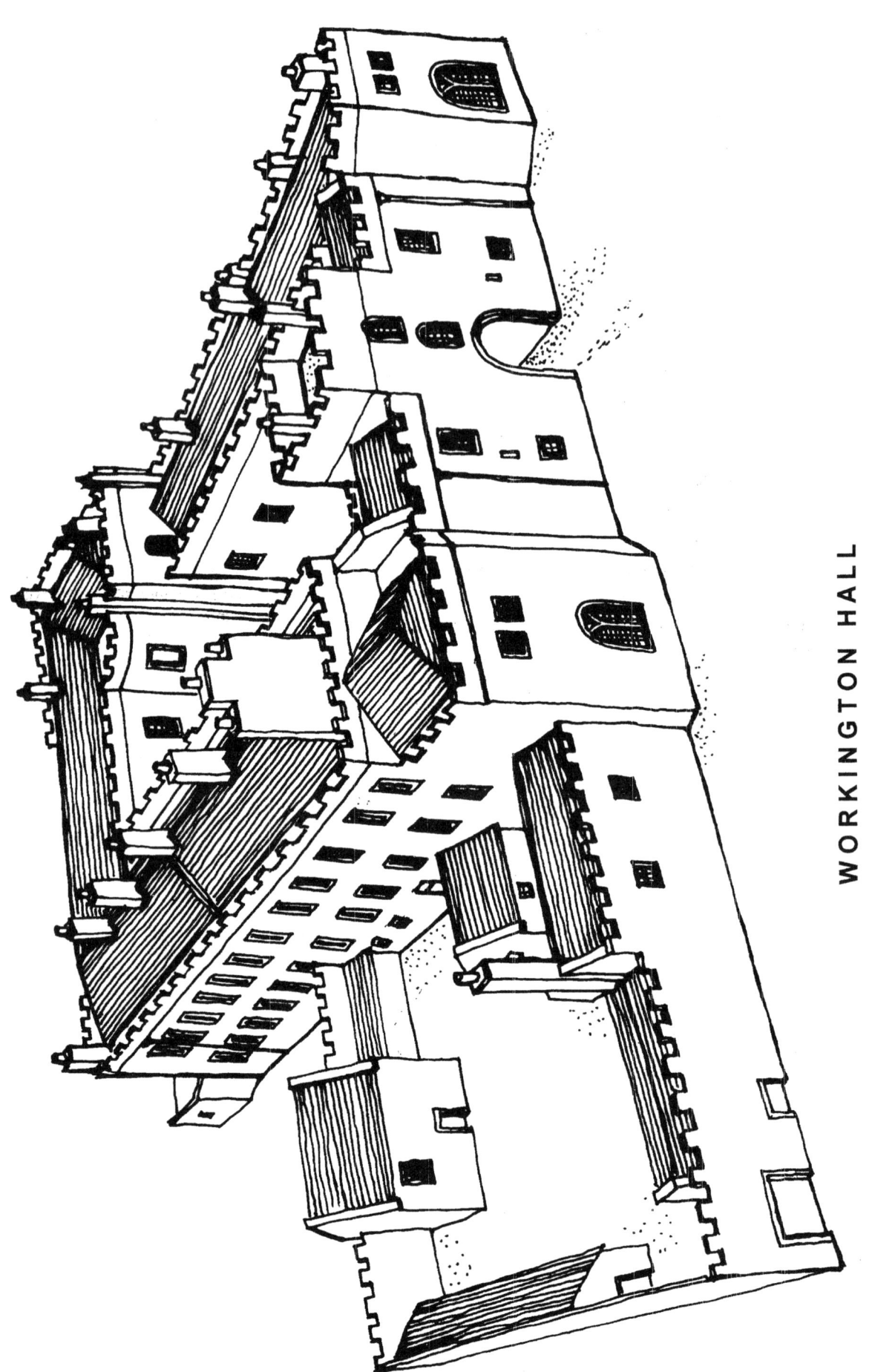

WORKINGTON HALL

This sketch (looking almost due north) shows us how the hall would have looked throughout the timeframe of this book, upto its transfer to the Borough Council in 1947. The last major building work had been undertaken around a century and a half earlier, at the end of the eighteenth century. The drawing clearly shows the hall's extensive roof and gives us an indication of the many tons of leadwork and flashings that would have been required to keep the structure watertight. Once this lead was stolen or stripped for safe keeping, severe penetrating dampness, wet and dry rot quickly prevailed. ■

❧ CHAPTER SEVEN ❧

WORKINGTON HALL

FOR AT LEAST the last quarter of the nineteenth century with his father Edward Stanley Curwen now preferring to live at Cowes, Henry Fraser Curwen became the principle resident of Workington Hall. But following his death in 1900, the Curwen ancestral home was to remain unoccupied for long periods of time. Although possession passed to his second son Alan De Lancy Curwen, he continued to use Belle Isle on Windermere as his main residence. When he did come to Workington he would only usually spent the odd couple of nights beneath the roof of the ancient hall.

We do know the Ellen Patricia Curwen [01] stayed there around the 1920s. Often accompanied by Alan De Lancy's daughter Isabel Mary Curwen, who is thought to have been something of a companion to her unmarried aunt. But after Isabel Mary's marriage in 1923 and Ellen Patricia death the following year, once again the hall was seldom visited by the family. The only occupants were usually the caretakers, Mr. and Mrs. George Morton. This trusted couple, originally from Bulwell in Nottingham were appointed by Alan de Lancy Curwen. Their son, J. W. Morton was also employed by the family at Belle Isle.

Even after Isabel Mary (now Isabel Mary Chance) inherited the hall following her father's death in 1930, she would continue to live mainly at Carlisle. In my earlier volume of Workington's history, there is an account of the last major alterations to the fabric of the Hall. These were carried out by John Christian Curwen at the end of the 1790s. And we know that in 1925 much of its interior, including the contents and furnishings were still very much intact and was virtually as John Christian Curwen would have known it well over a century earlier. [02] The glorious plasterwork and decoration, including the ornate marble fireplaces were still in excellent condition. The original full length portraits of John Christian and Isabella Curwen, painted by George Romney still hung on the walls. And the priceless furniture made by Gillows of Lancaster still adorned the dining room and saloon.

Almost every room also contained artifacts and pictures, reminders of the families rich history. The small sixteenth century agate cup said to have been given to

Readers are referred to chapter nine of *History of Workington (Earliest Times to AD 1865)* for more details of the history and layout of Workington Hall. Here you will find a lengthy description of the building and its contents, together with floor plans and photographs of the once elaborate interior. ■

[01] Ellen Patricia Curwen (1868-1924) was the unmarried daughter of Rev. Alfred Francis Curwen, brother of Henry Fraser Curwen. It is know she spent a great deal of time in the Hall's well-stocked library. ■
[02] In August 1925, a detailed account of the interior of Workington Hall was published in weekly instalments in the Workington Star. ■

the family by Mary Queen of Scots, and sentimentally known as the *"Luck of Workington"* was displayed in a glass case in the saloon or billiard room. It was even claimed that the actual bed in which Mary slept on was then still in existence. Located in a spare room off the drawing room the *"full tester"* bedstead still had it's tapestry hangings. The library was also *"incased"* floor to ceiling with a valuable collection of books. Elsewhere were displayed the Viking sword found at Northside and John Christian Curwen's solid silver salver, presented to him by the Workington Agricultural Society in 1810. The remainder of the families collection of George Romney paintings and numerous not so famous family portraits still hung within the Hall.

Yet no further records exist to suggest any major renovation and repair work to the Hall since the time of John Christian Curwen, and he died in 1828. A century in the life of any building is an extremely long time and it is inconceivable that some major decay and deterioration of the structure did not occur. During this long period of neglect, the once glorious Hall must have begun to look run-down and quite shabby. This may explain why later Curwen generations appeared reluctant to occupy the once-grand old historic building and preferred to lived elsewhere.

As time progressed, so the repair cost of the dilapidated building escalated. The once very wealthy Curwen family could no longer afford anything more than the very basic repairs. In 1936, Isabel Mary Chance hinted that she would accept a *"serious offer"* to purchase the Hall. And it is known Workington Borough Council then made an abortive effort to acquire the building. As WW2 approached, it was also proposed to turn the mansion into a hostel to accommodate 100 pupils from Mill Hill School in London. They were to be evacuated from the city to West Cumberland. It was planned to send them to St. Bees School. A survey carried out at this time by local architect R.A.C Simpson tells us *"dampness is coming in badly in various places, particularly on the north west wing, overlooking Hall Brow"*. Some very basic repair work was carried out at this time, but Jonathan Saul (Simpson's partner) recorded it was *"a mere flea bite compared with what ought to be done"*.

The arrangement to house the school pupils at the Hall, eventually failed to materialise and the entire building was soon requisitioned by the Military authorities. From 1939 and for much of the war, troops were billeted within the historic building. The family had previously cleared the Hall of all its valuable contents,

"Later generations of the Curwen family were certainly no longer as wealthy as they had been in the late eighteenth and early nine-teenth century. And simply could not afford anything more than the very basic repairs."

but during this period its elaborate interior did suffer some damage. The most significant of which was a fire within the dining room, at the north corner of the Hall [01]. A great proportion of the highly decorative *"Adam style"* plasterwork was extensively damaged, particularly the ceiling and cornice. The fire also damaged the rooms above and some roof timbers. Although some basic repairs were carried out, this area was never restored to it's former glory. It is also suggested elsewhere that the troops also *"looted"* the Hall, removing some of the elaborate door furniture and other ironmongery.

Long before the death of her husband in 1946, we know Isabel Mary was contemplating the future of the vacant Hall. A decade had passed since she first considered selling the property. Now she faced the prospect of a significant demand for death duties on her late husband's estate. This appears to have prompted the Lady of the Manor to gift the entire building to the Borough Council. Her particular wish was that it be converted into a Town Hall, and this initially was made a condition of the transfer. The large elegant saloon, with it's fine columns and Adam style plasterwork was to become the council chamber. And the *"Corporation may at last have a mayor's parlour"* possibly accom-modated in the equally fine dining room.

Months before the formal transfer of the Hall to the *"Mayor, Alderman and Burgesses of the Borough of Workington"* was completed in June 1947, the Council had appointed architects and surveyors to carefully examine the run down building. Extensive dry and wet rot was now rampant throughout the structure. They also reported that much of the priceless decorative plasterwork in the dining room had deteriorated further, following the fire damage during military occupation. Vandals had also broken many windows and caused further major damage to the vacant building. With hindsight perhaps the Borough Council should then have respectfully declined the gift of the Hall. Certainly, they were aware that the *"quite significant sum"* of at least £30,000 was required to repair and convert the building to a Town Hall. They should have also know or been properly advised that such work was very unlikely to be sanctioned by the Ministry of Works in these austere post WW2 years. Yet, after much debate in the council chambers where worries and reservations were clearly voiced, they still voted to accept the historic building.

Very soon afterwards, tenders were invited to re-roof the hall, in an attempt to make it watertight and halt further any deterioration. The cost of this work would be just

"Councillors should really have also known or been properly advised that such work was very unlikely to be sanctioned in those austere post WW2 years."

[01] See chapter nine of *History of Workington (Earliest times to AD 1865)* for more details of the dining room at Workington Hall. ∎

over £5,500, but not surprisingly Westminster would not sanction this spending either. However, a very basic amount of work was undertaken, but this proved barely adequate. The hall stood empty and unmaintained for a further couple of years. During this time the untreated dry rot spread further throughout the structure. Vandalism continued to be a problem and the large quantities of lead were systematically stolen from the roof of the vacant building. This included *"irreplaceable"* lead down pipes and a significant amount of lead flashings and guttering. They also stripped the lead floor of the verandah above the vinery and conservatory, which ran along the southern wall of the building. [01]

This *"wanton"* theft and vandalism now left the hall extremely vulnerable to the elements. Any previous penertrating dampness and dry rot problems were merely multiplied and compounded. In June 1950, council workers from the Parks Department patrolled the Hall grounds, in an effort to deter the theft of further lead. But things were not to improve, as the Council somewhat foolishly instructed the Borough Surveyor to *"strip and store all remaining moveable leadwork"*. The Corporation were already facing a bill of *"many hundreds of pounds"* to replace the stolen lead, and were anxious not to lose everything. Reflecting on this course of action half a century later, this is exactly what they did lose.

Although for many decades the Hall had been obviously neglected by its previous owners, in the three years after it had been taken over by the Corporation it's condition had declined quite dramatically. To the great embarassment of those councillors who had supported the scheme in the first place, the townspeople now began to openly question their actions. In an effort to progress matters they appointed prominent architects *Cordingley and McIntigre* (of Manchester) to prepare a further report. In January 1951, Professor Cordingley stated *"the Hall is at a critical stage of dilapidation, already it has gone so far as to make restoration of some parts, impractical, uneconomical and unjustifiable.....Decay will continue with cumulative rapidity"*.

The *Ancient Monuments Division of the Ministry of Works* also visited the Hall in November 1952. Although they highlighted the medieval parts of the Hall, such as the pele tower, vaulted rooms and kitchen as having the *"most rewarding features"*, they contradicted Cordingley somewhat by stating the building was *"sound structurally"*. They also felt the Georgian dining room, saloon, library and entrance should be retained and fully restored as *"they contained fine examples of John Carr's work"*.

"The important features of Workington Hall have been lost through Municipal indifference and neglect"

J. T. Smith
Royal Commision for
Historic Monuments
1965

[01] We know from the Curwen papers that the conservatory measured around 57' long by 17'2" wide. (17.4m x 5.2m). Records point to it being erected sometime after Nov. 1890. Old engravings of the Hall suggest it is likely to have replaced another similar structure.

■

But funding any remedial work would still be an insurmountable problem, as no major grant aid was available.

The Borough Council now, albeit in private appear to have began questioning the whole issue of converting the Hall into a *"Town Hall and Municipal offices"*. And despite Cordingley's report, they avoided all pressure to at the very least halt any further decay of the building. Or was that the plan, did the same councillors who foolishly voted to acquire the Hall, now wish to see it fall into such a state of disrepair that demolition would be the only alternative. Certainly for the next ten years, they tried very hard to disassociate themselves from the entire project.

Finally in March 1961, the Borough Council made contact with Isabel Mary Chance and requested her to release them from *"clause four in the Deed of Gift"*. This stipulated the building should only be converted into a Town Hall. Council files show she appears to have somewhat reluctantly agreed. Further surveyors reports in 1965 clearly indicate that *"much of Carr's fine plasterwork"* had now been lost forever and the majority of the structure had *"virtually decayed beyond repair"*. The estimated cost of even the most basic conversion had now rocketed to over £100,000. When funds were sought from the County Council to carry out some works, the Borough Council received a very blunt reply stating *"they could not be party to the attempted restoration of this moribund relic"*[01].

In 1778, the will of Henry Curwen tells us there was once between 40-50 deer grazing freely in Low or Hall Park. And a century later we know the general public were allowed to freely *"take walks"* within the private wooded grounds of Workington Hall. These visitors were only permitted to enter and leave the grounds by the Park End Lodge, at the top of Ramsey Brow. Unfortunately, following *"several cases of misbehaviour"* the privilege was later withdrawn by Henry Fraser Curwen. Prior to May 1942, the entire grounds was surrounded by a high stone wall, almost eight feet high. Much of this was removed by Isabel Mary Chance, possibly because it too fell into disrepair. The Council minutes record the lowered wall now *"affords passers-by a splendid view of the Hall and Park grounds"*.

On 4 February 1944, Mrs. Chance offered to the *"Corporation and the Burgesses of Workington the gift of Low Park - that is the park below Workington Hall, as an open space for the town."* The Borough Council

"If no suitable or economic use can be found for the Hall. It would impose a burden on the ratepayers of the town".
Borough Council
Report 1965

[01] The adjective *moribund* is seldom used today, but simply means *"at the point of death"*. ∎

In October 1954, a model railway track (800 ft or 234m long) was completed in the grounds of the Hall. Jack Miller took his steam train, the *"City of Carlisle"* around the track to formally open the narrow gauge line. Almost half a century later, it is still located on the Ramsay Brow side of the park, and used regularly by local model rail enthusiasts. ■

without hesitation "unanimously" accepted the gift at it's next meeting. And it's *"Title Deeds"* were formally handed over to the Corporation at a special meeting in the Carnegie Council Chamber on 11 October 1944. On receiving the documents, the Mayor, Alderman William Armstrong "Yankie" Walker, spoke of how the new park would *"provide healthful pleasure and recreation for the people of Workington"*. The 45 acres of park land, originally part of Schoose Farm, was officially re-named Curwen Park in July 1945.

In December 1945, rugby and football posts were erected in Curwen Park and a hockey pitch was also laid out. The old laundry buildings within the hall grounds were used to store the sports equipment used in the park. Some of the remains of these now demolished buildings, which were built into the bank at the foot of Hall Brow, can still be seen. During the early nineteenth century, at the time of John Christian Curwen they were also used as a small brewery. From August 1946, annual Agricultural Shows were also reintroduced to the town and held in the park.

Cuckoo Arch [01] crossing the Stainburn Road to the east of the entrance to Workington Grammar School (now Stainburn School) was demolished on Sunday 25 October 1931. The structure had deteriorated into a *"dangerous condition"* and with the rapid increase in traffic along this busy road to Cockermouth, its narrow semi-circular opening became something of a hazard. The work was carried out by local contractor Tom Johnston. Explosives were used to remove the bulk of the bridge in order that

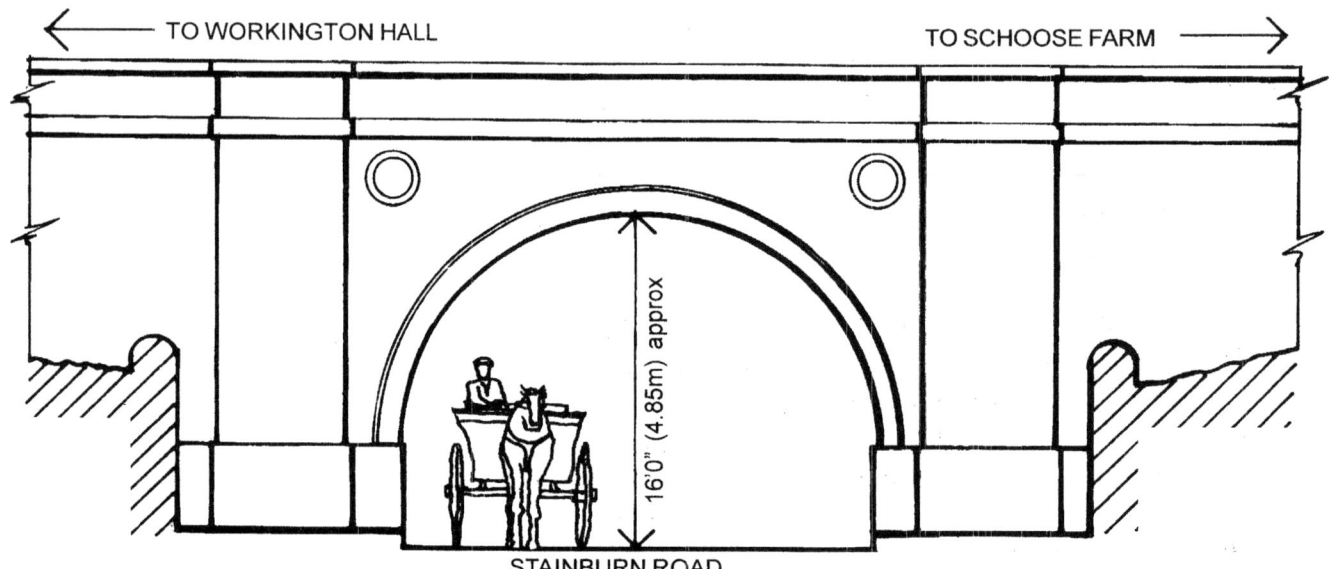

ABOVE - South west elevation of Cuckoo Arch. The semi-circular stone built bridge which once spanned Stainburn Road and linked Workington Hall with Schoose Farm. Built around 1795 by John Christian Curwen. ■
[01] See page 197 of *History of Workington (Earliest times to 1865)* for more information on Cuckoo Arch. ■

the road could be quickly reopened. These were set by demolition man Jim Renney, assisted by Bob Hucknall and George McManus.

Just moments before the blast, a dark dog was apparently seen *"streaking"* over the bridge. The demolition was immediately halted and a hunt was made to ensure the dog was safe. After an unsuccessful search, one local onlooker is said to have told the explosives men of *"a phantom dog"* which was often seen crossing the arch. Through the years, many people profess to have seen similar ghostly apparitions. Even in recent times, the dog is still said to be seen crossing the road where Cuckoo Arch once stood. The true identity of the dog may never be known, some suggest it was John Christian Curwen's black labrador, frantically searching for his master who died in 1828.

Other legends surround the once-prominent land-mark, which was featured on countless old picture postcards and has been painted by numerous artists. One suggests that the ghost of Galloping Harry who died in 1725, is also seen crossing the arch on his famous stallion *"Curwen Bay Barb"*. Another tells how John Christian Curwen who built the arch, wagered that he *"would ride over"* the rival landowners the Lowthers (of Whitehaven). So he put up the bridge and won the bet.

Sadly in recent months, with the construction of the Stainburn bypass the final remains of the bridge support to the south side of the road have been removed forever. However, a large proportion of Cuckoo Arch still remains on the opposite side of the road extending into the woods of Hall Park. ■

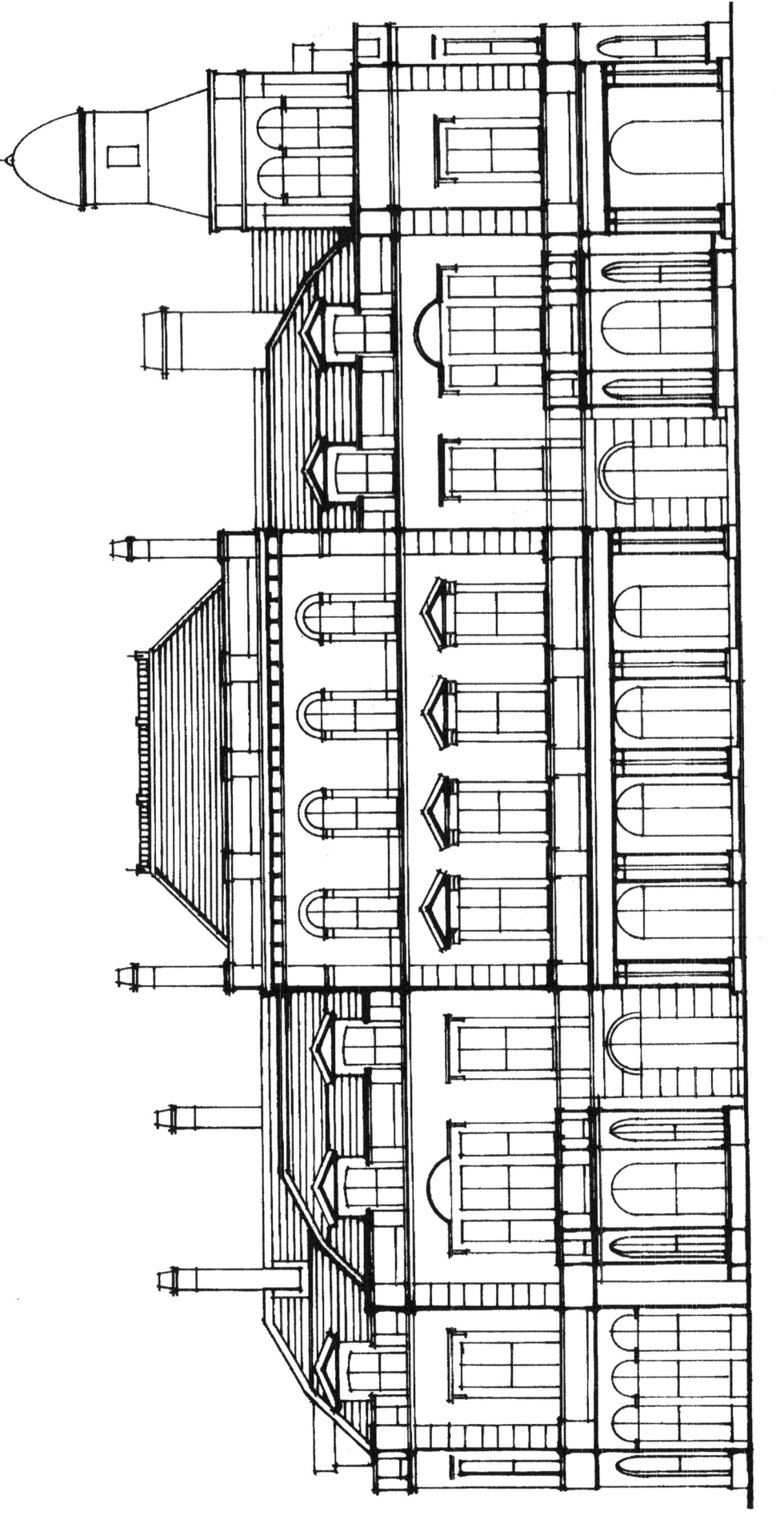

BANKFIELD, WORKINGTON - ELEVATION TO THE SOUTH WEST

❧ CHAPTER NINE ❧

BANKFIELD

THE ELEGANT MANSION of Bankfield once stood in its own extensive grounds, high above Banklands. The main entrance to the estate was at the south end of Bank Road, through the gates near the front of St. Michaels R.C church. Whilst the rear of the house could also be reached from the tradesman entrance off Newlands lane. Completed in October 1876, it was built for prominent ironmasters Peter Kirk and Charles James Valentine, by building contractor Richard W. Schofield (of John Street). The Kirk and Valentine family were related by marriage, Charles Valentine having married Peter Kirk's sister Annie. Valentine later became the Member of Parliament for the Cockermouth constituency, which then included Workington.

The enormous property was essentially two semi-detached houses, with separate entrances at each end. The floor plans were very similar, but at the north end was a tall tower. Across the entire top floor of the mansion was a single room, used as a ballroom or function room for special occasions. It was reached from one of two ornate staircases, within each residence. Throughout the years, this vast ballroom witnessed many elaborate celebrations, perhaps the most prominent being the silver wedding anniversary of Mr. and Mrs. Valentine in March 1886.

Following Peter Kirk's departure to the east coast of America, he commissioned local auctioneer John Jenkinson to sell his Bankfield furniture and fittings. The three day sale in June 1887, attracted a very large attendance, with some good prices being achieved. The sale particulars are quite informative and we can piece together something of the ironmaster's life within the mansion. His half of Bankfield had an elaborately decorated entrance hall, dining and drawing rooms and a library, with at least five large bedrooms and a nursery on the upper floors. The walls were adorned with pictures and paintings, there were also a number of bronzes in the house, including two large ones in the hall. Here also prominently displayed were two full-size suits of armour. Almost everything in the house was offered for sale from the huge spanish mahogany dining table with twelve richly carved chairs, to the chamber pots in the bedrooms and even a cow in the garden. There was also Kirk's two

"The landmark occupies one of the most commanding sites in the town"
Mike Burridge

The enormous property was essentially two semi-detached houses, with separate entrances at each end.

horses, *Charley* who pulled his carriage and *Black Points* who was ridden by the ladies of the household. One wonders what has happened to the hundreds of items sold and where they are today? Particularly the *'handsome carved walnut bookcase'* measuring a massive 15ft 6in (4.72m) long by 8ft 6in (2.59m) high, which once belonged to the Marquis of Hastings.

The 1891 census reveals that the Kirk family's end of Bankfield was occupied by Joseph F. Hodgson and his wife Elizabeth. The 'partially deaf' wine and spirit merchant had just agreed to sell his Old Market Place business, to the Workington Brewery Company. He later moved to Storrsholme at Windermere, where he died in November 1912. Charles J. Valentine and his family then still occupied the other half of the large property.

By 1895, Peter Iredale (also of Workington Brewery) took *"up residence of the beautiful mansion"* at Bankfield, which he had acquired from ironmaster Charles J. Valentine. Exactly how much he paid for Bankfield is yet to be discovered. But we do know Iredale was by then certainly a very rich man, having sold the family brewery to the newly formed Workington Brewery Company Limited in 1891. Iredale shared the large house with his family. One end was occupied by James Lawrence Smith (the manager of Workington I&SCo.) who had married the brewer's eldest daughter Mary in February 1891. The 1901 census reveals that both families were still living in the large property. Both households were still obviously ran quite independently from one another, as each employed it's own cook and housemaids. Within the decade, Peter Iredale now had three young granddaughters and a grandson, living next door with his daughter and son-in-law. It's quite interesting to imagine these small children dancing around the enormous ballroom across at the top of the mansion.

After the death of Peter Iredale in November 1906, Bankfield passed to his son Frederick William Iredale (1879-1943). He was also employed at his father's brewery, later rising to the post of managing director by the 1930s. In August 1916 during WW1, Peter Iredale's grandson Reginald Iredale Smith (1896-1916) was killed in action on the Somme. He was a second lieutenant with the 10th Argyle and Sutherland Highlanders. At this time, much of Bankfield was utilised as a military hospital to care for soldiers injured returning from the front. The Smith's had vacated Bankfield and now resided at Rayrigg Hall, Windermere. Quite soon after, the *Bankfield Military Hospital Charity* was launched by the local townspeople, they rallied round to help the makeshift

PETER IREDALE
(1828-1906)

Peter Iredale was the son of John and Mary Iredale, who moved to Workington from Keswick in November 1839. Taking over the High Brewery at the top of Hall Brow.

Following his fathers retirement, the brewery passed to Peter and his brother Thomas, and the business traded until 1891 as Iredale Bros. Thereafter, it became the *Workington Brewery Company Limited.* ■

hospital. Within Harrington Road Cemetery are a number of gravestones standing as a poignant reminder of the hospitals existence.

In 1944, the Borough Council agreed to purchase Bankfield along with the 17 acres of adjoining park land, from the family of the late F.W. Iredale [01]. His widow Jane, was allowed to *"rent back"* the eastern portion of the house for £60 per annum. The remainder was requisitioned by the War Department who remained there until March 1946. A few months later Jane Iredale also vacated her part of Bankfield. The Corporation now approved in principle proposals to convert Bankfield into a new Town Hall. A. B. Cooper, the Borough Surveyor commenting that *"it would achieve the civic dignity so necessary for effective administration"*. There was even plans to make Cross Hill the new "town centre", demolish the Royal George public house and form a new "grand entrance" up to Bankfield. But soon after the Council were also gifted Workington Hall. [02] This obviously lead to great conflict within the council chamber. They now had to choose which of the two grand houses would be transformed into a new town hall. They failed to agree and eventually both buildings suffered gross municipal neglect and were lost to the town forever.

In 1947, Bankfield was subsequently let to the National Coal Board on a ten-year lease. It was used as office accommodation for the next twenty years or so. The NCB vacated the property in October 1968, and asked the Borough Council to be released from their lease. Correspondence suggests that large sections of the building were in a *"dilapidated condition"*. Now some twenty three years after first considering converting Bankfield to a town hall, the Corporation looked again at the proposal. They engaged local architect R. Craig Graham (who had his offices in Thompson Street) to carry out a thorough survey and feasibility study.

His report makes interesting reading and gives us further important details of Bankfield. *"Internally, the building is commodus, having several principal rooms of quite substantial proportions...In general these are so large, that it is difficult to accommodate them economically. Externally, the building appears to be structurally sound, though much of the building is weatherworn and will require a fair amount of repair and reinstatement. All the facades are embellished with a well proportioned mixture of pillars, pilasters, rusticated work, tracery, cornices, ballustrading, turrets, windows etc. - giving the general impression is ponderous and institutional"*. The cost of the repairs and conversion to a Town Hall was

[01] Frederick William Iredale (1879-1943) was the son of Peter Iredale, and eventually succeeded his father as managing director of the *Workington Brewery Company*. He also served on Workington Borough Council, as a councillor and alderman for over twenty years. As well as being Chairman of the Town's Magistrates. He is buried in Harrington Road Cemetery. ∎
[02] See chapter seven for more details of Workington Hall.∎

then estimated at £150,000. Despite the cost, there was much concern that Bankfield was really too far from the town centre, and eventually the scheme was dropped.

The NCB lease was later assigned to Cumbria County Council in December 1971. They used the building as *"alternative classroom accommodation"*, whilst repairs were being carried out at Harrington Junior School and Newlands School. In 1979, the County Council surrendered the lease back to the District Council. Soon after, Allerdale District Council decided to advertise this once grand building for conversion to offices or a hotel. Hoping to persuade a developer to take the premises on a long 125 year lease. But at the same time they also sought permission from the Secretary of State to demolish the property.[01] Approval for the latter option arrived first, and in the meantime no one had shown any real interest in adapting the building.[02] In April 1980, Allerdale invited tenders for the demolition of Bankfield.

In August 1980, it took Carlisle based contractor Rod Long a month to demolish Bankfield. It was discovered to have been constructed almost *"entirely of ancient concrete, incorporating ironworks slag"*. No doubt transported in hundreds of small carts up the long hill from Kirk's Moss Bay ironworks. This made the structure extremely strong, and Long had to resort to explosives to bring down parts of this once proud house. Eventually, removing forever another symbol of the town's rich industrial past. ■

[01] The Dept. of Environment made Bankfield a "Listed Building" in 1977-78. ■

[02] Thomas Armstrong Limited (of Cockermouth) did express an interest in buying and demolishing Bankfield, to build new housing. After much debate, Allerdale decided that private housing on the site was inappropriate. ■

PORT & HARBOUR

LONSDALE DOCK on the north side of the Derwent, was constructed in 1861-2 by the William, Lord Lonsdale. But within a decade or so it was considered *"altogether too small for the present traffic"*. The size of visiting vessels had also increased dramatically and by the mid 1870s the present entrance on the north bank of the river was described as *"tortuous"*, Long steamers were unable to even enter the dock, due to insufficient room in the narrow channel, except at high tides. Much trade was being lost to the neighbouring ports of Maryport and Whitehaven.

One newspaper report from April 1882, tells us the Lonsdale Dock was *"crammed full with many large steamers from Spain with iron ore, together with a large barque and several other sailing ships and smaller steamers"*. The Dock workers were also being employed *"night and day, with the cranes continuosly used"*. A considerable portion of these vessels, carried pig iron, steel and plates, from this port to all parts of the world, whilst iron-ore was imported from Spain and North Africa. Many meetings were held with interested parties to consider *"increasing the dock accommodation"*.

The trustees of Lord Lonsdale did obtain an Act in 1882 for making a new *"Deep Water Dock"* at Workington, this was extended seven years later, but had expired by 1896. In 1898 and 1900, two attempts were made by Workington Corporation to obtain parliamentary powers to build a new larger dock facility at the mouth of the Derwent. The first attempt was unsuccessful and although the latter was approved, they failed to raise the neccessary capital. The Council's Dock Commitee had offered Lord Lonsdale £100,000 for dock and harbour estate, and all plant and machinery. £20,000 to be paid in cash and remaining £80,000 to bear interest at 3 per cent, secured on first charge on the dock and harbour estate.

Eventually, Cammell Laird and Co. negoiated the purchase the dock from Lord Lonsdale and their first scheme was approved by Parliament, on 13 February 1905. Yet it would be another two decades before the dock was finally enlarged and its entrance re-located facing

"Workington is one of the workshops of the world. Yet how badly equipped it is to make good use of the natural advantages it enjoys. The lack of deepwater shipping facilities has handicapped the town at every turn"

West Cumberland News
Sept 1924.

The new "first class deep water" dock being achieved through the hard work of United Steel Company, *"is to improve and consolidate the position of Workington in the iron and steel industry."* *(1924)*

due west. In 1919, the *Workington Dock and Harbour Board*, under the control of Cammell Laird and Co., applied again for *"powers to construct the new dock"* at Workington. The Borough Council who unable to *"raise the necessary capital"* themselves, activily supported the application. However, they would have preferred to build the new dock themselves, had it not been for the post war sanctions on borrowing. It was anticipated that it would cost £½million and the work would take around two years. Work commencedon site in 1922,

On 30 June 1927, His Royal Highness the Prince of Wales (later King Edward VIII) formally opened the new dock, after whom it was named. Accompanied by Mayor A. Baines and Mr T. Jackson he performed the ceremony with a pair of *"gold sissors"*. Prior to his arrival in the town, the Prince had visited Cleator Moor and Haig Pit at Whitehaven. The entrance to the new dock is 70 feet wide, with a depth of upto 33'6" at high spring tides. It measures 975 feet long, and 350 ft wide at is widest point, and will accommodate vessels upto 12,000 tons.

The harbour now also had a more direct rail link to the iron and steel plants, to the south of the Derwent. The private railway of the United Steel Co. then passed across the River Derwent esturary, over a swing bridge. This could be opened to allow larger vessels to still enter the tidal harbour of the South Gut. In 1981, it was replaced with a modern fixed railway bridge, but we can still see the remains of the old swing bridge supports, rising out of the river.

The Workington Harbour and Dock Board operated the Prince of Wales Dock, until the end of 1957, when it was transferred to the United Steel Company. They created a subsiduary company called the Workington Harbour and Dock Co. Limited, to manage the facility.

Upon the foreshore to the south of the Derwent estuary stood the folly, known affectionately as Billy Bumley house. Although technically it was not a house, as it had no doors or windows and was used simply as a navigation for vessels using the port. From the white painted circular structure mariners could take bearings to prominent landmarks such as St. Bees Head, the Peak of Ally and Borough Head and easily plot their course to and from the harbour. It is possible that the structure was named by virtue of it's likeness to a beehive. But the writings of William Dickinson (of Thorncroft) in his dialect dictionary may suggest something quite differnt. He tells us that one of the Cumberland dialect word for bailiff or sheriffs officer was "Bumbaily". Perhaps in the past it was once also used by the locals to describe the customs officers that patrolled the shoreline, seeking out smugglers.

For many years, I was a little puzzled by the actual location of the Billy Bumley house. I have studied several early plans of the old glebe lands around the foreshore, some dating back to 1777. All seem to show it as being situated well to the west of Shore (or Store) House, a good point of reference. But more recent maps and certainly the many photographs suggest Billy Bumley as being located more to the east, and much closer to the western boundary of Williamson's shipyard. Then I stubbled across the 1930s writings of Joseph Scott, who taught at Victoria School for fifty years. Everything fell into place when he revealed there were actually two Billy Bumley houses. The octogenarian clearly remembered the foundations of an earlier structure closer to the shoreline, whilst the later one was *"nearer the town"*. Sadly what Joseph Scott didn't reveal was some vital information about the plan of the previous structure. As well as serving as a navigation reference, was it perhaps also a *"watch house"* for the excise men. Lending some credance to the theory that it did derive it's name from the dialect word *"Bumbaily"*.

Exactly when the more recent folly was built has yet to be determined. We know it was before 1860 when the first OS plan of the town was surveyed. We also know this familar landmark was demolished on Friday 24 June 1960, by the WI&SCo. [90] Although at the time the company claimed that the old structure "had now become quite unsafe".

Readers should not confuse these original Billy Bumley navigation points with the similar structure (which still exists today) to the north and almost opposite the entrance to the Prince of Wales dock. Although later generations have now become accustomed to also calling this quaint circular stone building by the same name. We know this later structure actually served a tidewatchers look out, and was not built as a navigation aid. When Williamson's used this area of the south bank of the estuary as a shipyard, it was often dwarfed by large vessels under construction.

[90] There is a photograph of the partially demolished Billy Bumley

ABOVE - The large gilded baldachino (or canopy) over the altar to the west end of St. Johns Church. Supported on four massive columns, this forms a magnificent focal point guiding the congregation's attention to the sanctuary as they enter the church. Designed by Sir. J. Ninian Comper it was installed in 1931. Praised by the *National Committee for the Care of Churches*, who described the baldachino as *"the finest classical altar in England"*. ∎

⁂ CHAPTER TEN *⁂*

CHURCHES & CHAPELS

A PLACE OF WORSHIP has existed on the site of St. Michaels Parish church since at least the ninth century. But the structure of this church has changed several times. Up until 1887, there was a Georgian church here built in 1770. Bulmer (1901) tells us this *"was destroyed by fire in September 1887, and was rebuilt on the same lines"*. The joint architects for the replacement church were Bassett Smith (of London) and James Howes (of Workington).[01] Their design was *"unanimously"* selected from seven entries in a competition to rebuild the fire ravaged church. The estimated costs were stated to be around £5,500, although this did not include the cost of raising the main tower. This would require around a further £1,500 to complete the project. By 1888 a local newspaper revealed about £5,000 of the total sum required had already been raised.

Generally, the exterior dimensions of the new church were very similar to that of the old Georgian building. However, pointed gothic tracery windows replaced the rather plain round-headed openings, and more decorative pinnacles, parapet walls and buttresses were added to reflect more the Early English style. The interior of the church having been totally destroyed, was more radically altered. Instead of the typical Georgian double row of columns, one over the other supporting the roof, the architects opened up the nave by using arches over larger pillars, placed further apart. Less emphasis was placed on the galleries which became *"subordinate"* to the design. The walls of the old tower were slightly raised and adorned with battlements and pinnacles. Bulmer added that *"the pulpit is a very handsome one of Caen stone and marble, erected to the memory of Miss M. Dickinson. There are several fine stained-glass windows, beautifully alike in design and execution"*.

On 30 December 1885, the new parish rooms and caretakers house were completed in Dean Street. Although they were not officially opened until 8 March 1886. The final monies to cover its cost were raised by a huge bazaar. Held on 9 Dec. 1885 it was opened by Mrs. H. F. Curwen. Within the parish rooms services were held during the rebuilding works to the main church. A *"commodious"* choir vestry was also added to the new

Pointed gothic tracery windows replaced the rather plain round-headed openings, and more decorative pinnacles, parapet walls and buttresses were added to reflect more the Early English style.

[01] James Howes (1845-1903) had his offices at 13 Bridge Street. ■

When the Georgian church was first re-built in 1770, several of the oldest headstones from the graveyard were re-laid as flag-stones in the north and south aisles. One of note read *"Here lyles! of women and wives: the best, Bereft of F by Death; who's now in Bliss at Rest - Elizabeth Benson, died April 12 1685".*

ABOVE - St. Johns Church in Washington Street, built in 1823. ∎

church in 1897 as a Jubilee memento costing around £300.

On 26 August 1895, St. Michaels lost it's longest serving rector, Rev. Henry Curwen. He had taken over the post in 1837, and served a remarkable 58 years. Henry was the third son of Henry [iv] Curwen, and brother to Edward Stanley Curwen of Workington Hall, Lord of the Manor from 1860-75. After his death aged 82 years, he was interred at Windermere. Other rectors included 1895-1905 Rev. Herbert Ernest Campbell and 1905-47 Rev. Stanley Patricius Lamplugh Curwen.

In 1954, the now obsolete graveyards of St. Michaels and St. Johns, were both designated by the Borough Council as *"Open Space"*. The Parochial Church Councils then conveyed their interest in the churchyards to the Corporation. Soon after with the help of funds from the Helena Thompson Trust, they were later both improved. This involved removing many stones, to make grass cutting and routine maintenance much easier. At St. Michaels, there was once over eight hundred gravestones, recording the family history of many generations of townspeople. Today (2001) there are around eighty.

As detailed in my earlier volume of *History of Workington* when St. Johns Church was originally built the interior was dominated by a very large *"three-decker"* pulpit at its west end. In 1866, this was eventually removed by Canon Thornley, to provide a more clear view of the altar. By 1877, it was reported that the fifty-five year old church was in a state of *"decay and dilapidation"*. It was subsequently closed for two months while essential repairs were carried out. The interior was also redecorated, the walls were painted *"french grey"*. Behind the altar the text of the commandments, the creed and the Lords prayer were boldly painted in the old English typeface, with *"richly ornate"* illuminated capitals.

Further minor alterations followed until 1903, when the first of two major re-arrangements of the interior of St. Johns were commenced. This was carried out under Canon Greene, who made no secret of the fact that he considered the layout of the church *"neither beautiful or adapted to Public Worship"*. The chancel was moved to the east end of the nave, below the tower and all the seating was reversed. Whilst work progressed the services were held in the Drill Hall in Edkin Street, or the parish rooms. On 25 July 1904, the church was reopened and re-dedicated.

In 1914, Canon John R. Croft, succeeded Rev. Greene and became one of St. Johns most influential incumbents. Previously, he was curate of Whitburn, and had been instrumental in building St. Andrews Church, near Marsden Colliery. After an appointment at St. Hilda's College in Durham, he was appointed Vicar of St. Aidan's in South Shields, from here he moved to Workington. In addition to his clerical work, Canon Croft took an active part in the town's community affairs. After acting as Chaplain to the Border Regiment and witnessing first hand the horrors of WW1 in France and Flaunders, he was one of the founders of the Discharged Soldiers and Sailors (now Veterans) Club. He was also responsible for finalising the designs of the bronzes, set into the Vulcans Park War Memorial. Holding several meetings at the Vicarage with the sculptor, Alexander Carrick A.R.S.A. Among numerous other appointments, Croft represented Cambridge University, as a Governor of the town's Secondary and Technical Schools, and was Chairman of the Helena Thompson Museum committee. He was also one of the earliest members of Workington Rotary Club, of which he was president in 1932.

It was Canon Croft who was responsible for the interior of the church we see today. In 1931 after electric lighting and power was installed, he implemented Sir. J. Ninian Comper's 1915 restoration scheme. Comper was an authority on the neo-classical style and planned the reversal of the church once again. The altar was returned to its original location at the west end and the large impressive gilded baldachino (or canopy) erected. Supported on four massive columns, this formed an magnificent focal point guiding the congregation's attention to the sanctuary as they enter the church. This major work was made possible by the bequest of the late Mrs. J. Yeowart, wife of John L. Yeowart. Later, these alterations were praised by the *National Committee for the Care of Churches*, who described it as *"a model of the proper treatment of late renaissance churches"*. Making St. John's *"a church of which the Diocese can be justifiably proud,"* its altar being *"the finest classical altar in England"*.

In 1923, Canon Croft also inaugurated a Centenary Fund, in order that extensive and essential repairs to the tower and roof could be carried out. During the same year, the south churchyard was laid out, by the *"generoisty"* of Miss Helena Thompson of Park End.

In April 1881, the church received approval to demolish the original rooms to the rear of St. Johns, and build a new parish room. Designed by William Deighton,

It was Canon Croft who was responsible for the interior of St. Johns church we see today.

the large hall measuring 27 x 77 feet (8.3 x 23.5 m), and included other rooms for the Sunday school. This addition which cost £580, could hold about 400 people. The new church hall was used for religious services on weekday evenings, as well as literary lectures. The vestry on the north side of St. Johns was also added in 1883.

Also at this time, the organist at St. Johns was Jonathan F. Scurr a music teacher who lived in Brow Top. One of his friends later wrote of *"an amusing incident"*, telling of a *"bet of a cigar"* that the organist could not play *"Pop goes the weasel"* during the morning service. Scurr won the bet by playing the tune of the nursery rhyme *"very slowly, like Bach or Wagner"*. One wonders what the vicar and his congregation thought, if at all they noticed.

The vicars of St. Johns Workington included 1856-61 Rev. John Irving, 1861-62 Rev. John Thomas, 1862-71 Rev. James Pearson, 1871-92 Canon John J. Thornley, 1892-1914 Rev. Robert Sanders Greene, 1914-59 Canon John R. Croft.

Throughout this book there are many references to the massive influx of new families into the town, with the relocation of Dronfield's Charles Cammell works, around 1883. To cater for their religious needs, a mission church was established at Westfield, under the care of Rev. Alfred Spence, the curate at St. Johns Church. From September 1886, the first services together with a Sunday school were held in the Westfield Board School.

In December 1889 as this community developed, St. Marys Church was opened. It was consecrated by Dr. Harvey Goodwin, the Bishop of Carlisle, and remained a chapel-of-ease and under the "charge" of St. Johns until 1952. The church was first designated a *"conventional district"*, before becoming an independent parish.

Holy Trinity Church at Northside (or West Seaton as it was then called) was erected in 1891 mainly through the *"liberality"* of Mrs. Catherine Blanshard, lady of the manor of Camerton, on a site given by the Earl of Lonsdale. Bulmer tells us *"the edifice is designed in the early geometrical period of Gothic architecture, and consists of nave, chancel, transepts, organ chamber, and vestries. Standing on elevated ground and surmounted by a square massive tower rising to a height of 52 feet, the building forms a prominent feature in the district"*.

In 1925, Rev. James Herbert Fish arrived to begin 31 year ministry in charge of Holy Trinity. As he travelled around his parish by bicycle, he is remember by many as the *"cycling cleric"*. When he left Northside, he retired to Wallasey in 1957 and died in 1975.

One of Jonathan Scurr's friends later wrote of *"an amusing incident"*, telling of a *"bet of a cigar"* that the organist could not play *"Pop goes the Weasel"* during the morning service.

The present Our Lady and St. Michael Roman Catholic Church on Banklands, was formally opened on the 21 September 1876. It replaced the much smaller chapel which was retained and later used as a school. The attractive Early English style church is based on the designs of architect, Edward Welby Pugin. The famous designer of *"some of the noblest Roman Catholic ecclesiastic edifices in the kingdom"*. Edward was the son of Augustus Welby Pugin, another prominent architect who had himself developed a fervent passion for Catholic architecture, based on the gothic revival style. Pugin the elder, had also assisted Sir Charles Barry, with the design of the Houses of Parliament.

The Banklands church is cruciform in plan, about 130 feet long by 70 feet wide. It was built at a cost of around £10,000 by Liverpool contractor Hugh Yates. The Right Rev. Dr. Chadwick (Bishop of Hexham) laid the corner stone in October 1873, and construction work took almost two years. A contemporary account of the church from 1876, tells us that the external walls are *"red ashlar sandstone, quarried from St. Bees, Aspatria and Lazonby"*. Although the historical notes in the 1976 centenary booklet, seems to suggest that *"the outside and some of the inside is Cheshire Red Sandstone"*. At the east end facing onto Bank Road, the belfry rises to around 90 feet. There are several similarities between this Roman Catholic church and those at Whitehaven and Cleator Moor, all based on the designs of Edward W. Pugin.

Internally, the panelled and arched roof and clerestory is supported on ten massive pillars of polished granite. This was supplied by Robinsons Goraghwood quarry in Newry, Northern Ireland. *"So it is said that the church is supported by ten strong Ulster men"*. Upon each pillar is carved an impressive stone figure of an angel. Within the north-west and south-west walls, are two handsome circular rose windows. The pews of the nave are *"Baltic"* timber. Whilst the later choir stalls are of English oak, built and carved by Robert Thompson (1876-1955). He was more commonly known as *"Mousey Thompson"* or as the *"Mouse man of Kilburn"*, whose pieces are usually hallmarked by the inclusion of a carved mouse. It is said that when Thompson had started his joinery firm, he was *"as poor as a church mouse"* and thereafter the mouse reminded him of his humble beginnings. Beneath each seat Aesops fables is beautifully carved on the misericord. It was 1882, before the altar and chancel area of the new church were finally completed.

Much has been written about the *"spirit and energy"* of Abbot Vincent Cuthbert Clifton, who was the long-

"It may fairly be said to be one of the finest specimens of this style of architecture in the county, as it is unquestionably by far the finest in Working-ton".

Bulmers Directory 1901.

OUR LADY & ST. MICHAELS

The beauty of our church my tongue cannot tell,
the beholder can see none can excel,
Her pillars are granite, polished so fine,
Surmounted by figures of angels devine.

The altar is marble, the finest of stone,
And on it a tabernacle, the seat of God's throne,
The windows represent angels and saints,
And the rays of the sunshine their beauty it paints.

Anne Malone White
poem written in 1876
(original had 16 verses)

serving parish priest from 1844-91. Without whom the new church may not have been completed. For when insufficient funds were available to pay the contractor, records suggest that he himself contributed a significant sum. He also introduced into the town, the nuns of the *"Sisters of Charity of St. Paul"* (from Selly Park). Their convent just a short distance from the church on Banklands, was opened in August 1876, only a few weeks before the new church. The first Mother Superior was Sister Catherine M. Rowe, and the duties of the nuns was to teach in the local RC schools, visit sick and housebound parishioners, as well as care for the church. A century later, the convent was still serving the Roman Catholic community in the town.

Cuthbert Clifton was believed to have been related to the Duke and Duchess of Norfolk. There was at least one account of their magnificent yacht berthing at Workington, so they may visit the Abbot. He died on 5 December 1891, and is buried within the graveyard on Banklands. A large obelisk-like stone marks the burial plot, and is one of the few gravestones still remaining in this cemetery. To mark the golden jubilee of the late Abbot Clifton, an imposing stained glass window was installed above the High Altar. The central panel depicting *"Our Lady Star of the Sea and St. Michael the Archangel"*.

In 1905, Fr. Clement Standish replaced Fr. Elphege Duggan as parish priest at Banklands. He was not new to the church, as he had been their curate since 1900. In total Clement Standish served the Workington congregation for over 38 years and is best remembered for *"acquiring and building"* the first part of St. Joseph's School on Harrington Road. He also established the *"Sister's of Poor Clare"* convent in the town. From around 1930, this was located at Thorncroft on Park End Road, the former home of William Dickinson. [01] Other parish priests at Banklands include 1844-91 - Cuthbert Clifton, 1891-1903 Denis Firth, 1903-05 Elphege Duggan, 1905-38 Clement Standish, 1938-47 Clement Hesketh, 1947-52 Dunstan Pozzi, 1952 Sigbert D'Arcy.

In 1879, Banklands Cemetery above Our Lady and St. Michaels church was opened, the acre site adjoining the original catholic burial ground. The first interment in this new cemetery was a Mrs. Mayhollam (1798-1879) whose funeral took place on the 4 March 1879. Little further is known of this old lady who is thought to have lived in King Street.

The existing Wesleyan (now Trinity) Methodist church, at the junction of Vulcans Lane and Finkle Street was built between 1889-90 and replaced the earlier

FATHER CLEMENT STANDISH

[01] See chapter two for more details of William Dickinson and Thorncroft.■

Georgian church [01] destroyed by fire. The architect for the new church was Charles W. Bell (of London) and the new building cost in excess of five thousand pounds. Although the original church was well insured the congregation still had to raise about 40% of this figure. The foundation stone of the new church was formally laid by Henry Fraser Curwen (then mayor) on 26 September 1889, just five months after the fire. During the rebuilding works the old Sunday School rooms in Tiffin Lane and the nearby Queen's Jubilee Hall were used for worship.

A glance at the church today, reveals a large stainless steel illuminated cross dominating its facade, together with wide glazed entrance doors and (rather un-sympathetic) green slate panels above. These are of course much later additions added in 1965. Early photographs also reveal that like the original Georgian church, it was once surrounded by an ornate iron railing. Like much of the ironwork throughout the town, these were removed during WW2 and recycled for the war effort.

In 1883, the present substantial Sunday School buildings were added to the rear of the old church, these suffered only minor damage in the fire of April 1890. Interestingly six memorial foundation stones were built into this building in a ceremony in March 1883. Church records praise the *zealous efforts* of the Sunday School Superintendent John Parker (d.1892) in pushing forward the project to completion. Prior to the construction of this new building the Wesleyan Sunday School Rooms were situated in the old Wesleyan chapel in Tiffin Lane. Perhaps the first, and certainly one of the earliest Sunday School Superintendents was William Wildridge (1810-1897) who served till 1877. By profession, Mr. Wildridge was a tinman (or plumber) and along with his wife Jane is buried in Harrington Road cemetery.

It appears that the first Wesleyan Methodist mission chapel at West-field (or Moss Bay as it later became known) was opened in February 1883. The small chapel accommodating a congregation of up to 160 people. Around six years later a new chapel was built, the memorial stones being officially laid in June 1889. The baptisms register for this methodist chapel is deposited in Whitehaven Record Office, and covers the period from 1893 (until its closure in 1988).

The Wesleyan Methodists also had a mission church in Queen Street. The exact date it was established is unclear, but we know their baptism register covering the years from 1896 to 1949 are again deposited at White-haven Record Office. In the spring of 1951, *Workington Amateur Operatic Society* were granted change of use of the former Methodist Church Hall in Queen Street. One other methodist chapel existed at Barepot and is often

"The Wesleyan Church is a large handsome building, with tower, and was erected on the site in 1890".

Bulmers Directory
1901

"Methodists still adhered to the old-fashioned tenets; smoking and drinking were frowned upon, and frivolity and casual-ness in dress were looked down upon."

Norman Appleyard
remembering 1948
(Trinity Methodist Centenary
booklet 1890-1990)

[01] See pages 87-89 of History of Workington (earliest times to 1865) for more information.■

referred to as the *"Derwent Wesleyan Mission"*. This chapel was opened 29 June 1899, although its baptisms register only covers the period from 1903 to 1963, when services ceased.

In 1932, the various branches of the Methodist church were united under one banner. The Wesleyan Methodist Church was now more commonly referred to as *South William Street Methodist Church*. With the Methodist Church in John Street, becoming *John Street Methodist Church*. Despite the union it would be 1965 before both groups were finally amalgamated under one roof. Then to became known as simply the *Trinity Methodist Church*.

A list of the Superintendent Ministers at the Wesleyan church includes 1871 Rev. Robert N. Barret, 1880-81 Rev. S. Cooke, 1881-83 - Rev. Thomas Dicken, 1883 Rev. H. Owen Rattenbury, 1889-92 Rev. J. Bourne Jones, 1892-95 Rev. J. Bond Charles, 1895-98 Rev. E. S. Banham, 1898-1901 Rev. C. H. Gough, 1901-04 Rev. W. W. Walton,

RIGHT - The Wesleyan Methodist church, at the junction of Vulcans Lane and Finkle Street was built between 1889-90 and replaced the earlier Georgian church destroyed by fire. The architect for the new church was Charles W. Bell (of London) and the new building cost in excess of five thousand pounds. ■

1904-07 Rev. P. J. Cocking, 1907-10 Rev. M. L. Camburn, 1910-13 Rev. J. J. Smith, 1913-15 Rev. J. J. Sutton, 1915-18 Rev. Bramwell Brown, 1918-21 Rev. J. Walker Clarke, 1921-25 Rev. W. Towers Garrett, 1925-28 Rev. Avon Walton, 1928-31 Rev. A. G. Tuck, 1931-33 Rev. H. H. Symmonds, 1933-40 Rev. Mark H. Earl, 1940 Rev. Evans, 1940-41 Rev. Neville Ward, 1941-46 Rev. Walter Reed, 1946-49 Rev. E. Owen Lane, 1949-54 Rev.Frank Leach, 1954-58 Rev. G. Leslie Wilson.

As mentioned in the first volume of the town's history, [01] very little is really known of the town's earliest Primitive Methodist chapel. Bulmer's 1901 directory suggests that its *"congregation was founded in 1823"*. Its first chapel was built in the upper part of John Street around 1826, and served the congregation for around fifty five years. By May 1875, the old chapel was obviously quite run down, when it was advertised for sale in the local newspaper. The Rev. John Day Thompson was the minister, and it is thought services were held elsewhere due to the poor condition of the building. No serious purchaser appears to have been forthcoming, as it was eventually renovated in the autumn of 1880. But less than two years later, it was described once more as *"dilapidated and unsafe"*.

In June 1882, the old chapel was demolished and work began on a new church building. A month later amidst much ceremony, the foundation stones for the new church were laid. Instead of a single memorial stone, there were actually four. These were laid by Henry Bowes, George J. Snelus, Charles J. Valentine and Dr. T. S. Dodgson. Each simply bore just their name and were placed at the foot of the four sandstone buttresses, on the John street facade. The new church was designed by local architect William G. Scott, who was also responsible for much of St. John's Board schools on the opposite side of the street. The exterior was red dressed stonework and window arrangements were typical of the decorated gothic style, so popular in Victorian architecture. Above the centrally placed entrance doors was a "handsome" stained glass window with stone tracery.

The entrance to the church was reached by five broad steps, either side of which were stairs descending to the basement level. This large *"well-lit"* lower level room extending below the main church, accommodated the Sunday School of 250 children. In it's later years, it was also used as a lunchtime canteen for the pupils from nearby St. Johns Junior School. Internally, the main church was 58ft x 31ft, around 16 feet (4.9m) larger than

"My Mother and Dad walked to church each Sunday, Dad in his silk high hat and walking stick and Mother in her bonnet, bustle and curly hair".
Agnes Whitfield

[01] See pages 89-90 of History of Workington (Earliest times to 1865) for details of the earlier Primitive Methodist Church, in the town. ■

The Primitive Methodists formally merged with the Wesleyan Methodists of South William Street, in 1965 and became known as the Trinity Methodist Church.

the old 1826 chapel. It was galleried on three sides, reached from staircases either side of the entrance. The new church could accommodated about 500 people comfortably, and cost of construction was around £2000. The contractors for the new church were Lancelot Ferguson and Robinson Fox.

The new church was opened on 8 July 1883. The first wedding performed in the new church took place on the 31 May, 1884. When Joseph Smith of Cockermouth, married Miss Wilson. Several Workington born men trained to be Primitive Methodist preachers, notably John Sharpe and John Magee. In the early 1880s, they were ministers at Barnard Castle and Durham respectively. Other ministers at the John Street church include - c.1862 - Rev Adam Dodds, c.1875 - Rev. John Day Thompson, c.1880-83 - Rev. Matthew. P. Davison, 1907-11 Rev. Frederick Jesse Hopkins.

As previously mentioned, the Primitive Methodists formally merged with the Wesleyan Methodists of South William Street, in 1965 and became known as the Trinity Methodist Church. They vacated the John Street Church and it was another victim of Workington Borough Council's new town centre redevelopment. Money received from the sale of the premises was used to finance the alterations to the South William Street church.

One former Workington church which is often overlooked is the United Free Methodist Church at the end of Victoria Road, close to the corner of Bolton street and Blackburn Street. The memorial stones for the new building were laid in October 1890 and the church formally opened in June 1891. It's baptisms register deposited at Whitehaven Record Office, shows that the chapel served this part of the town for over 43 years.

In 1934 after the union of several branches of the Methodist religion, the chapel closed and it's congregation merged with the Wesleyan Church in South William Street. The old United Methodist Chapel on Bolton Street, became the Town Band Rooms. During the early 1930s, Workington Town Band under conductor Robert Atkinson (1869-1934) was particularly prominent in the town. In October 1934, they competed in the National Championships for the first time at Crystal Palace. Gaining a very credible 24th place out of the *"finest bands in the country"*. Sadly, Robert Atkinson (of Guard Street) who had died in July that year, never got to proudly lead his band at the championships. At his burial in Salterbeck cemetery, the *"massed bands"* of Workington, Cockermouth, Maryport, Clifton and Broughton played at his grave side.

In April 1935, the Workington Town Band gave their first live radio performance, broadcast to the nation by the BBC. A further radio broadcast followed in March 1936, with the band under the conductorship of Henry Sutcliffe. Sutcliffe also gave a memorable cornet solo, said to be the highlight of the programme.

Records suggests that the congregation of the Presbyterian Church was formed in 1742, and the first chapel built in Sanderson Street in 1750. This was enlarged in 1858 to accommodate about 300 worshippers. In 1888, the building was totally replaced by a new *"Early English Gothic"* style church designed by architect Charles W. Eaglesfield (of Maryport). This was officially opened in May 1889. The best feature of this building is its neatly balanced facade, constructed mainly of red sandstone, with coursed ashlar stonework. The pointed gothic windows having finely detailed mullions and tracery.

Before WW1, one interesting feature of this church was the use of hydraulic (water) power to *"blow the organ"*. Council minutes reveal that the Corporation charged the church *"ten shillings per quarter"* (50p) for the water used. A similar powered organ was also used in the town's Roman Catholic church. In 1873, a *"commodious"* Sunday school building was erected in St. John's Court for the Presbyterian congregation. Designed by local architect W. G. Scott, the building was consecrated on Christmas day 1875. This building still exists close to the parish rooms of St. Johns Church.

In 1972, the Presbyterian Church merged with the Congregational Church to become the United Reform Church, based in South William Street. Recently, it was confirmed that the Sanderson Street church now occupied by the Workington Christian Fellowship or Pentecostal Church (Assemblies of God) is to be demolished to make way for the further redevelopment of the town centre.

The Congregational Church was situated opposite the Wesleyan (now Trinity) Methodist Church in South William Street. It was built in 1884, replacing an earlier building on the same site. The new church has six memorial or foundation stones, laid at a ceremony on 9 August 1884. Between the rear of the church and Vulcans Lane is a small burial ground. Rev. James Rennie was minister at the Congregational Church from 1858 to his retirement in December 1883. The long-serving pastor

The best feature of the Presbyterian church was its neatly balanced Early English gothic facade, constructed mainly of red sandstone, with coursed ashlar stonework.

died the following year and is buried alongside his wife Martha, within this graveyard. He was succeeded by Rev. Charles Burrows who moved to the town from Dronfield, along with the hundreds of steelworkers who relocated with the Charles Cammell works. As a result the congregation of the church was greatly swelled by those who had previously worshipped with Rev. Burrows in Derbyshire.

The Congregational ministers included 1858-1883 Rev. James Rennie, 1883-06 Rev. Charles Burrow, 1906-10 Rev. F. C. Rollin, 1911-17 Rev. Samual Frow, 1918-23 Rev. Henry Threllfall, 1924-25 Rev. Ernest Elliott, 1925 Rev, Frank Jones.

In October 1879, we know that one of the first attempts to form a Baptist Church in the town, took place at a meeting in Daniel Harkness's School. How successful this was is unclear as Bulmer's 1901 directory tells us that the Baptist church was eventually established in the town after *"many fruitless efforts on the part of a few zealous members"*. It would appear that up until at least 1888, the Workington Baptists may have worshipped as a branch of the larger Maryport Baptist church.

Their first chapel (or mission room) is though to have been the premises on the south side of Edkin Street, facing up Thompson Street. This was opened in February 1882, the Rev. Hugh Singleton (of Rawdon College) being appointed it's first minister. We know this property was

BELOW - The Baptish church on Harrington Road, built in 1886. ∎

not new, but simply adapted for use as a mission room. All of Edkin street was of course demolished in the late 1960s to make way for the new town centre re-development.

Within a few years and particularly after the congregation was swelled by the influx of the Dronfield steelworkers into the town, the small mission room was to prove totally inadequate. Plans were now put in place to build a large new church on the corner of Harrington Road and Gray Street. The memorial stones of which were laid on 9 March 1886. The new completed church being formally opened on the 23 September 1886.

This new church (demolished in the early 1980s) was built predominantly from red ashlar sandstone, in neat horizontal courses and bands. It's facade was dominated by two tall hexagonal lead roofed "pepper pot" towers at each corner. Between these towers was an slate roofed porch supported by three arches. Above the wider central arch was the date stone, reading "AD 1886". The main entrance to the church, beneath this porch was raised some five or six steps above the street level. Between the church and the corner of Gray Street was an open piece of ground, surrounded by iron railings. The present modern single-storey Baptist church rooms now occupies much of this grassed area.

By April 1882, we know the Baptist Chapel had started a successful Sunday school. Within six months there were around 170 pupils and 14 teachers. Records show that their Edkin Street hall was "frequently crowded", particularly after the influx of the steelworkers and their families from Dronfield. In 1890, a new Sunday school was built on the corner of Gray Street and Hartington Street, to the rear of the new church. The building capable of holding upwards of 500 children, was designed by W. G. Scott and cost around £820. In December 1893, their old Edkin Street premises was taken over by the Salvation Army Citadel.

Plans for the Emmanuel Church on Vulcans Lane, almost opposite the main entrance to the park, were approved by the Borough Council in September 1931. This neat little predominately brick built church was officially opened in February 1933, by Mr. and Mrs. J. H. Fisher of Staveleigh, Workington.

During the early 1880s, the very popular Salvation Army held their meetings in the Assembly Rooms in Portland Square. Newspaper reports tell us that very often the large congregation would *"spill out into the cobbled square"*. By 1884, they had acquired one of the vacant

This Baptist church was built predominently from red ashlar sandstone, in neat horizontal courses and bands. It's facade was dominated by two tall hexagonal lead roofed *"pepper pot"* towers at each corner.

The Salavtion Army held their meetings in the Assembly Rooms in Portland Square.....very often the large congregation would *"spill out into the cobbled square"*.

building plots in Duke Street. Here they built a large mission hall, the foundation stone being laid on Good Friday, 11 April 1884 by James N. Carr (of Carlisle). The building was designed by local architect W. G. Scott.

Of the remaining religious groups in the town, the Free Church or Christ Church had a chapel on the south side of Edkin Street, almost opposite the entrance to the Drill Hall. It certainly existed here in 1888, and appears to have still been in use until the 1960s. In 1878, the Christian Workers' Association Mission Hall was opened in Bell Street. It is believed that they had acquired, renovated and converted the former YMCA rooms. Around this time, the Scottish National Church are known to have held services in the Good Templars Hall. In 1901, the Christian Brethren held their meetings in the Dent Hall on Fisher Street.

In September 1885, it is thought that the Church Army was first established in the town. For many years, it was based in the small mission church on the west side of King Street. This small red sandstone chapel was built in 1885. Few records of this organisation appear to remain, although we know that St. Johns Church (on Washington Street) greatly assisted their evangelical work. In the early 1880s, we know the Seamans Christian Friends Society had a small chapel in Falcon Street. Exactly when this was established is unclear. By 1893, this old chapel was replaced with a new Seamans Bethel which still exists today.■

❧ CHAPTER ELEVEN ❧

EDUCATION - SCHOOLS & LIBRARY

TODAY, WORKINGTON'S SCHOOLS are administered by the County Council's Education Authority. But the majority of the town's Victorian schools were built and managed by a locally based School Board. This committee (of nine members) officially formed on 11 March 1873 consisted of local councillors, the clergy and prominent members of the community. Workington had eight Board schools. St. Johns at the upper end of John Street, St. Michaels in Station Road, Victoria School in Victoria Road, Guard Street, Marshside or Lawrence Street school, Westfield (Moss Bay), Northside and Siddick schools.

In August 1903, the School Board was replaced by the *Borough of Workington Education Committee*. It now had around fifteen members, again appointed from the local councillors, clergy etc. In these early days it met every month at its office in Guard Street. By the 1930s, the Education committee had moved to Mossdale House at 149 Harrington Road.

In the autumn of 1926, Cumberland County Council had suggested that the Workington schools be amalgamated into the County Education Committee. Workington unanimously declined to transfer powers to the County authority. Their eight well equipped and maintained schools were then valued at over £100,000, and some form of compensation could not be agreed. However eighteen years later, responsibility for the town's education was finally passed to the *Cumberland Education Authority*. Workington becoming part of the Western area, but was still administered from the same Harrington Road offices.

St. Johns school was first opened on 30 March 1860, the buildings were subsequently extended on two occasions. Like St. Michaels School, it was originally built and maintained by the parish church, supported by annual subscriptions and government grants. In 1873, both schools were handed over to the newly formed Workington School Board. St. Johns was located at the upper end of John Street, on the east side of the road. The two-storey school and this section of the street eventually disappeared when St. Johns Precinct was built in the late 1960s. Initially St. Johns was known by the somewhat

During the 1880s Workington had eight schools managed by the School Board. These were -

St. Johns in John Street.
St. Michaels in Station Road.
Victoria School in Victoria Road.
Guard Street School.
Marshside or Lawrence Street.
Westfield (Moss Bay).
Northside.
Siddick.

In August 1903, the School Board was replaced by the *Borough of Workington Education Commitee*.

The headmaster of St. Johns was James Fielden, a Yorkshireman and strict disiplinarian who frequently punished latecomers with *"two strokes of the cane across the hand"*.

lengthy title of *"Workington Church of England Schools (John Street)"*. But in August 1874, the school's name was simplified to just the *"St. Johns Board School"*.

St. Johns was first extended in 1882, the plans were prepared by Workington architect W. G. Scott [01], whilst the local contractor Richard H. Hodgson carried out the work. By 1901, Bulmer tells us the school consisted of a *"spacious block of buildings and contained three departments"*. There was a mixed infants school, with the older boys and girls being educated separately. The girls section was located at the Pow Street end of the school. In the centre of the building was the headmasters house, with a front garden running towards John Street, enclosed by a high wall. In later years this garden became part of the playground. St. Johns accommodated nearly 850 pupils (302 infants, 541 older pupils).

For many of these early years the headmaster of St. Johns was James Fielden, a Yorkshireman and strict disciplinarian who frequently punished latecomers with *"two strokes of the cane across the hand"*. He was succeeded by Mr. Mawson, who in 1894 handed over the headship to his son Ernest William Mawson. Mawson junior had previously taught at both the Westfield (Moss Bay) and Victoria schools. That same year, James Fielden's son Herbert (who had been born in the school house) started work at St. Johns as a pupil teacher. When Mawson eventually retired in 1924, Herbert Fielden returned to become the head himself following in the footsteps of his father. Another prominent pupil teacher at St. Johns was John Carruthers Beattie (b.1867). He was the grandson of Thomas Beattie, who lived in King Street. John Beattie achieved fame surveying the Cape-to-Cairo railway. And from 1918-1937 he was the principal and vice-chancellor of Capetown University.

Fielden's notes in the school log make interesting reading, giving us an indication of the level of attendance and Victorian discipline imposed. Frequently the cane was very much in evidence. Schools in James Fielden's day relied heavily on their average attendance figure to qualify for a school grant. If the figures dropped their *"precious grant"* was in danger. Up until 1891, parents still had to subsidise their children's education. Each pupil had to bring *"school pence"* with them. This related to about six shillings a year (or 30p), slightly less than *"three old ha'pence a week"*. Fielden's notes in the log tell us that after they *"opened the school free of fees; there was a great influx of children and considerable improvement in attendance"*.

Opened at the same time as St. Johns, over the years

[01] William Graham Scott (b.1837) had his architectural practice in William Street, and was also responsible for designing much of Workington's better quality Victorian houses. Such as Frostoms Road (1902) Craig Road (1903) and Highfield (1903). ■

St. Michaels School (in Station Road) has also been extended and altered on several occasions. The first school buildings were built on the corner of Falcon Place (Hagg Hill) and Station Road. Again the older boys and girls were all taught in separate classes. In 1882, William G. Scott designed a new infants school for St. Michaels. This new detached block contained one large schoolroom, with two smaller classrooms to the rear, each room having gallery-type seating for the pupils. One feature of the main hall was the substantial king-post roof trusses. Records suggest that this new infant school was formally opened in April 1883.

During the mid 1890s, St. Michaels was also said to accommodate upto 850 students (396 infants, 241 boys and 241 girls), although it's average attendance was 660 pupils. Joseph Wood was then the headmaster. At the beginning of WW1, the headship was held by J. H. P. James, who later became the secretary of Workington's Education Committee.

Up until the late 1920s, all the scholars at the Board schools sat closely side by side on bench seats in galleries (or tiers) of long desks facing their teacher. A 1926 report on the Workington schools revealed that *"hundreds of new dual desks"* had now been provided to replace these galleries in classrooms. St. Michaels was apparently one of the last to receive these new modern cast iron and timber desks.

Built in 1884, Victoria School on the south side of Victoria Road was named in honour of Queen Victoria. Designed by local architect, George Dale Oliver (off 44 Pow Street) the large single storey building again had separate classes for the older boys and girls, and a mixed infant school. Like other Board schools in the town there was also a masters residence, on the same site. Victoria was probably the largest of the Workington Board schools and was said to be capable of holding over 900 pupils. Although seldom did the attendance exceed 800. Joseph Scott was one of the schools earliest headmasters, having moved to Victoria from St. Michaels. When he retired Mr. Scott claimed to have taught some four generations of many families in the town, in a career lasting *"half a century"*. With the construction of Islay Place Junior School during the mid 1950s, Victoria school became a girls only school.

In October 1997, dangerous levels of methane gas were discovered within the classrooms of the aged Victoria School. It was thought by many to have been leaking from the many abandoned mine workings below the town, some at a level of around 300ft (91m). But con-

Up until the late 1920s, all the scholars at the Board schools sat closely side by side on bench seats in galleries (or tiers) of long desks facing their teacher.

Built in 1884, Victoria School on the south side of Victoria Road was named in honour of Queen Victoria.

sultants believed the gas was not emulating from the old pits, but occurred naturally underground. As the school was closed for three weeks, efforts to draw off the gas proved unsuccessful. Finally after much debate the decision was taken to demolish the old school buildings and replace them with a new school.

The Lawrence Street (or Marshside) Board school was erected in 1876. It was located in Lawrence Street, which ran off Stanley Street. The single storey school held a total of 560 pupils (153 boys, 159 girls and 250 mixed infants). It is believed that William Charles Lewis was the first headmaster at Lawrence Street, where he lived in the house attached to the school premises. By the 1890s he had left the post and become a private tutor and music teacher, living in Murraydale Terrace (off South William Street). Lawrence Street school was demolished when the Marsh and Quay area was cleared by the local authority in the 1970s.

During 1883, as the influx of the Dronfield steel working families settled in the Westfield area (now more commonly known as Moss Bay) a further Board school was built. The new school capable of holding around 500 pupils (130 boys, 130 girls and 240 infants) was opened in 1884. This school would serve the less prosperous Moss Bay community for over seventy years. With the further development and expansion of the local authority housing estates at Salterbeck and Westfield, a new junior and infant schools were opened in November 1954. These new schools being located just off Westfield Drive and the old school building was vacated.

The Northside (or West Seaton) school was built in 1878 on the east side of the main road north to Maryport, adjacent to the Holy Trinity Church. The school drew the majority of its pupils from the iron and steel working families who lived in the nearby rows of terraced properties at Oldside and Northside. The single-storey school was then said to accommodate around 300 scholars (164 boys and girls and 133 infants). Although the school roll reveals the average attendance was usually around 185.

In December 1900, the Borough Council approved plans for a further Board School at Siddick. This village with it's rows of terraced properties had only recently sprang up to house the miners employed at the nearby St. Helens Colliery. Eventually opened in 1902, Siddick school on the east side of the main road was built to accommodate just over 300 pupils, although its average attendance was around half this figure.

Up until the turn of the century, the School Board also ran an infants school for around 100 pupils in the

During 1883, as the influx of the Dronfield steel working families settled in the Westfield area (now more commonly known as Moss Bay) a further Board school was built.

old Guard Street school. These buildings on the south side of the road, almost opposite the foot of Pinfold Street, were formally occupied by the town's School of Industry, endowed by Thomas Wilson in 1831 and 1845. After the infants school closed, the premises became the Higher Grade or Standard school. It educated around 500 older scholars, upto the statuatory age of 14. Although some could stay on until 16, in order to take their school certificate examinations. They were taught *"Science and Art, Technical Instruction and Manual subjects"*. At this time there was also a Pupil Teachers' centre at Guard Street, where new prospective teachers were trained before being employed in the Board schools.

In February 1902, a new Grammar School was opened at Guard Street. Although Guard Street is really considered the town's first secondary school, there was an earlier public higher grade school operating in St. Johns Court (off Jane Street) known as the Workington Academy. This establishment was not controlled by the school board, but by a management committee, its chairman being local architect W. G. Scott. Benjamin J. Whitaker, who lived in Washington Street was the principal or head master. This private school attracted around 115 older pupils and is thought to have existed till at least the outbreak of WW1.

The original Guard Street school buildings were extended in 1882 and 1899. The latter alterations being

BELOW - Sketch of the front elevation of Guard Street school, first opened in 1831. The dotted line around the central block reveals the extent of the original school, later extended. ■

Another private school was the Garfield School in Carlton Road ran by Mr Daniel Harkness.

carried out in preparation for opening the new higher grade school. During the work to the new science building, builder John Murchie (1864-1899) fell 30 feet and was fatally injured. He was the son of William and Jane Murchie, confectioners in Pow Street, and was buried in Harrington Road Cemetery.

The higher grade school later became known as Central School, and a 1926 report tells us Guard Street Schools contained two domestic subject centres, two manual instruction departments and a *"splendidly equipped room"* for practical science. After the new senior school was built in Newlands Lane, it became known as New Central School. In February 1951, Guard Street School was renamed Wilson Secondary Modern School, in honour of its founder some 120 years earlier.

Another private school was the Garfield School in Carlton Road ran by Mr. Daniel Harkness. [01] It was located in a purpose built single storey building, plans for which were approved by the Council in December 1881. There was one very large schoolroom (50ft x 25ft) and two smaller classrooms. A year or so later, Mr. Harkness built himself a house, beside his school on the corner of Carlton Road and Ramsey Brow, the property became known as Garfield House.

Before 1931, Dr. Young is known to have purchased the house and later extended the property. Early in 1953, this property is thought to have been converted to a Nurses' hostel for those employed at Workington Infirmary. Much later it became the Garfield Hotel, today we know it as the Hall Park Hotel.

The Garfield School later became known as the *"Little Theatre"* and Janet Thompson (daughter of Hudson Schofield) remembers as a child attending Miss Wegulin's dancing classes there in the late 1940s. Miss Wegulin, a small lady with *"beautiful red hair"* was an Hungarian refugee and brother of Mr. Wegulin a solicitor in the town. In 1954, the old school building was acquired by the County Council, and used as a Civil Defence headquarters.

We know there has been a Catholic school at Banklands since the start of the nineteenth century. But in Victorian times the St. Michaels Roman Catholic School in Bank Road, adjacent to Our Lady and St. Michael RC Church was not managed or controlled by the town's School Board. The church itself built, equipped and ran the school. From 1876, lessons were taught by the nuns of the *Sisters of Charity of St. Paul* (from Selly Park). The school had two departments, one infant and one mixed class for older scholars. Although it was said to

[01] School master, Daniel Harkness was born in Abbey Holme in 1841 and lived with his wife Annie, at 7 Christian Street, before moving to his newly built house in Carlton Road. ■

accommodate upto 750 pupils, its attendance was generally around 550.

In November 1900, the Borough Council approved plans for a second Roman Catholic School in South William Street, and two years later St. Patricks was completed. Like Banklands School there was an infant and mixed primary classes, with the majority of classes being taught by nuns. Records suggest St. Patricks could hold nearly 600 pupils, but the average attendance was around two thirds this figure. It is thought that the first part of St. Josephs Roman Catholic Secondary School on Harrington Road was built in 1930, and first extended about nine years later.

Guard Street Higher Grade and Grammar School was opened as a result of the Borough Council adopting the Technical Institutions Acts of 1889 and 1891. But these acts of Parliament also gave Local Authorities the powers to establish Technical Schools or Colleges to further educate their older students. Rather than go it alone, the various local councils in the district formed a special committee to plan and build a new Technical College for West Cumberland. Their first meeting was held at the Globe Hotel in Whitehaven in June 1901. Within a month, the Borough Council extremely keen to have the new college built in Workington, offered to provide a suitable site free of charge. Initially, the Town Clerk was instructed to offer Field House (later the Town Hall) or the vacant site on the corner of Vulcans Lane and Finkle Street (later used for the Carnegie Library).

Little was achieved in the ensuing six years or so, the proposal to use Field House was rejected as the site was considered too restrictive. Records also show that Bankfield was also offered by it's owners as a possible new technical school. But *not withstanding its fine position* it was felt it would cost too much to adapt for the new college. Finally in April 1907, it was agreed to use part of the land purchased by the Borough Council for it's new public park, off Lowsa Lane (later re-named Park Lane).

As the formal purchase of the park land was completed by the Borough Council, the first governors of the new Technical College were appointed. Canon H. D Rawnsley and local man Richard H. Hodgson (formerly of Field House) were included in the seven members representing the County Council. While Miss Helena Thompson, Councillors Herbert Thompson, Patrick Walls and Frederick Hall represented the Borough of Workington. The final governor was seconded from the University of Cambridge. The actual site of the new

ABOVE - Canon H. D. Rawnsley, one of the first governors of Workington Technical College. ■

College was formally conveyed to the County Education Committee in April 1909.

In October 1910, the Borough Council formally approved the plans for the new college, and construction work began on the new building. The attractive red brick buildings, with yellow sandstone detailing was completed during 1911-1912. Initially the college had just twelve classrooms, with accommodation for around 300 pupils. There was also several workshops for practical work, a dining hall and administration block. The first principal was G. H. Woollatt, the second master was A. B. Coles.

Essentially, the new Park Lane building was both a secondary school and a technical school or college (offering day, afternoon and evening classes). The town's grammar school moved to the new premises, the youngest pupils were 12 years old. From 1912 to the summer of 1929, the school was known as the Workington County Technical and Secondary School. Up until 1945, it's name was changed to the West Cumberland Secondary School and Cumberland Technical College. Thereafter it became Workington Grammar School and Secondary Technical College. Following the opening of the town's new grammar school at Stainburn in 1954, the name was changed once more to the Workington Technical College.

During 1933-1934 the college was considerably enlarged, the new buildings included laboratories, workshops, classrooms and a mining school (funded by the Miners Welfare Fund). In May 1951, plans were also approved by the Borough Council for a new Motor vehicle workshop at the college. This was located close to the Park End Road entrance, along the boundary with Vulcans Park.

By the spring of 1928, a site on the corner of High Street and Newlands Lane was chosen for a further secondary school in the town. The Borough Council purchasing the 3.5 acres of land for £2,000, from the executors of the late Peter Gibson Quirk. This included the nine cottages and a stable which then fronted on to the west side of High Street. At this point the main road out of the town was then very narrow. When building the new school the council also took the opportunity to widen the road to it's present width. In January 1929, the adjoining field below Newlands House, was also purchased from the United Steel Company.

In April 1930, the Borough Council formally approved the plans for the new school, the estimated costs of construction were nearly £31,000. Opened in 1931, the school was first named the New Central School. It

Essentially, the new Park Lane building was both a secondary school and a technical school or college (offering day, afternoon and evening classes).

was then a mixed secondary school, but initially both sexes were taught in separate areas, with a strict *"never the twain should meet"* policy. By 1949, the New Central School became a girls only school and was re-named Newlands Girls Secondary School.

Not too long after WW2, the existing grammar school within the technical college complex was considered out-dated and inadequate. By 1947, it was decided to build a totally new modern grammar school on part of land belonging to Schoose farm, fronting on to Stainburn Road. It's playing fields were accommodated on what was once called Mire Meadow, off Cross Hill. On 10 July 1952, the foundation stone for the town's latest secondary school was laid by John Mitchell Cusack. The existing grammar school pupils left Park Lane and transferred to the new school, which was formally opened on 30 September 1954. This co-educational school capable of holding 650 pupils was then described as "spacious and functional with outstanding facilities for advanced and scholarship work". Today, we know the school as Stainburn Comprehensive School.

As more and more local authority housing was built at Salterbeck and Westfield, it was identified that another new secondary school was required to the south of the town. The site for what was to become Salterbeck School was selected in January 1953, and was purchased for around £2,700.

The existing grammar school pupils left Park Lane and transferred to the new school, which was formally opened on 30 September 1954.

In July 1890, the Corporation opened a newsroom on the upper floor of the Savings Bank building in Pow Street. Followed by a new lending and reference library in November 1891. The premises were those previously occupied by the town's Mechanics Institute, being rented from the bank's trustees for £20 per annum. The bank itself continuing to trade from ground floor offices.

The town's first librarian was W. E. Jones, appointed in August 1891. Four years later, he was succeeded by J. W. C. Purves. We know from Mr. Purves' notes that the premises were always *"only intended as temporary"*, and by 1899 the library had *"completely outgrown the accommodation"*. The library was then funded by an additional *"penny"* on the rates, generating around £258 per year. There were around 6,500 books available to borrowers, with just over 39,800 books issued annually.

In November 1901, Mr. Purves [01] requested that the new Library be built on the corner of Vulcans Lane and Finkle Street, but the Borough Council could not immediately concede to his request, as the site had in the meantime been one of those offered to the County Coun-

[01] J. W. C. Purves, was appointed the librarian in October 1895. He was also secretary and treasurer of the Northern County Library Association from 1900-02. ∎

cil for the new Technical College. Amongst, those other sites considered for the new library were Tuscan Villa and the site of the present Bus Station, in Oxford Street. The latter was actually their first choice, but its owner Henry McAleer [01] refused to sell the Council the site. The Finkle Street site was then selected as a second option. It had been acquired by the Corporation in order to widen Finkle Street, and was previously the site of the old Appletree Inn, the stone yard of Robert Brown and a row of eight small cottages.

In 1902, Andrew Carnegie[02] gifted £7,500 for the town's new library, on the condition the Council *"supply the site free"*. In June 1902, the Borough council sent a letter to Mr. Carnegie expressing their *"grateful thanks for his munificent and noble generosity"*. Like many other municipal projects of the time, several architects were invited to submit designs for the *"new library and lecture hall"*. This open competition attracted some seventy-four entries, the winners being Messrs. W. A. Mellon and George Wittet of York. In May 1903, locally based contractors, Messrs. J. I. Wilson and Co's submitted a tender of £6,894, which was accepted by the Council. Alderman R. E. Highton formally laid the foundation stone for the new building on 10 September 1903.

The new building was formally opened on 6 October 1904 by Alderman R. E. Highton. Who was given a silver key to mark the occasion. The process of borrowing a book from the library was then quite different than today. All the books for *"lending"* were kept behind a counter, and borrowers had to request the title by asking an assistant. There was also a reference library, together with a newsroom and magazine room. Adjoining the library, in what we now know as the Carnegie theatre was a lecture hall.

In January 1946, H. V. Chandler (formerly of Merton and Mordon) was appointed Workington's librarian. Interestingly, Daniel Hay, the librarian and curator at Whitehaven was also interviewed for the post. One of Mr. Chandler's first improvements was to open a Children's (or Junior) Library, at the Finkle Street library. A carefully structured selection of books was now available for children upto the age of eleven. By October 1950, the shelves of the junior library had 16,000 books and nearly 1,900 members. ■

[01] Henry McAleer who lived in Pow Street, and had a thriving boot and shoe shop. He was actually an Alderman of the Borough Council and member of the School Board. ■

[02] Andrew Carnegie, born in Dunfermline, had emigrated to America with his parents and settled in Pitsburg. After a visit to Scotland in 1868, he founded the Pitsburg Union Mills, for the manufacture of steel rails. In 1901, when his Carnegie Steel Company was later taken over by the American Steel Trust, its capital exceeded 28 million pounds. He would use this great wealth for many charitable purposes, principally providing local libraries and church organs throughout the world. The philanthropist is estimated to have donated around £8 million on libraries alone. ■

WATER, GAS & ELECTRICITY

WORKINGTON'S FIRST WATERWORKS was established in 1859 by *the Workington Waterworks Co. Limited*. The town's water was raised by two large steam engines directly from the River Derwent and stored in an underground reservoir close to Stainburn Old Hall. Following the town's adoption of the 1864 Local Government Act, the Local Board subsequently acquired control of the town's water supply, through the outright purchase of the privately owned company that built it.

Unfortunately, the original engineers who designed the waterworks, failed to really anticipate the rapid rise in the town's population and the subsequent enormous increase in water consumption. Soon the waterworks were running at full capacity, so much so that the Local Board struggled to maintain even a basic supply. In March 1878, an explosion occurred at the Stainburn pumping station, depriving the entire town of water for almost two days. Both the ageing boilers were extensively damaged by the blast. The supply was only restored when railway contractors Robert Ward & Sons, who were building Navvies railway bridge over the Derwent, provided two large portable steam engines.

Obtaining healthy drinking water from the River Derwent also proved far from satisfactory. The river was heavily polluted with sewage and industrial waste from the towns and villages upstream of the town. Several reports particularly highlight the *"damage done to Workington's health, by receiving the sewage of Cockermouth in it's water"*. The lack of good clean drinking water contributed greatly to at least two cholera epidemics in the town, during the 1870s. After several years of negotiation, Workington joined forces with the Cockermouth Local Board and the Cockermouth Urban Board [01] to obtain a new water supply from Crummock Water. This lake was selected because *"almost 16,000 acres of mountainous land drains into Crummock Water basin, which is around 321 feet (97.8m) above sea level.....There is on average about 85.12 inches (2.15m) of rainfall annually.....The daily requirements of Workington is 800,000 gallons, yet the lake itself is capable of holding around 505 million gallons of water"*.

The River Derwent was heavily polluted with sewage and industrial waste from the towns and villages upstream of the town.

[01] These two local authorities later became known as the Cockermouth Rural District Council and Cockermouth Urban District Council. ■

Frequently the domestic supply was totally turned off at eleven in the evening till six the next morning, in order to supply the ironworks. This often left the entire town without any water supply whatsoever.

In 1878, the *Cockermouth and Workington Water Act* received approval and the work on laying the new water main commenced. The total cost was about £32,000, but because of their larger consumption and greater distance from the lake, Workington agreed to contribute 67% of the cost. The two Cockermouth Boards paid the balance and were permitted to take a supply for their own townspeople. All maintenance and any later improvements would also be jointly funded by these authorities. In August 1879, the new *"bright, clear and pure water"* supply was officially turned on by Mrs. Susie Curwen, wife of Henry Fraser Curwen. The original timber four-spoked wheel used during the ceremony, is now displayed at the town's Helena Thompson Museum. Fixed to its centre is an inscribed silver plaque commemorating the event.

At the beginning of the 1880s, the Local Board had a major problem supplying trade water to the various iron and steelworks which established themselves in the town. Anxious not to lose the considerable revenue, the increased demands for trade water could only be met at the expense of the domestic customers. Frequently the domestic supply was totally turned off at eleven in the evening till six the next morning, in order to supply the ironworks. This often left the entire town without any water supply whatsoever. With the news of Charles Cammells takeover of the Derwent Ironworks and their major expansion plans, the situation would be unlikely to improve.

In 1883 as the new Derwent steelworks was nearing completion, a further Act of Parliament was passed enabling the Local Board to take trade water directly from the River Derwent. The work on this new 28" main, laid from an intake in Falcon Street was carried out by Richard H. Hodgson. By September 1883, the pumping station on the Cloffolks was nearing completion. The cost of the scheme was £22,000, and the pipe was capable of carrying a quantity of 5 million gallons daily. Although some thought the main should have been larger, it was estimated Moss Bay I&SC alone were using around 1 - 2½ million gallons of water a day. The large investment in this scheme by the Borough Council was also met with a considerable amount of *"violent opposition"*. Many fearing such an enormous outlay would never be recovered. But gradually over the years the cost was recouped and the scheme eventually generated a considerable annual profit.

Still Workington's population continued to grow at a frightening rate, particularly as Cammell steelworks brought an influx of hundreds of families from Dronfield. To meet this ever increasing demand for domestic water it was decided to enlarge the water main from Crummock Water. But the two Cockermouth authorities, partners in the original scheme were still perfectly satisfied with the old arrangement and *"had as much water as they required"*. Not surprisingly, they declined to spend any further monies *"for the sole benefit of Workington"*. As Workington sought parliamentary approval to upgrade the supply, their Cockermouth neighbours opposed the scheme. Finally after much negotiation, it was agreed that Workington Borough Council would take sole control of the entire Crummock water main, and make a charge for supplying the other two districts. They subsequently spent a further £60,000 on upgrading the water main.

The inlet pipe from Crummock Water was then 24" (600mm) in diameter, until the pipeline reached Scale Hill Bridge near Cockermouth, thereafter it reduced to 21" (535mm) for the remainder of its route to Workington. The Stainburn reservoir held 213,000 gallons and water consumption by the town per head of population averaged 23.5 gallons per day, including that for trade use. In March 1903, a new waterworks was formally opened by Henry Howard (the Chairman of the County Council).

We know that the Crummock water main was replaced again in 1929. The town Mayor Joseph Goss officially turned on the supply using the same wheel used by Mrs. Curwen in 1879. Around 125 years later, Workington's domestic water is still drawn from Crummock water.

By 1866, Workington had two separate gasworks, the more modern plant on Stanley Street and the original Harrington Road works. Both were owned and operated by the Local Board, who were solely responsible for supplying gas to virtually all the town's domestic and trade consumers. Gas was traditionally produced by coal carbonisation, a method superseded by the widespread use of natural gas we know today.

Between 1883-98 as the town's population rapidly increased, the Stanley Street works were gradually extended to meet the rising demand. Initially a new 220,000 cubic feet gas holder was built at Clay Flatts at the end of Bolton Street. Erected by Messrs. Moulson (of London) and costing around £9000. It was supplied by a new underground "trunk main" laid from the gasworks. Then a further £2,500 was spent on a new boiler (supplied by Lowca Engineering Co.), a purifying house, two travelling cranes for removing purifier covers and a new

During the winter of 1892, the Borough Council visited 4,314 households in the town and their report makes interesting reading. There were 20,543 residents, 11,816 water fittings, 6,803 inside taps, 584 outside taps, 3,896 water closets, 544 baths, and 222 trough closets and 692 defective or leaking water fittings. There was only around one bath to every nine homes, and obviously some dwellings shared toilet facilities.

"She worked harder than ever, cooking on an open fire and a wood stove with an oven attached. Four men had big appetites and her days were busy ones as she gathered wood on the beach and carried it home for kindling. They could get coal cheaply".
Agnes Whitfield Knapp
writing about her mother
Catherine Whitfield
who lived in Meadow View.

"In 1930, the Corporation's gasworks in Stanley Street, produced 181 million cubic feet of gas, from 8,845 tons of coal".
Mike Burridge

[01] Fifty-three new coke ovens had recently been erected at the Workington works, and were soon producing around 5,000 tons of coke a week. ■

lime shed. The contractor for these works, completed in September 1893 was J. I. Wilson. In 1894, a new office was built on the corner of the former Derwent Rolling Mills site. In 1898, an additional gas holder was built at Clay Flatts. This was very much larger than the earlier one, with a capacity of 550,000 cubic feet. By 1885, the now obsolete Harrington Road gasworks was closed, although the gas holder in Peter Street would remain in use until at least 1922.

In 1914, the Borough Council had purchased a further 1½ acres of land in Stanley Street and extended their gasworks once again. Erecting an entire new carbonisation plant, built by Woodall-Ducklam. Once completed the Borough Council had *"built and equipped one of the best and most up-to-date Gas works in the country"*. This served the town for the next twenty years.

Long before there was a domestic electricity supply in the town, meals made at home were either cooked on a coal fired range or using a relatively modern gas cooker or stove. From as early as 1895, we know the Corporation would regularly purchase large numbers of gas cookers. These were offered to the poorer householders on a hire purchase basis, eventually *"handed over to consumers as soon as the rental equals the value of the cooker"*. By October 1904, the Borough Council were renting out over 500 cookers to homes in the town. In order to make gas more accessible to almost every household, the first prepaid gas meters were also installed around 1894.

From around 1884, regular exhibitions of gas cookers, fires and lighting were also hosted by the Corporation in several halls in the town. An integral part of these events were the cookery demonstrations to tempt the housewife to rent their gas stoves. They also opened their first gas showroom at 47 Pow Street. By early 1925, they built a *"fine new showroom"* at 21 Finkle Street. This was located next to what was once the main post office and it is presently occupied by the Tourist Information office. At the rear of the showroom was a workshop for the gas fitters. The more gas cookers and other appliances it placed in homes, the higher the consumption of gas and the bigger the return for the Corporation.

By December 1937, the production of gas by the Corporation ceased and was replaced with a supply from the new coke ovens at United Steel's Derwent Works [01]. The arrangement to use this coke oven gas from the steelworks had mutual benefits for both United Steel and the Borough Council. In real terms, the gas was simply a by-product of the coking process. The waste gas had to be disposed off somewhere, selling it in bulk to the local authority was an obvious solution. Furthermore, it relieved the Corporation of any further major investment in their own ageing gasworks. Because of the outbreak of WW2, the now obsolete Stanley Street gasworks were not immediately dismantled but retained *"for stand-by purposes"*.

In September 1938, work started on a further 330,000 cubic feet *"two lift spiral guided"* gas holder, built by Drummond and Co. The Mayor (Alderman J. Poole) marked this occasion, by driving home the first rivet into the steel tank. With the two existing gas holders at Clay Flatts, the town now had a gas storage capacity of over one million cubic feet. In May 1949, the gas industry was nationalised and Workington Corporation's gasworks and holders were incorporated into the newly formed Northern Gas Board. Thereafter the Borough Council had no further responsibilities for the gas service in the town. Workington I&SCo. continued to supply bulk gas from its coke ovens to the newly formed company.

Although Cockermouth had experimented with installing electric street lighting as early as 1881, they had reverted back to gas soon after. Several of the local works were already lit by electricity, produced from steam powered generators. We know the *West Cumberland Iron and Steel Works* and *St. Helens Colliery* had used *"electric lighting"* since 1887. Reports in the local newspapers, also tell of a well-attended lecture given by George Snelus (the manager of the West Cumberland Works). The lecture in January 1888 entitled *"Electric Lighting"* was illustrated with various *"arc-light"* apparatus and equipment used at the steelworks.

The matter of supplying Workington with electricity was first seriously discussed by the Borough Council in 1899. The proposed West Cumberland Electric Tramway Bill would effectively bring electric cables into the town, allowing a private company to also supply individual businesses and households. The Corporation who already managed the successful gasworks, believed they too should also control and benefit from any electricity supply in Workington. They refused to grant concessions to the privately owned tramway company, and strongly opposed their application to Parliament. At the same time they themselves, applied to the Board of Trade for *"powers to supply electricity throughout the Borough"*.

The tramway proposals subsequently faltered and the Borough Council received approval to supply the town with its own electricity. But it was June 1903, before they

"Candles and paraffin lamps were the only lights and her brothers were put to bed by candlelight in winter".

Agnes Whitfield Knapp
writing about her mother
Catherine Whitfield
who lived in Meadow View.

again seriously investigated *"generating a supply"*. One suggestion was to install turbines in the mill-race through the Cloffolks. But this scheme was soon abandoned when it was discovered that it would generate just 5% of the electricity required for *"Workington's lighting needs"* only. Using the whole flow of the River Derwent was also considered impossible because of the need to seek approval from the *"several interested parties involved"*.

During the next twenty years, several other reports were prepared and adopted by the Borough Council. But it always appeared more than a little reluctant to actually implement any of these reports. If we look closer at the Borough Council accounts perhaps we can see why, for we find that they regularly made a large annual profit exceeding £1000 from gas production. Of course the events of the First World War could have delayed the project, but Whitehaven had it's own electricity supply since the end of 1917. Some have suggested that the Corporation actually *"dragged their feet"* because they

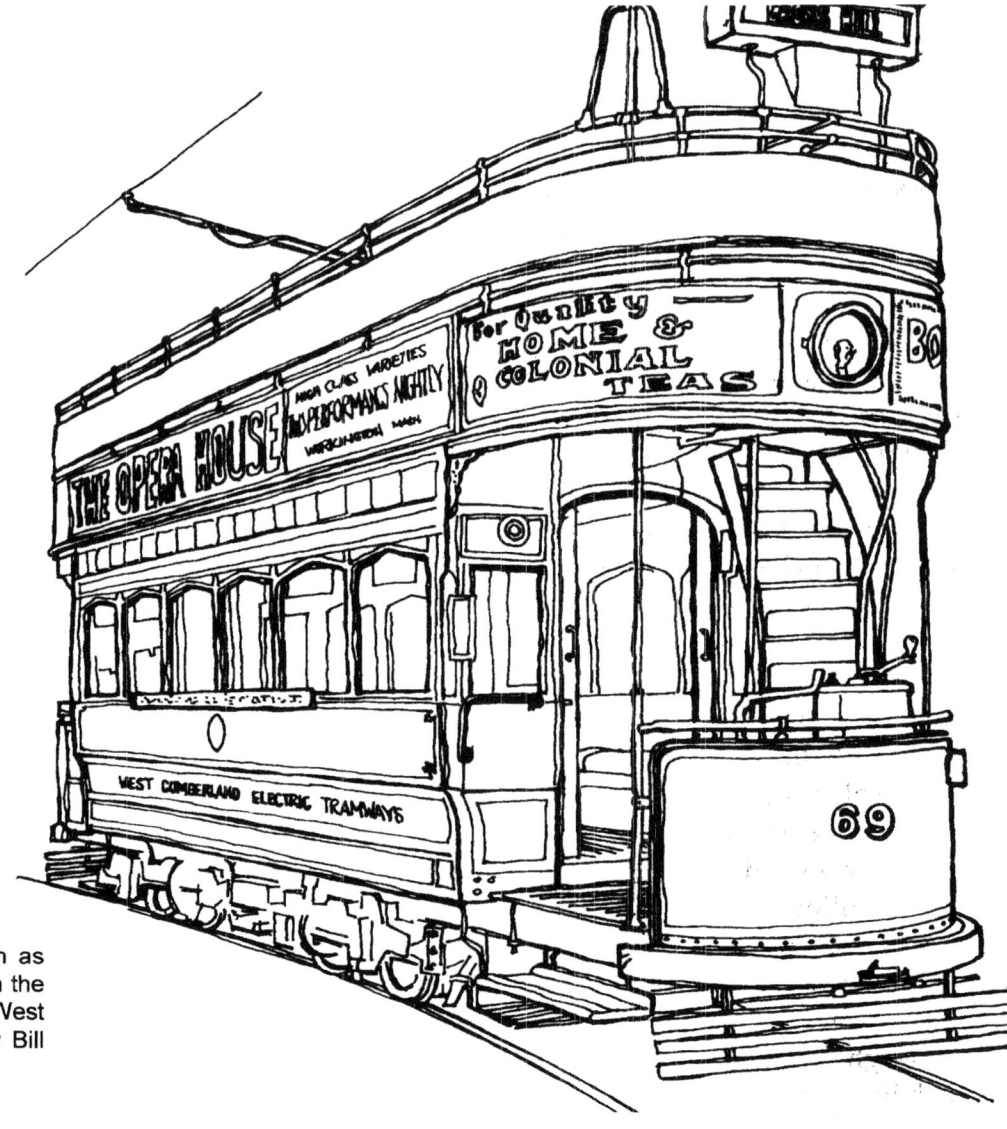

RIGHT - Victorian trams such as these would have been seen in the streets of Workington had the West Cumberland Electric Tramway Bill been approved. ■

"owned and controlled" the town's gasworks. Described in 1921, as *"one of the best and most up-to-date Gas works in the country"*.

In 1919, they revised their plans and now obtained parliamentary approval *"to purchase electricity in bulk and distribute the same"*. But it was almost four years later before they took the first hesitant steps to establish electricity in the town. First, they advertised in the local press *"with a view to ascertaining the number of those prepared to take a supply of electricity"*. They received over 140 favourable replies from potential consumers. Later that year, Mr. Edward Cross, an electrical engineer of Rotherham, was asked to report on supplying the Borough with electricity. He considered that an electricity scheme was *"no competition to the Corporation's Gas Works as it has universally been shown that there is room for both methods of supply"*. The following summer his scheme to obtain a supply from St. Helens Colliery at Siddick, was implemented by the Council.

The electricity at St. Helens was generated from *"waste heat"* produced from its coke ovens, and this option was considered much more cost effective than the local authority building their own new power station. However the directors of St. Helens Colliery must receive some credit for being able to make the service available in the first place. Had it not been for their foresight and investment in building a power station capable of generating electricity far beyond their own requirements, Workington would have had to look elsewhere or commit greater investment in building their own plant.

The town's first sub station was in Finkle Street and a cable was laid the 2,700 yards (2,500 metres) from St. Helens, a transformer station was also built in Stanley Street. [01] The *Workington Electric Power Company* administered the supply for St. Helens and sold bulk electricity to the Council for 1d (0.5p) a unit. They in turn resold the electricity to the townspeople for 6½d (2.7p) for lighting, 3d (1.25p) for heating, 3½d (1.45p) for picture houses and 2d (0.8p) for power. This developed into a comfortable arrangement which appeared profitable to both sides.

Very soon after the work of laying new cables throughout the town commenced, the Council also began to canvas householders in each street to take a new electricity supply. By April 1925, the cables had been laid and tested by the *Hackbridge Cable Co.*, the sub station was completed and the switchgear installed at St. Helens. Fifty eight consumers had signed upto the scheme when it was officially switched on. A couple of months later

[01] This sub-station was thought to have been built by G. H. Chambers. ∎

the number of consumers had trebled, and early records suggested that around 68% of the electricity was being used for lighting purposes.

Within two years the number of consumers had risen to nearly 350. By 1930, the town had 1,197 consumers, and the following year this figure rose by a further 50%. About a thousand of these households benefiting from the Borough Councils *"assisted wiring scheme"*.

At the beginning of 1931, the Council gave the *Workington Electric Power Co.* twelve months notice that they wished to terminate their contract. Exactly why is not clear, but we do know there was some negotiation with the larger Central Electricity Board around this time. The Corporation later renegotiated a new contract with their old supplier and a new three year agreement was signed with the St. Helens company in March 1931.

In September 1933, it was the *Workington Electric Power Co.* who gave notice to the Corporation that they wished to cease supplying the town. There were *"developments contemplated at St. Helens"*, and it would now be almost impossible to continue the supply. Over the next year, a contract with the *Central Electricity Board* was successfully completed. With the change-over to the new supplier taking place at midnight, on the 28th February 1935. By February 1937, there were 3,168 electrical consumers in the town.

Plans to centralise the town's *"Electricity Department"* in Oxford Street, were also pushed forward. The new purpose-built showroom, substation and offices, was officially opened on 20 June 1935, by Alderman F. W. Iredale . Much of these premises on the north west side of the street (above the bridge over the old railway line) are today occupied by Cumbria County Council, although the substations are still in use to the rear of the site. Within this new showroom, consumers could now for the first time, see permanent displays of the very latest in electrical appliances. Companies such as Hotpoint and Burco who would later become household names, arranging demonstrations of these almost magical new cooking and washing machines, to crowds of upto 200 people.

During the winter of 1929, a national electricity grid was first proposed to cover almost all of England and the Borough Council had petitioned for West Cumberland to be included. The town was then still supplied by the Central Electricity Board. By April 1948, the electricity companies were nationalised and thereafter Workington received its supply from the North Western Electricity Board (later to be known as Norweb). At this time, Workington had in excess of 4,000 consumers. ■

In December 1942, seventeen years after they had first supplied Workington with electricity, roles were reversed when the Borough Council agreed to supply St. Helens Colliery.

By 1943, Workington's streets were *"still not lit by electricity"*, despite a report being prepared many years earlier.

SPORT

NEWSPAPER RECORDS suggest that Workington Rugby Union Football Club, or the *"Zebras"* [01] as they are commonly known, were first formed during the autumn of 1877. Playing their first home game against Whitehaven on Saturday 15 December of that year. Whitehaven narrowly won the *"closely contested"* match staged at the town's cricket ground. The progress of the club in these early years is somewhat vague, for a report in the *Cumberland Pacquet* of 30 September 1879 suggests that attempts were being made to form another or perhaps reform the original club. Either way a rugby union side continued to represent the town, playing the bulk of its home matches at the cricket ground until the early 1890s.

In December 1884, Workington Rugby Union Football team which drew with Eden Wanderers at Carlisle were J. Hunter (Capt..) - back, J. Fielden and W. Irving - three quarter backs; Joseph Wilson and A. James -half backs; James Lawrence Smith, P. Hayton, D. Blackburn, John Wilson, C. Smith, T. Longcake, W. Hodgson and T. Fell - forwards.

With the opening of Lonsdale Park, the Zebras are thought to have moved across the Cloffolks and began playing their home games at the new stadium. In 1896, they won the Cumberland Shield for the first time. The club is thought to have remained at Lonsdale Park until the Ellis Sports Ground (on Moss Bay Road) was opened in September 1925. There is a little confusion over the origin of the name of this new stadium. Some believed that it was named after William Webb Ellis, the young Rugby school pupil who in 1828, is said to have *"picked up the ball and ran with it"* - so creating the game of rugby football. However, the sports ground is in fact named after Joseph Valentine Ellis (1874-1935) a director of the *United Steel Companies Limited* and *"enthusiastic follower of rugby union"*. Had it not been for his sheer hard work and personal donation of much of the funds, the sports ground may never have been built. The stadium which then had seating for 2,200 and a total capacity of 30,000 [02] was said to have cost in excess of £10,000.

Joseph Valentine Ellis was the son of Joseph Ellis (ironmaster) who lived at Ashfield House, in High Street.

"Although Joseph Valentine Ellis is buried at Crosthwaite Church, there is no doubt that his real monument is at Workington. In the steelworks, the Prince of Wales dock and his sports ground, his memory will long be honoured here."
West Cumberland Times

Workington Zebras Rugby Union Club records for the period 1920-77 are presently lodged at Whitehaven Record Office.

[01] Legend has it that the club aquired their "nickname" soon after the Boar War. It is said a group of returning soldiers were quite disillusioned by the performance of the black and white clad rugby team. So much so that they accused them "of running around like a herd of zebras". ■

[02] In January 1934, when Workington Reds were drawn against Preston North End in the fourth round of the FA Cup, it was speculated that the match maybe played at the Ellis Sports ground. Newspaper reports tell us that the capacity of the Ellis was 30,000, with around 2,200 seats. The match however was eventually played at Lonsdale park. ■

He followed his father into the iron and steel industry, first starting work at Oldside. In 1903, he moved to London as the representative of the *Workington Iron and Steel Company*. Returning to the town in 1910, to take up the post of commercial manager at the Workington works. Between 1923-8, he served as a director of the United Steel Companies, and helped to secure the loan from the *Trades Facilities Board* for the building of the town's Prince of Wales dock. He was buried on 27 June 1935 at Crosthwaite Church, Keswick.

If we read the sports reports in the old local newspapers from around the 1880s, we see many references to *football* being played in and around Workington. However, a closer examination reveals that this was actually *rugby union football*, which was then commonly reported simply as *football*. We actually need to look for references to *association football*. Soccer as we know it today, was a relatively new game and an offshoot of rugby football. The popularity of which, had grown steadily since the introduction of the FA Cup and International fixtures between the 1870s and 80s.

Yorkshire (or more particularly Sheffield) was one of the main centres for the game. So it was no surprise that several *association football* teams were formed in the town, following the major influx of steelworkers from Dronfield. Perhaps the first local reference to the game is a brief report of a match between Dronfield (Workington) and Wigton, played in January 1884. Later the same year we read that a new football club *"has been formed under the association rules, principally for those living in the Westfield District"*. We know that the Moss Bay Road area was then known as Westfield, and this was where the majority of the Dronfield families had settled. This new club (formed in October 1884) became know as *Workington Association Football Club* and is the origins of the club we know today.

A fixture list in the *Maryport and Workington Advertiser* suggests that Workington's first competitive match is likely to have been an away fixture at Newcastleton, on Saturday 29 November 1884. During that season, which ran from late November to mid March, they also played sides from Distington, Barrow, Wigton and Dumfries. The venue for the early home games seems to have been Schoose Meadow (or Highclose).

In its early years the team dominated the Cumberland County Cup, introduced in 1885-86. Despite losing the first final to Carlisle. They later won the trophy on five consecutive occasions between 1887-1891. After their

---

WORKINGTON (ASSOCIATION) FOOTBALL CLUB.

LIST OF FIXTURES.

Saturday, November 29.—Newcastleton, Newcastleton.

Saturday, December 20.—Distington, Distington.

Monday, January 1.—Barrow-in-Furness, Workington.

Tuesday, January 2.—Newcastleton, Workington.

Saturday, January 31.—Wigton Athletic, Workington.

Saturday, February 28.—Wigton Athletic, Wigton.

Saturday, March 14.—Distington, Workington.

Dates not yet fixed :

Dumfries at Dumfries, and Dumfries at Workington.

ABOVE - Perhaps the first competitive fixtures of Workington AFC, taken from an 1884 newspaper. ■

fourth success, a large silver shield was presented to the club by local ironmaster James Duffield. This commemorative shield is presently displayed at the Helena Thompson Museum, and proudly lists the players who represented the side in each final. There is also a 1891 Workington team photograph, taken by Mr. Atkinson. From these surnames it is clear that the backbone of the side were steelworking families, many of whom had their origins in Dronfield. In May 1888, the side also played host to the famous Preston North End, in a benefit match in aid of the St. Helens pit disaster fund.[01] The Lancashire side had a massive reputation, having reached the final of the FA Cup that year, and the semi-final in the previous season. The game played on what we know today as Curwen Park, naturally attracted a massive crowd. Preston North End comfortably winning by seven goals to nil.

Up until 1910-11 season, Workington lifted the Cumberland County Cup on seven further occasions and are known to have competed in the Cumberland Senior League, the Lancashire League, the Lancashire Combination and the North Eastern League. In January 1910, they also narrowly lost 2-1 to First Division Manchester City, in the first round of the FA Cup. The match played at Lonsdale Park attracted a large crowd of 5,233. However in July 1911, the club was disbanded and went into voluntary liquidation, withdrawing from all competitions. In the period upto the beginning of WW1, three other football clubs were formed in the town. *Workington Central* played for three seasons from 1911-14, with *Workington United* and *Workington Athletic* both operating for much of the 1914-15 season.

Many of the early soccer matches were played either on the Cricket Field, at Ashfield, or Lonsdale Park. Before Borough Park was laid out, records suggest another football pitch may also have existed on the east side of the New Bridge approaches, as early as 1902. Here the Black Diamonds football team are known to have played some matches. By October 1903, after the Borough Council had agreed to purchase the Cloffolks from Lord Lonsdale, the site was subsequently used as a tip for *"household refuse and ashes"*. During 1919, with high unemployment in the town, the Council employed many of the jobless to cover this refuse tip with topsoil. As the year came to a close, a deputation from the football club approached the Council wishing to start playing their matches again on the Cloffolks. Unfortunately, the Council then *"ploughed the Cloffolks for cropping"*, to aid the post war food shortage.

Reds narrowly lost 2-1 to First Division Manchester City in the first round of the FA Cup. The match played at Lonsdale Park attracted a large crowd of 5,233.

[01] See chapter four for more details. ■

"The Preston right back that day was Bill Shankly, later to be Workington Reds most famous manager".

Billy Watson

In the spring of 1921, Workington AFC was *"reborn"*, and successfully elected to the North Eastern League once again. Steve Durham in his various club notes states *"We spent twenty-five years at this level, finishing runners-up in the league on one occasion, and lifting the North Eastern League Cup twice from three appearances in the final"*. During this period the team also scored *"over a century of goals a season"* on no fewer than eight occasions. Perhaps their most exceptional year being 1933-34, when they netted 147 times. This was also a memorable year when the team achieved it's best run in the FA Cup, reaching the fourth round proper. Workington were eventually defeated 2-1 by Preston North End, in a exciting match played on Lonsdale Park. As former Reds groundsman Billy Watson remembered *"the Preston right back that day was Bill Shankly, later to be Reds most famous manager"*. The town was invaded that day by around 3000 "Prestonians" and Lonsdale Park was filled to capacity.

Up until the start of the 1937-38 season, virtually all Reds home matches were played at Lonsdale Park. Even after 1933, when the stadium was converted for greyhound racing the arrangement continued. In May 1928, J. W. Mason approached the council on behalf of the football club, seeking permission to play their home matches in the recently opened Vulcans Park. Unfortunately, the council members refused to entertain such an option for their then *"jewel of a municipal park"* with its neat and well maintained flower beds. Seven years later, the Borough Council did agreed to lease the former Education Committee playing fields on the Cloffolks to the Reds. This was the site to the east of the New Bridge Road, again part of the land purchased by the local authority from Lord Lonsdale in 1904. Within weeks the football club, submitted ambitious plans for a new grandstand to the west side of their new ground.

During the summer of 1938, Mr J. C. McCulley (the secretary of the Reds) asked the Borough Council to help fund the erection of two new further covered areas at Borough Park. These were built by *William Sandham & Sons*. The football club then entered into a hire-purchase agreement to repay the Council over a seven year term. Everything was obviously completed by June 1939, as the grandstand was used in the film *"The Stars Look Down"*. [01]

Following the outbreak of WW2 just after the start of the 1939-40 season, almost all football was suspended again and the teams disbanded. Borough Park was one of the town's buildings re-quistioned by the War Depart-

[01] see chapter fourteen for more details about the film. ∎

ment. As the ground was no longer available to the team, the Council agreed to postpone all loan repayments for the foreseeable future. It would be February 1944, before the stadium was returned to the club. Competitive matches resumed at the start of the 1944-45 season, with Workington competing in the West Cumberland League. In the following season they rejoined the North Eastern League.

At the beginning of the 1950-51 season, the Borough Council approved plans to provide addition shelters at Borough Park. In preparation for their first season in the Football League, new screen walls and turnstiles were also added to the Borough Park ground. An old redundant railway carriage was also lifted into position, close to the entrance to the ground, to be used as a *"temporary storeroom"*. This became something of a permanent feature, being later adapted as a supporters club shop and remained in place well into the 1970s.

The summer of 1951 was a memorable time for the Reds, who were elected to the Third Division (North) of the Football League [01] replacing the Merseyside club, New Brighton. At this time there was no automatic promotion or relegation to and from the Football League. Clubs that finished the season in the lower places of the old Third Division (North and South) had to seek re-election. The election process was decided by a vote, involving all the ninety two League clubs at their Annual meeting, usually held during June of each year. Non-League clubs could then apply to join the league and be included in the vote. Prior to the meeting, the Reds directors (led by Ernest. D Smith) activity canvassed the other league clubs. To some extent it is acknowledged that their cause was helped greatly by the national publicity of Workington Town's rugby league championship achievements. In those days of course, the Reds and Town both played their matches at Borough Park.

On 18 August 1951, Workington Reds played their first ever match in the Football League, away to Halifax Town at the Shay. John Maxfield scored their first League goal, but Reds eventually lost the game 3-1. Four days later, they played their first home match at Borough Park. Defeating Chesterfield by the same score, with goals from Danny McDowall (2) and Ted Cushin. Under the guidance of manager Bert Flatley, Reds struggled to come to terms with life in the higher division, gaining something of a reputation as the *"whipping boys of the league"*. They won only eleven matches in their first season and finished bottom of the league, with just 29 points.

"Workington Reds have a Rugby League stronghold to combat and their actual election to the Football League was rather surprising in view of the club's modest achievements."

Stuart Shaw *Soccer Star*
April 1964

[01] The English Football League in 1951, was then (as today) made up of four divisions - there was the First Division (now referred to as the Premier League), then a Second Division (now equivalent to today's First Division). The other two leagues were known as the Third Division (South) and Third Division (North). In 1958-9, these two lower divisions were re-structured to form a Third Division and Fourth Division. Today, after the introduction of the Premier League, we refer to them as the Second and Third Divisions respectively. ∎

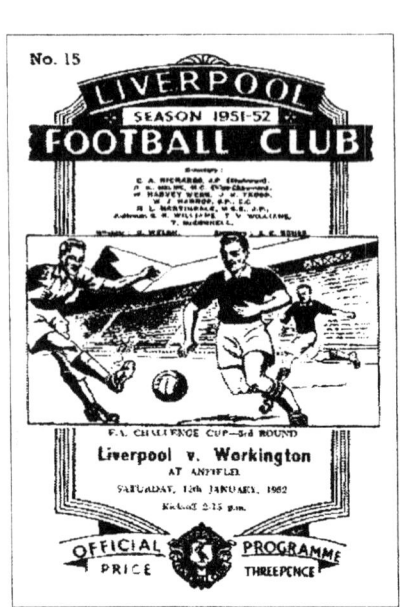

FA Cup Third Round
Anfield 12 January 1952

Liverpool   1:0   **Workington**
Payne 78
HT 0:0   Attendance 52581

ABOVE - cover of the original match day programme from the Anfield fixture. ■

[01] Bill Shankly, who began both his playing and managerial career at Carlisle, moved to Workington Reds from Grimsby Town. In December 1959, he became the manager of the faded, run-down and half-forgotten Liverpool side. Over a twenty year period, he brought the Merseyside club many League, FA Cup and European successes, and laid the solid foundations for later success. ■

During their first season, they did have some success in the FA Cup, reaching the third round proper. Their reward was a dream trip to first division Liverpool. In the weeks prior to the game, almost the entire town was captivated by cup fever. Several thousand enthusiastic Cumbrians travelled to Merseyside for the game, played on Saturday 12 January 1952. In front of 52,581 spectators at the famous Anfield stadium (a record attendance for any match featuring the Reds - that still stands today) the Workington side were certainly not intimidated by the occasion. They were much the better side for long periods, and were very unlucky to lose by a single goal to nil. Red's captain that day, George Dick remembered the referee disallowing a Reds goal and the pain of missing an open goal after Andy Mullen had rounded the Liverpool goalkeeper. Chris Simmonds also netted the ball for Reds a split second after the referee blew the final whistle. Things could have been so much different and many felt the team's performance certainly warranted at least a draw. Then of course the mighty Liverpool would have had to face a replay at Borough Park.

Following their poor performance during the 1951-52 season, Reds were successfully re-elected to the league. During the close season, Ted Smith replaced Flatley as manager, but results failed to show significant improvement. They ended their second season in 23rd place, next to bottom, and facing the prospect of seeking re-election once again. Results again improved only slightly in the subsequent season (1953-54) when they finished 20th, narrowly avoiding a third and perhaps final application for re-election. It was during this season that legendary Bill Shankly [01] took over as manager at Workington, and is credited with taking Reds to a much more respectable eighth position in 1954-55.

Without doubt, the little scotsman who was later to become a legend at Liverpool, was Workington's most famous manager. Between 1953-55, he spent nearly three seasons in charge of the Reds. Soon after his arrival at Borough Park, he brought about huge changes in the way the club was ran. Despite the obvious lack of funds he made many shrewd signings, adopted imaginative and constructive tactics and gave his players a special belief in their own abilities. Throughout Tom Allen's excellent book, *The Team Beyond the Hills* which profiled many of Reds ex.players, Shankly's man management techniques were frequently highly praised and the respect he commanded was clearly obvious. Jackie Bertolini (1953-1958) commented *"I will never forget the two years he worked with the team. Earning praise from Shankly was all I ever aimed for. A wink and a thumbs up sign from him gave me a tremendous lift".* Whilst Norman Mitchell (1953-58) echoed his views *"He made me a better player because he filled me with confidence and was always saying positive things to me about my play. With his guidance and a real team effort we managed to avoid having to apply for re-election".*

Borough Park's long-standing groundsman Billy Watson also remembers the charismatic manager with great affection. *"Bill Shankly was unique, a great man and a really good friend. I'd spend hours just listening to him talk about football, because he was so fascinating. He was a tremendous enthusiast and that enthusiasm got through to the players, and to all who came in contact with him."* In December 1955, Bill Shankly left Workington to take over the manager's position at Huddesfield Town. Before joining Liverpool in December 1959. Above all he is credited with making the Anfield club the footballing legend we see today. In August 1980, the little scotsman returned to Borough Park for the last time to open the Reds Social Club (named in his honour). Sadly he died just thirteen months later.

Encouraged by Shankly's success the directors of the football club applied to the Borough Council for a further loan of £3000, to fund the building of new shelters at Borough Park - to be repaid over ten years. The plans for the work were prepared by local architect Jonathan Saul. In September 1955, the Council did agree to extend the existing shelter, to the Popular side (adjacent to Lonsdale Park). They accepted a tender of £730, from Robert Fraser & Sons, of Hebburn.

Although rugby league began in Cumberland as early as 1898, no senior side existed in the county until after WW2. However we know it was still a very popular sport and by 1946, upwards of 600 amateur players were playing for the numerous junior clubs. And despite the lack of a first-class team, sides still produced many fine players, who moved south to join many of the leading clubs. On several occasions the Cumberland team also overcame the might of Yorkshire and Lancashire to win the County Championship. Workington was always well represented at county level, particularly in the early days as Joseph Huntrods was the first president of the Cumberland County Rugby Football League, serving until 1901.

Almost half a century later Workington Town Rugby League club was formed and elected into the senior league

"That the Reds were scarcely ready for the rigours of the League soccer was evident from their first two seasons within the sphere, when they had to apply for re-election on both occasions".
Stuart Shaw *Soccer Star*
April 1964

"I took to him immediately, Bill Shankly had a tremendous presence and I had instant respect. We were two different sports but the affinity was remarkable".
Jim Brough
Workington Town manager
1981

[01] In November 1944, the Borough Council granted permission to Workington Reds F.C., allowing Workington Town R.L.F.C. to play their home matches at Borough Park. The Reds leased the stadium from the local authority. ■

for the first time. This rugby league side has always been known as the "Workington Town", whilst the football team is simply known as Workington AFC or the "Reds". Over the years confusion has arisen from people outside the area, who often also refer to the soccer side as "Workington Town". Much to the annoyance of the fans of each code.

It is acknowledged that without the efforts of George Plummer, the hard working Cumberland representative on the Rugby League Council, the rugby league side may never have been elected to the national league. In January 1946, the board of Workington Town, under the leadership of Mr. Meageen began the search for a manager to lead their newly-formed side. They soon appointed Gus Risman (1911-1994) a welshman and former member of the famous all-conquering Salford side. It was a big decision for the full back to leave Manchester, but he saw it as an ideal opportunity to learn the managerial side of the game. He eventually joined Town as player-manager at the start of the 1946-47 season, after leading a victorious Great Britain side on a highly successful tour of Australia.

In the early years, things were extremely tough for the new Rugby League club. Finances were tight and as Workington was so far displaced from many of the other clubs, travelling expenses in particular were an enormous burden on the fledgling club. They also played all their home matches at Borough Park, [01] sharing the ground with Workington Reds soccer side. Often reserve teams would have to play their games on nearby Lonsdale Park pitch, both games taking place at the same time. As there was then no high perimeter wall surrounding Borough Park, spectators on the Popular side could chose to watch either match from the top of the bank, which separates the two grounds.

Around the time Risman agreed to join Town, the ambitious Rugby League club also approached the Borough Council, seeking land to build their own stadium. Within weeks they were offered and accepted a site on the west side of the Cloffolks, adjacent to the Workington to Maryport railway line. This was another portion of the Low Cloffolks purchased from Lord Lonsdale. It's proposed use as a sports ground clearly met the *"recreational use only"* condition imposed when the original sale was completed in 1904. As previously mentioned, this area close to the mouth of the River Derwent would have once been almost submerged at high tide. But for almost half a century the site had been used as a council refuse tip, and it's level was now very much higher and ready to be landscaped. In September 1947, long before construction work [01] began on the proposed new pitch, it was officially named *Derwent Park* by the local authority. In June 1951, when the new stadium was almost completed the lease was formally signed and approved by both parties. Initially, this lease was for only 20 years but was later extended after negotiation.

Much has been written about the difficulties of ground sharing Borough Park with the football club. Especially in recent years as Allerdale Borough Council embark on their ambitious proposal to build a single new stadium to combine the now dilapidated facilities at Borough and Derwent Parks. Former Reds captain (and later manager) George Aitken recalled many a heated argument between Gus Risman, Town's coach during the early 50s and the Reds manager, the legendary Bill Shankly. *"Gus wanted the pitch narrowed, whilst Bill wanted it widened, groundsman Billy Watson found himself in the middle of it."*. In practise the two sports sharing the same ground is something of a logistical nightmare, fraught with major difficulties. Imagine how those wet boggy pitches would be "chewed" up in the winter months by virtue of the number of matches to be played. Whilst rugby can be played on such a pitch, it does not really bode well for good flowing football.

Borough Park's long serving groundsman Billy Watson, also remembered a particularly hectic and *"gladly unique"* day, during the time Reds shared Borough Park with Town. On Saturday 15 March 1952, the football club were already scheduled to play a home game against Oldham Athletic, when the Rugby club found they had also been drawn at home to Warrington in the quarter final of the Rugby League Challenge Cup. Both games were played at Borough Park on the same day. Reds kicked off first, the groundsmen then had around half an hour to change the goal posts and prepare the ground for the rugby match. The terraces and grandstand also had to be quickly cleared of the football fans, before the rugby fans could be admitted.

One of Gus Risman's first tasks was to strengthen the enthusiastic young local side by introducing a couple of really experienced players. Two influential signings being Australian's Tony Paskins and Johnny Mudge. Gradually Town settling down to life in top flight, match by match the team improved and so did their league position. In their first three seasons they finished 19th, 11th, then fifth in 1948-49 (or 1949-50) just below a Championship play-off place. The following season was

George Aitken recalled many a heated argument between Gus Risman, Town's coach during the early 50s and the Reds manager, the legendary Bill Shankly.

[01] Please see photograph on page 44 of *Workington from the Air (Past and Present)* by the same author, for aerial photograph of Derwent park under construction in 1954. ∎

even better, in an incredibly short time Town had become one of the game's strongest sides.

In the semi-final of the Championship play-offs, Workington received a very tough draw away to Wigan, at Central Park. It turned out to be a sensational game which highlighted the stupidity of the old *'play-the-ball'* rule, [01] a rule that was changed shortly after this memorable match. The game was played long before substitutes were permitted, and when Town's Bill Ivison was injured in the first half, they were reduced to just twelve men for the remainder of the game. Although Workington's task looked pretty hopeless against a very powerful Wigan side. George *'Happy'* Wilson did manage to go over for a try, Johnny Lawrenson kicked the goal and Town amazingly lead 8-5. With fifteen minutes remaining Gus Risman instructed his team to retain possession at all costs. Each player would hold onto the ball until they were tackled, making use of the play-the-ball rule and never risk a pass or attempt a kick. The match ground to a virtual halt, the frustrated Wigan supporters booing and jeering Town's negative play. But they held out to win the game, making no mistakes and keeping possession of the ball.

Despite being loudly booed off the pitch, depleted Workington had simply exploited a poor law of the game to advantage. As Risman later commented *"The chips were stacked against us and there was really nothing else we could do"*.

The Championship final against Warrington, played at Maine Road, Manchester (then the home of Manchester City Football Club) was so very different. As a result of the negative publicity received after their dour semi-final, Town were determined to show the world that they were capable of playing excellent Rugby League. The game turned into a classic and despite being reduced to twelve men Warrington led marginally at half time. But within five minutes of the re-start, Town regained the lead and ran out 26-11 winners. In front of a vast crowd Workington had won the Championship. Risman described it as *"one of the finest Rugby League games"* he had ever played in.

When Risman had first embarked on the task of building a successful Rugby League club at Workington, he predicted it would take at least five seasons to build a team capable of winning honours. In his autobiography he tends to suggest that this was something of a chance remark which he had soon forgotten. But the Town supporters did not look at it that way, they thought it a serious forecast and were looking forward to major

Gus Risman described it as *"one of the finest Rugby League games"* he had ever played in.

[01] The old play-the-ball rule greatly favoured the team with possession of the ball. By making no attempt to pass the ball whatsoever, they could retain possession for long periods of time and virtually kill the game. As soon as a tackle was made the game stopped, the tackled man is then allowed to stand up and then usually plays the ball back to a colleague, no opposing player was allowed with three yards. He in turn retained possession, never risking passing the ball or attempting a kick, until he himself was tackled, and so on. ∎

success in 1951. And that's exactly what they got - Workington Town ended the 1950-51 season as league champions. (the first and only time they have ever achieved this feat).

But the Town fans had even more to cheer and shout about in the following season. Workington had suddenly become one of the game's most prominent powers and reached the final of the Challenge cup for the first time in 1951-52. On the road to the final, Town had beaten York over both legs in the first round, before defeating the mighty St. Helens and Warrington at Borough Park. In the semi-final they again met local rivals Barrow, at Wigan's Central Park. In front of 37,206 fans they won a hard fought 5-2 victory, booking a place in their first ever Wembley final. Risman later wrote of subsequent enthusiasm in the town. *"Almost every man, woman and child in Cumberland seemed determined to go to London to support us on the great day."* There was a *"mass exodus"* from Workington to Wembley.

So on the 19 April 1952, Workington Town met Featherstone Rovers in the final of the Rugby League Challenge Cup. That Saturday afternoon the town's streets fell virtually silent as everyone who couldn't afford the long trip or was unable to travel crowded around their television sets and radios. Wembley was bathed in glorious sunshine as the teams lined up in front of 73,000 spectators. Town with eleven internationals were actually *"red-hot favourites"*. By comparison Featherstone had finished that season in 22nd place in the league. It was also Rovers' first visit to the twin towers of Wembley and they fought out a classic final. The West Cumbrians were certainly ready and if not a little complacent. But within two minutes of the kick off, Captain Gus Risman settled any nerves with a 35 yard penalty goal.

Despite Rovers fighting *"hard and gallantly"*, Town's right-winger Johnny Lawrenson scored the game's first try after sixteen minutes, with Risman adding the conversion. But by half time Featherstone had reduced the arrears to just three points with two penalty goals. The game continued after the break at a pulsating pace. Rovers pinning back Town in their own half for quite long periods, before grabbing an equalising try through Eric Batten. After the re-start, all the pressure was again coming from the Yorkshire side. But in the 50th minute, Workington's loose-forward Billy Ivison sent Australian Johnny Mudge away and he raced across the pitch to score a *"stunning"* try at the corner flag. Seven minutes later, Johnny Lawrenson intercepted the ball well inside his own twenty-five-yard line. He raced three-

"Playing at Wembley is as much a burning ambition with all Rugby League players as it is with soccer players."
Gus Risman
Workington Town player manager
1946-54

R. L. Challenge Cup Final
Wembley 19 April 1952

Featherstone 10:18 Workington

t. Batten, Evans	Lawrenson 2, Mudge, Wilson G.
g.	Miller 2, Risman 3
(HT 4-7)	Attendance 73,000

Workington RLFC team sheet
Gus Risman (Capt.),
Johnny Lawrenson,
Tony Paskins,
Eppie Gibson,
George Wilson,
Jack Thomas,
Albert Pepperell,
Jimmy Hayton,
Vince McKeating,
Jimmy Wareing,
Johnny Mudge,
Bevan Wilson,
Billy Ivison.

quarters of the length of the pitch, to score another amazing try under the posts. His captain later described it as *"surely the greatest try seen at Wembley"*. Risman easily kicked the conversion they led 15-7, and the hard-fought game had swung once again Town's way.

Featherstone were stunned and never really recovered. Town passed the ball with confidence and it was no surprise when they scored again through George "Happy" Wilson, with around fifteen minutes left. Every Town fan, wherever they were, be it on the sunny terraces at Wembley, or watching at home huddled around a black and white television set or listening on their radio, suddenly realised Workington Town were actually going to win the Challenge Cup. Those anxious faces relaxed a little, some even dared to smile. Despite a consolation try from Featherstone, you can imagine the scene as the final whistle blew, signalling Town's finest hour. Workington Town's player-manager, a clearly elated Gus Risman, followed closely by Bill Ivison and the rest of his exhausted heroes, climbed the famous Wembley steps. He received the Rugby League Challenge Cup from Sir Anthony Eden, and raised it aloft to a mighty cheer. As rugby league historian Robert Gate recently wrote *"It was a sight West Cumberland's rugby league fans had never seen before - and never would again"*.

One important addition to the 1953-54 Town side, was the signing of Theodore Cecil Thompson from Hunslet. Although he was more commonly know as Ces Thompson, or even *"Darkie"* Thompson, for at the time he became Workington's first black player. After two remarkable games for Hunslet against Town in the previous season, Gus Risman signed the forward the moment he became available. Between 1953-60, Ces ultimately played 193 games for Town, scoring 55 tries, captaining the side on many occasions. In Thompson's highly readable 1995 autobiography *Born on the Wrong Side*, he explained how Risman was such an inspiration to both him and the team. He also told how *"Workington Town were an impressive club at that time. Almost every member of the team was an international"*. Although Workington was a relatively small town, they *"regularly attracted gates of 15,000 to our home games"*.

Sadly at the start of the 1954-55 season, the vibrant Gus Risman resigned after a dispute with the Workington directors, and subsequently joined Batley. He was the Town's *"first genuine legend"* playing 301 games and scoring a total of 1,539 points. Ces Thompson later described him as *"magnificent, a handsome and athletically built 6-footer.. the greatest player ever to grace British Rugby League".* Risman continued to live at Cockermouth and ran a sports shop in Workington. That season, Town under the new management of Jim Brough, did return once more to Wembley in May 1955. Where they met neighbours Barrow in the Challenge Cup final, unfortunately only to lose 12-21.

The present Workington Cricket Club is said to have been formed in 1873. During the summer, matches were played nearly every Saturday against neighbouring clubs. We know they were then contested upon the "Laundry field", to the upper or east end of the Cloffolks. The first cricket pavilion at this ground was opened on 6 July 1899. It was located on the west side of the field, backing onto the C&WJR line. The new timber building was presented to the club by their captain, Mr. Herbert Spencer who fittingly also performed the opening ceremony. This pavilion served the club until 1955, when it was replaced with a new brick-built structure to the south of the cricket ground.

In September 1879 we know that the club lost four of its most prominent players, when Joshua Branthwaite, Sim Whitehead, Robert Fisher and John Brown all emigrated to New Zealand. Robert Fisher appears to have eventually moved on and settled in Australia. He developed into *"quite a fine"* wicket keeper, and subsequently represented New South Wales. Interestingly, in those early days they appear to have played thirteen a side in Australian cricket.

During WW1, the club temporarily disbanded and their cricket pitch was laid out as allotments to grow fruit and vegetables. However, after the ceasation of hostilities cricket returned to the town in 1920. During the following year, Jakey Madden the club's professional, played against Australia at Whitehaven.

Workington Golf club owes it's creation to Dr. John Highet, the town's Medical Officer of Health. Although in it's earliest days it was more generally known as the West Cumberland Golf Club. The well-researched history of the club tells us that in February 1893, Dr. Highet called a public meeting at the Green Dragon Hotel to determine the level of support for a golf course in the town. When the decision was taken to proceed the club's first greens were laid out to the north of St. Helens Colliery, at Siddick. Initially having just nine holes, the course was between the sea and the main Workington to Maryport road (A596), opposite today's Iggesund Paperboard factory (formerly Thames Board). Perhaps appropriately the first organised

"Gus Risman's great skill lay in assembling successful combinations of players, in building a team in other words. And he could read a game the way other men read a news-paper."
Ces Thompson
Workington Town 1953-60

The good old English game of cricket, at one time appeared to be on the wane in Workington - is now thriving again.
West Cumberland Times
June 1874

The Bread and Beer House once stood very close to the west side of the Workington to Lillyhall road (A596), almost at it's junction with the Branthwaite road.

members' competition in April 1893, was won by Dr. Highet himself. Sadly, interest declined in the club and by 1899 the windy and exposed Siddick course was closed.

The club was re-formed in September 1906, with around 130 members. Once again Dr. Highet was elected captain and another nine-hole course was laid out at Hunday. The land owned by Curwen Estates was sub-let to the club by the Furness family (of Scaw Farm). On 6 October 1906, Workington's Mayor Henry McAleer officially opened the new Branthwaite Road course. Until the spring of 1908, there *"was no club house"* and golfers would leave their clubs at the nearby Bread and Beer House.[01] No doubt they also assembled there after a round of golf for refreshments. The Bread and Beer House once stood very close to the west side of the Workington to Lillyhall road (A596), almost at it's junction with the Branthwaite road. Exactly, when this hostelry was established is not quite clear, but early maps suggest it was once a Lodge on the edge of Workington Common. Before these commons were enclosed in 1809, there was also a gate across the main road here, preventing livestock straying into the town. Early census returns appear to also record the building as *"Hunday Gate"*. [02] Tradition has it that the public house was used by the agricultural labourers who worked in the nearby fields. It was also a regular stop for the local carriers and cart owners, on route in and out of the town, a latter day *"transport cafe"*.

Despite the upheaval of WW1, the golf club operated until February 1918, when it entered another period of inactivity. In the latter years of the war, membership had seriously declined and the club found it impossible to continue. For the next few years, the greens of the Hunday course were once again returned to farming. Then in November 1922, local architect Harry Oldfield called a public meeting attempting once again to re-form the club. Within a month, sufficient members had successfully been recruited and he re-negotiated a lease on their old redundant golf course. Willie Andrews was appointed greenkeeper and the nine hole course was re-established. Soon after, a new club house was added, paid for with a share issue to members. Today, much of this original building, with it's double-hipped roof still exists, although it is flanked either side by more modern structures. As membership rose, additional land north of the road upto Hunday was also rented from the Curwen Estates. By 1927, a new eighteen hole course was created, under the guidance of five times Open Champion, James Baird.

[01] William Walker and his wife are known to have kept the Bread and Beer House around 1881. Wallace Ritson seemed to suggest that the Walkers had previously lived at the old school house at New Yard. The same building once used as a Roman Catholic chapel.■

[02] See the 1810 map of Schoose and Moorclose Farms on page 200 of *The History of Workington* (Earliest Times to 1865). ■

Canon H. D. Rawnsley said *"Wrestling, Warstling" or Wrustling"*, as it has been called, is *"indigenous to Cumberland and Westmorland"*. The noble art of Cumberland and Westmorland Wrestling became very popular in the late 19th century. Even the odd challenge bout attracted several thousand spectators. The sport was often also extremely rewarding, with the winners "purse" being amazingly high. In 1880, when former Workington wrestler Jackey Barnes entered a contest at Manchester, the winner received £110. Quite a handsome sum, when an ironworkers weekly wage was barely 15/- (or 75p). Cumberland and Westmorland wrestling was then well supported by the local gentry, such as Lord and Ladies Lowther and Muncaster, Canon Rawnsley and W.D. Heelis (husband of Beatrix Potter).

George Lowden, *"a monster of a man weighing around eighteen stones"* won his first major wrestling titles at Cleator Moor Sports in 1876 and at the Derwentwater Regatta in 1878. He then took the heavy weight (over 14st.) championship at Grasmere Sports in 1880. Thereafter he successfully defended his title in 1883, 1884, 1885, 1886, 1891 and 1894. He was also runner up three times to the famous George Steadman (who won the title at Grasmere 17 times). In 1897, Lowden again defeated Steadman at Grasmere, in a special *"over 16 stone"* category. He successfully defended his title the following year, his last success at Grasmere. Perhaps the peak of his career was winning the Cumberland & Westmorland Wrestling 'world championships', held at Carlisle in 1881. Although he was known to have *"wrestled in many styles and against representatives of various nations"*.

George Lowden (1849-1906) was born in Keswick, and was first employed as a iron ore miner at Frizington. He then moved into the licenced trade and managed the Station Hotel on Yeathouse Road in Frizington. Before moving to Workington taking over the Black Lion in Washington Street. By 1901, he had moved again to the Royal Hotel, on the corner of Fisher Street and William Street (now the Labour Club). When Lowden retired, he went to live at Branthwaite where he died in 1906. In November 1935, his magnificent array of trophies were gifted by his nephew John Haile to the Borough Council. These were originally proudly displayed in a cabinet within the entrance to the Carnegie Library. Today, only a handful of the original 24 cups, 7 belts and 3 shields are still displayed at the Helena Thompson Museum.

The town boasted another champion Cumberland and Westmorland wrestler in Hexham Clark. He was born in

Perhaps the peak of George Lowden's career was winning the Cumberland & Westmorland Wrestling 'world championships', held at Carlisle in 1881.

204

In August 1928, horse racing was also staged on Lonsdale Park. There were five races on the card and special trains ran from as far away as Cleator Moor.

Seaton in 1857, and was employed as an engineman at the Barepot tinplate works. Along with Steadman and Lowden, the trio dominated the sport for nearly thirty years. Although Clark was perhaps a *"couple of stones lighter than both his contemporaries"*, the six foot tall man, still weighed 15st. 2lb. and had a 46 inch chest. He won the heavy weight title at Grasmere on six occasions in 1897, 1898, 1899, 1901, 1902 and 1904. Several interesting photographs of both Lowden and Clark, each wearing the traditional wrestling costume of a silk vest and cotton trunks with a centrepiece of velvet (often decorated with embroidery), appear in Hugh Machell's 1911 book *Some Records of Grasmere Sports.*

As previously mentioned Lonsdale Park opened around 1893, and has over the years played host to rugby union, rugby league and football. We also know that from the turn of the century it was used by the *Workington Athletic Sports Club.* Each August they would stage their annual sports in the ground. On 20 August 1910 as an added attraction to the large crowd, the committee of the sports club arranged for Aviator L. N Barnes to land his monoplane within the stadium.

In August 1928, horse racing was also staged on Lonsdale Park. There were five races on the card and special trains ran from as far away as Cleator Moor, to bring spectators to the town. But the stadium is most famous for greyhound racing. It all began in the early 1930s when the ground was thought to have been leased to White City Sports Stadium (Preston) Ltd. One of the first meetings was held in June 1933, the Workington Star reporting a *"small crowd watching the attractive"* greyhound racing. The official opening of the *"Greyhound Racing stadium"* did not take place until February 1934. The ceremony was performed by Alderman Frederick W. Iredale, then the deputy mayor.

For well over half a century before the establishment of a greyhound track in the town, greyhounds were raced at coursing meetings. Shepherd Sewell (1824-80) of Workington Hall Mill had a kennel of *"highly prized"* greyhounds, who had achieved *"notable brilliant success"*. During Victorian times the sport was very popular, and a course was laid out on Curwen Moor. In 1888, regular *"rabbit coursing"* events were also held each month at Calva Farm. There was three classes of dog - 16" bonofide fox terriers, 16" rough haired terriers and 32" large dogs. With the races over a straight course, usually measuring 200yds (183m).

In 1936, the greyhound track at Lonsdale Park was now operated by West of Scotland Greyhounds Ltd. Although it had no mains supply of electricity, and everything was powered by generator. In fact, it is thought the venue didn't have mains electricity until after WW2. Despite the war, it is clear racing still continued as they remained registered with the Borough Council, under the Betting and Lotteries Act.

After the war, greyhound racing at the Cloffolks stadium was continued by the Moffat family. First Alexander Moffatt took over the track and was later joined in the business by his grandson Harry Moffatt (1926-1999). After Alexander's death in 1971, Harry became the managing director, assisted by his brother Graham. Just prior to Harry's death, the track was leased to Jan and Ernie Little. But although the couple are thought to have invested heavily in "revamping" the facilities, greyhound racing ceased at Lonsdale Park after almost sixty six years, in February 1999.

Finally during the 1930s, speedway or dirt-track racing was also staged at Lonsdale Park. It is believed the first track measured 439 yds (401m) was laid out in 1931, and a number of open licence meetings were held that season. The first of which is thought to have taken place on 15 August 1931. Records suggest that there was then a break of several years before, the track was re-established and used again during the 1937-38 season. Speedway did not return to the town until 1970. Then of course meetings took place at Derwent Park.

Despite the Borough Council's wish to adopt the *1899 Baths & Wash Houses Act*, it would be 35 years before the townspeople enjoyed a *"municipal swimming baths"*. Carlisle had build baths in 1884, and Whitehaven had purchased theirs from a private company in 1901.

In 1932, the Council made enquiries about the vacant Artillery Riding School property, to the rear of the Conservative Club on Oxford Street. This obsolete building was subsequently purchased for £2000, and converted into the town's first baths. In November 1934, the 75ft by 30ft (22.9m x 9.15m) pool and slipper baths [01] was opened by Thomas Cape (the town's MP). Swimming sessions for the town's school children proved extremely popular. In February 1935, Sir Samuel Kelly (of Belfast) presented the town with a large swimming trophy. Until the 1980s, Workington's secondary schools competed annually for this magnificent shield, more commonly referred to as the *Kelly Shield*.[02] ■

"Although Harry Moffatt was not a dog owner himself, he really enjoyed greyhound racing and was facinated by it. He was quite an expert on it and used to do all the handicapping and timing, knowing the business inside out".

Graham Moffatt
1999

[01] As well as the swimming pool, the building also contained two separate areas for male and females to take a bath. At this time the majority of homes had no proper bathroom facilities, and the slipper baths afforded people the opportunity to ensure their personal cleanliness. Records show that even in the 1950s, upwards of 10,000 baths were taken at the John Street facility annually. ■

[02] The Kelly Shield is currently displayed at the town's Helena Thompson Museum. ■

APPENDIX

WORKINGTON ASSOCIATION FOOTBALL CLUB

FINAL LEAGUE TABLES FOR THE REDS FIRST FOUR SEASONS IN THE FOOTBALL LEAGUE
(see pages 190-195)

LEAGUE DIVISION THREE (NORTH) 1951-52

	P	W	D	L	F	A	Pts
Lincoln City	46	30	9	7	121	52	69
Grimsby Town	46	29	8	9	96	45	66
Stockport Utd	46	23	13	10	74	40	59
Oldham Athletic	46	24	9	13	90	61	57
Gateshead	46	21	11	14	66	49	53
Mansfield Town	46	22	8	16	73	60	52
Carlisle United	46	19	13	14	62	57	51
Bradford PA	46	19	12	15	74	64	50
Hartlepools Utd	46	21	8	17	71	65	50
York City	46	18	13	15	73	52	49
Tranmere Rovers	46	21	6	19	76	71	48
Barrow	46	17	12	17	57	61	46
Chester City	46	17	11	18	65	66	45
Scunthorpe	46	14	16	16	65	74	44
Bradford City	46	16	10	20	61	68	42
Crewe Alex	46	17	8	21	63	82	42
Southport	46	15	11	20	53	71	41
Wrexham	46	15	9	22	63	73	39
Chester City	46	15	9	22	72	85	39
Halifax Town	46	14	7	25	61	97	35
Rochdale	46	11	13	22	47	79	35
Accrington S.	46	10	12	24	61	92	32
Darlington	46	11	9	26	64	103	31
Workington	46	11	7	28	50	91	29

LEAGUE DIVISION THREE (NORTH) 1952-53

	P	W	D	L	F	A	Pts
Oldham Athletic	46	22	15	9	77	45	59
Port Vale	46	20	18	8	67	35	58
Wrexham	46	24	8	14	86	66	56
York City	46	20	13	13	60	45	53
Grimsby Town	46	21	10	15	75	59	52
Southport	46	20	11	15	63	60	51
Bradford PA	46	19	12	15	75	61	50
Gateshead	46	17	15	14	76	60	49
Carlisle United	46	18	13	15	82	68	49
Crewe Alex	46	20	8	18	70	68	48
Stockport County	46	17	13	16	82	69	47
Chester City	46	18	11	17	65	63	47
Tranmere Rovers	46	21	5	20	65	63	47
Halifax Town	46	16	15	15	68	68	47
Scunthorpe	46	16	14	16	62	56	46
Bradford City	46	14	18	14	75	80	46
Hartlepools Utd	46	16	14	16	57	61	46
Mansfield Town	46	16	14	16	55	62	46
Barrow	46	16	12	18	66	71	44
Chester City	46	11	15	20	64	85	37
Darlington	46	14	6	26	58	96	34
Rochdale	46	14	5	27	62	83	33
Workington	46	11	10	25	55	91	32
Accrington S.	46	8	11	27	39	89	27

LEAGUE DIVISION THREE (NORTH) 1953-54

	P	W	D	L	F	A	Pts
Port Vale	46	26	17	3	74	21	69
Barnsley	46	24	10	12	77	57	58
Scunthorpe	46	21	15	10	77	56	57
Gateshead	46	21	13	12	74	55	55
Bradford City	46	22	9	15	60	55	53
Chester City	46	19	14	13	76	64	52
Mansfield Town	46	20	11	15	88	67	51
Wrexham	46	21	9	16	81	68	51
Bradford PA	46	18	14	14	77	68	50
Stockport Utd	46	18	11	17	77	67	47
Southport	46	17	12	17	63	60	46
Barrow	46	16	12	18	72	71	44
Carlisle United	46	14	15	17	83	71	43
Tranmere Rovers	46	18	7	21	59	70	43
Accrington S.	46	16	10	20	66	74	42
Crewe Alex	46	14	13	19	49	67	41
Grimsby Town	46	16	9	21	51	77	41
Hartlepools Utd	46	13	14	19	59	65	40
Rochdale	46	15	10	21	59	77	40
Workington	46	13	14	19	59	80	40
Darlington	46	12	14	20	50	71	38
York City	46	12	13	21	64	86	37
Halifax Town	46	12	10	24	44	73	34
Chester City	46	11	10	25	48	67	32

LEAGUE DIVISION THREE (NORTH) 1954-55

	P	W	D	L	F	A	Pts
Barnsley	46	30	5	11	86	46	65
Accrington S.	46	25	11	10	96	67	61
Scunthorpe	46	23	12	11	81	53	58
York City	46	24	10	12	92	63	58
Hartlepools Utd	46	25	5	16	64	49	55
Chester City	46	24	6	16	81	70	54
Gateshead	46	20	12	14	65	69	52
Workington	46	18	14	14	68	55	50
Stockport Utd	46	18	12	16	84	70	48
Oldham Athletic	46	19	10	17	74	68	48
Southport	46	16	16	14	47	44	48
Rochdale	46	17	14	15	69	66	48
Mansfield Town	46	18	9	19	65	71	45
Halifax Town	46	15	13	18	63	67	43
Darlington	46	14	14	18	62	73	42
Bradford PA	46	15	11	20	56	70	41
Barrow	46	17	6	23	70	89	40
Wrexham	46	13	12	21	65	77	38
Tranmere Rovers	46	13	11	22	55	70	37
Carlisle United	46	15	6	25	78	89	36
Bradford City	46	13	10	23	47	55	36
Crewe Alex	46	10	14	22	68	91	34
Grimsby Town	46	13	8	25	47	78	34
Chester City	46	12	9	25	44	77	33

CHAPTER FOURTEEN

THEATRES & CINEMAS

THE THEATRE ROYAL in Washington Street started life as the *Lyceum* and was probably built by George John Smith (1821-1906) sometime around 1866. He was born in Greenwich, and started his working life as a solicitors clerk, joining the offices of George Fry, his father's cousin. Around 1844, he left London and is thought to have moved to Whitehaven. Twelve years later, he married Hannah, the daughter of John Sherwood, who was a pawnbroker in Nook Street. John Skelton in his writings about the *Workington Playgoers' Club,* believed Smith loved the theatre, but found it difficult to become an actor himself, *"he would at least build a place becoming to the acting profession".* Capable of seating around 400, the little Victorian theatre was generally leased annually by it's owner, to a variety of different managers. Each winter season running from early September through to Easter.

"George John Smith is a fluent public speaker, has a ready fund of wit, and both as a useful public servant and a private citizen is generally well respected".
Maryport & Workington Advertiser
July 1884

LEFT - The Washington Street elevation of the Theatre Royal. Opened in 1866, the theatre was formerly called the Lyceum. ▮

There was the smaller Alexandra Music Hall, above the Bessemer Arms (in Church Street), but this was the Theatre Royal's only serious opposition.

Around Christmas 1874, the theatre's name was changed to the Theatre Royal. It was operated by J. B. Clifford and colourfully described in the local press as a *"little Thespian temple"*. Admission to the front boxes was 1/6 (or 7½p), the upper circle 1/- (5p) and the pit 6d (2½p). The following year the theatre was let to R. F. Smith, who was also the leasee of the Channel Island Theatre. He carried out extensive alterations at the stage end, sinking the orchestra pit, so it no longer interfered with the view of the stage. Despite the efforts of it's managers, the Washington Street theatre was not always a success. When Edward Fletcher (who also managed the Theatre Royal at Whitehaven) ran the theatre during 1876-7, he was forced to close midway through the season. Having incurred a substantial loss in excess of £200, he blamed it's demise on the poor and *"meagre support of the public"*.

During October 1879, a new gallery was completed, which increased the theatre capacity to 700. George Smith extended the stage again a couple of years later, and it was said to have been *"as large as any in the district"*. Up until the opening of the Opera House (in Pow Street), the Theatre Royal was Workington's only permanent theatre. There was the smaller Alexandra Music Hall, [01] above the Bessemer Arms (in Church Street), but this was the theatre's only serious opposition. Many prominent touring companies performed at the Theatre Royal, included the eminent tragedian W.C. Middleton. Bulmer (1901) tells us that the likes of Charles Matthews and Charles Dillion also trod the boards of the Theatre Royal. From around 1880, the Workington Amateur Dramatic Club also performed their plays there.

Between 1867-73, George Smith served on the Workington Local Board. At the age of 52 he took semi-retirement, and moved to Keswick. Although he is believed to have continued as proprietor of the theatre until his death in 1906. He made other improvements in 1888, but the extent of this work is unclear. Over the years the theatre was let to a long list of managers, including Mr. Mallalein (1882), H. A. Langlois (1883), Horace Hawling (1884), Mr. Wright (1897-1900).

The Theatre Royal subsequently became one of the first cinemas in the town. Mr. Skelton recorded that in 1907, *"Mac's Variety and Cinematograph Shows"* performed once nightly. In February 1910, Joseph Ellis (of 43 Devonshire Street) applied for the cinematograph licence [02] for the building. During the following years the licence was issued to Stanley Rogers. But live performances did continue at the theatre, one of the most

[01] See chapter two for more on the Alexandra Music Hall. ∎
[02] By virtue of the Cinematographic Act of 1909, each cinema had to apply annually to the Borough Council for a cinema licence. The Borough surveyor and the police then had to check the suitability of the premises before permitting films to be shown. ∎

famous performers during this period was Enrico Caruso, the Italian Operatic tenor. He was believed to have formed part of Mr. Turner's English Opera Company which visited the theatre in September 1912. Caruso was perhaps the first singer to achieve worldwide fame by virtue of the gramophone record. By the time of his death in 1921, he had made over 150 recordings. During his stay in the town, the opera singer is also known to have visited Workington Golf Club. Their visitors book is said to contain the entry *"Caruso (Opera Co.) Convent Garden"*. It's not known if he actually played a round of golf at the Branthwaite Road course.

During the early 1920s, Mr. J. Bayliff is listed as the operator of the Theatre Royal, till Issac Dockray Graves was granted the cinema licence for the premises in 1926. Graves then also held the licences for the Opera House and the new Oxford Cinema. The Theatre Royal continued as a *"picture theatre"* or cinema untill 1932, when it was closed.

The Workington Playgoers Club was the brainchild of local solicitor, Ieuan Montgomerie Banner Mendus, [01] which was first established in the early autumn of 1935. Through the energy and enthusiasm of its first 271 members, the club subsequently rented the empty and run down Theatre Royal. This was for an initial period of just six-months and cost £15. Records show that the Playgoers leased the property from Messrs. Graves and one newspaper report confirms that the theatre was then *"closed and was not likely to be re-opened"*. Their first public performance on 2 April 1936 was Sutton Vane's *"Outward Bound"*. Despite WW2, the club remained active and raised essential funds for local war charities such as the *"Tommies' Smokers Fund"*. Workington Playgoers were not the first amateur dramatic group in the town. For in July 1880, the Workington Amateur Dramatic Club gave its first theatrical performance.

Between 1949-52, the group spent nearly £1,100 installing a rake to the auditorium floor, re-seating and re-decorated the building. Almost a decade later, they eventually purchased the premises and have since carried out major improvements. Today, it seats just over 150 people, albeit in much greater comfort than it's earlier patrons who sat in the stalls on wooden bench seats. Despite numerous alterations and additions to the theatre throughout it's 135 year existence, much still survives of the original building. One feature is a tunnel, which runs from beneath the stage and under the auditorium, emerging at a trapdoor within the foyer. The windowless rooms

"The Theatre Royal idle for several years, is indeed a dismal sight seen in the dim light of a winter's afternoon".
Workington Star
Dec. 1935

"By our 10th Anniversary (1945) we were regarded as one of Workington's major cultural activities".
John Skelton
Workington Playgoers Club
1985

[01] Ieuan M. Banner Mendus was a solicitor with Milburn & Co., who then had their offices at 4-6 Nook Street. At this time his home was at 1 Irving Street (just off John Street).■

below ground level, midway along this tunnel are said to have been the original dressing rooms.

The Queens Jubilee Hall in Pow Street (on the corner of Ladies Walk and Tiffin Lane) was formally opened in July 1887, and is named in honour of Queen Victoria, who celebrated fifty years on the throne that same year. Over the years, the Jubilee Opera House has been known by numerous names, the Queen's Jubilee Hall, the Liberal Club Hall, the Jubilee Opera House or more recently simply the Opera House. It originally formed part of a larger complex built by Workington Liberal Club. The development covered a large site, and swallowed up around seven dwellings to the east side of Tiffin Lane. A number of shops and houses on Pow Street, including the home of music teacher, Charles Hooper. As well as the old Wesleyan Chapel [01] in Ladies Walk, purchased from the Methodist church in South William Street.

The building took over twelve months to complete. It's memorial stone was laid by Liberal MP, Sir Wilfred Lawson on 29 July 1886. The Jubilee Opera House, had its entrance in Pow Street. Theatre-goers entered the 2,500 seater public hall, through an elaborate stone arched doorway, and down a narrow passage between the two shops. At first floor level (above the shops) was a large

[01] For more details of this chapel - see page 87 of the earlier volume of the History of Workington (Earliest times to 1865). ■

BELOW - The Pow Street entrance to the Jubilee Opera House. On the first floor above the two shops was the Liberal club. Tiffin Lane ran down the left hand site of the property. ■

billiard room, with three full-sized tables and a reading room, all part of the Liberal Club. In 1894, the Opera House was managed by Messrs. Clark and Wood. Included in its New Year programme for that year was Arthur Kendall's *Saucy Dick Whittington* Burlesque Company.

In June 1903, when the Workington Liberal Club disposed of the building by auction the Opera House was described as being *"favourably known to the theatrical profession and many of the leading provincial touring companies"*. Exactly who purchased the hall is not clear, but we do know that James Bayliff ran the venue during WW1, perhaps even longer. From April 1911 some fourteen years before the town was supplied with electricity, the Pow Street entrance of the Opera House was lit by a huge arc light, powered from a private generator. By November 1923, we learn from the Council minutes that a John Bayliff now held a cinema licence for the hall.

On 1 November 1928, the Opera House and the shops facing Pow Street were almost completely destroyed by a devastating fire. William Wallace Penrice was the stage manager at the time, and afterwards he, his wife and their nine children moved to Ramsgate, and never returned to the town. By March 1929, the Opera House had been totally rebuilt by the Graves family. Newcastle architects, Percy L. Browne and Son (of Newcastle-upon-Tyne) designed the new theatre which then had one of the best and well equipped stages *"in the provinces"*, capable of staging very large productions. The new Opera House which was formally opened by the Mayoress, Mrs D. J. Mason was a major improvement on its predecessor. Each of its 1,300 seats was *"planned on generous lines, giving comfort and ease"* and everyone now had an unobstructed view of the stage. The theatre also had two entrances, for the balcony seats, patrons would use the front Pow Street entrance. Whilst those seating in the cheaper *"stalls and pit"*, would use the side door in Tiffen Lane.

Where the original Liberal Club building incorporated two shops either side of it's entrance. Montague Burtons, the tailors (later know as simply Burtons) built a single large store. When it opened in February 1929, one local newspaper described it's *"elegant facade"* as being *"practically a replica of their fine building"* in London's Strand. The new 1,300 sq. ft. shop, with a frontage of 50 feet on to Pow Street was obviously much smaller than it's London counterpart, but at the time was *"a handsome and striking"* addition to the town.

Built by local contractors, Messrs. J. Gilmore and

The Opera House was described as being *"favourably known to the theatrical profession and many of the leading provincial touring companies"*.

The rebuilt theatre was named the *New Opera House* and played host to a wide selection of famous or up and coming variety acts, such as Morecambe and Wise, Frankie Howard and Norman Wisdom.

Son (of 196 Harrington Road) with the steelwork supplied by Sandham's Marshside works. The front elevation boasted a large *"uninterrupted"* plate glass windows along its frontage, so as not to *"obstruct the view of the shoppers"*. Although this is something we take for granted today, it was perhaps the first shop of kind in the town. These windows were set into ornamental bronze frames, upon a polished granite plinth. The upper part of the front elevation was completed with white *"ceramo"* glazed terracotta tiles. Recently of course, Burtons closed their branch in the town, but many of these original features can still be seen on the property today.

The rebuilt theatre became known as the New Opera House and played host to a wide selection of famous or up and coming variety acts, such as Morecambe and Wise, Frankie Howard and Norman Wisdom. But the popularity of such acts waned during the 1950s and *"live theatre"* ceased at the Opera House in October 1957. When it closed it was listed as the last theatre in West Cumberland. It's owners were still Graves Bros., who planned to convert the premises into a permanent cinema. However, in 1963 after the new Betting & Gaming Act of 1960 became law, the building was transformed into the Opera Bingo and Social Club.

The Hippodrome on Hagg Hill (or Falcon Place) started life as a public hall built by James B. Whitfield in 1895. The Council minutes reveal that they granted permission for a large cast-iron *"portico"* projecting over the footpath at it's Hagg Hill entrance. Providing Mr. Whitfield paid them 1/- (or 5p) per annum easement. Like the Opera House, it was also part of a larger complex which included Whitfield's Arcade facing onto Station Road.

In 1909, Edmund Burrow[01] applied for perhaps the Hippodrome's earliest cinematographic licence on behalf of the late James B. Whitfield. Burrow is thought to have been the nephew and executor of James Whitfield who had actually died in 1900. The business continued to trade in it's late proprietors name for many years, until around the end of WW1. In March 1911, there is also a suggestion that Messrs. Relph and Pedley were now also involved with the running of the Hippodrome. It is likely Burrow may have let the cinema to this partnership.

Certainly in February 1921, the Borough Council approved plans to alter the Hippodrome, with Mr. William *"Billy"* Williams [02] now listed as the proprietor. He renewed the annual cinema licences thereafter until the 1940s. In 1931, a new projection room and new seat-

[01] In the 1920s, Edmund Burrow lived at Copstone House, on Brow Top. After his death in March 1928, his builders merchant business, in Oxford Street was continued by his son. ∎

[02] William *"Billy"* Williams, was the father of J. D. Williams the screen writer of Stars Look Down. ∎

ing were installed at the Hippodrome. The business now trading as Williams Cinemas Ltd., also ran the Hippodrome Dance Hall below the cinema. At this time the entrance to the dance hall was off South Watt Street, at the rear of the building.

The cinema and ballroom was later thought to have been acquired by Maud, Bailey and Crow (later known as M.B. Cinemas Limited). Although for a time it appears to have continued to trade as Williams Cinemas Limited. Eventually, the premises became the headquarters for the company which has numerous cinemas throughout the north west, stretching down to Morecambe. Following a major fire at the Hippodrome in 1955, the company thought long and hard about it's reconstruction. It even proposed building an entirely new cinema on the corner of Oxford Street and James Street. But although plans for the new site were subsequently approved by the Borough Council, the scheme was abandoned and the Hippodrome later rebuild.

In June 1939, Workington, Siddick's St. Helens Colliery and the terraced streets of Northside and Clifton formed the backdrop for the filming of *The Stars Look Down,* a major feature film starring Michael Redgrave [01] and Margaret Lockwood. Adapted from the novel of A. J. Cronin [02] and directed by Carol Reed [03], the film tells the moving and tragic story of a group of coal miners, who are buried alive by the greed of their pit-owner employer. The film was a great commercial success, described by many as *"one of the finest British pictures ever made"*.

Much of the pithead scenes were filmed at St. Helens, whilst the crowd and street scenes were shot at Northside and Clifton. Borough Park was also used to film the football match scenes. The relatively new ground was filled with a crowd of over 3,000 townspeople, who were admitted free to act as extras. Local footballers were also selected to take part in the match which formed part of the film. Over sixty years later, some of this film forms a valuable record of the town, particularly the brief shots of steam engines leaving Central Station.

Redgrave gave a memorable performance as a young idealistic miner's son who through determined hard work gains a place at university. Only to be forced to leave his studies and return to the village to support his father during a long and drawn out strike at the pit. Before filming began, he had visited the town to study pit-life at first hand. Causing quite a stir by going down the pit at St. Helens, *"donned in his miners clothes"*. He also surprised and delighted the crowds at the Hippodrome cin-

"Stars Look Down is generally an entertaining film....a well made social drama from a popular novel, with good pace and backgrounds".
Halliwells film Guide

"Dr. Cronin's mining novel has produced a very good film - I doubt wether in England we have ever produced better".
Graham Greene (1939

[01] An excited Michael Redgrave described his part in the *"Stars Look Down"* as a remarkable opportunity. Adding "that you might wait all your life for such a part". ■
[02] Archibald Joseph Cronin's fourth novel the *"Stars Look Down"*, was first published in 1935. The Scottish novelist also co-scripted the screen play with the well-known West Cumbrian journalist J. R. Williams. The release of the film was to gain him an international readership. Dr. Cronin's other important works include *The Citadel* and *The Green Years.* ■
[03] Sir Carol Reed was also responsible for a number of other important films, including *The Third Man* (1949) and *Oliver* (1968). Whilst in the town he paid tribute to the *"speck and span"* way the colliers wives kept their homes. ■

ema, by making a personal appearance on stage, during the screening of another of his famous films - the Hitchcock thriller *A Lady Vanishes.*

Work on building the Oxford Picture House (on the corner of Gray Street and Oxford Street) sometimes referred to as the Oxford Picture Hall or Oxford Picture Palace began in the autumn of 1919. The new cinema, with it's distinctive domed tower was built for Issac Dockray Graves. When it first opened in September 1923, it's manager was Louis B. Anisworth, who lived in Frostoms Road. He was the former manager at the Hippodrome, and his father had also helped run the cinema with Mr. Barnes. Within the *"arcade like"* entrance to the Oxford was a cafe. In it's early days it was open from 10 am to 10 pm. and was first let by Graves to the Stordy family. They also had a bakers and confectioners at 32 Fisher Street.

In September 1929, the Oxford Picture House screened the very first *"talking picture"* shown in West Cumberland. Nearly 1,500 people *"saw and heard"* the *Singing Fool.* In April 1932, the Graves family business became a limited company. Before 1932, the basement below the cinema was the Oxford Billiard Hall, operated by Holt Willie Limited (of Burnley). This large room with white ceramic tiled walls and stone floor, contained over a dozen or so full-sized tables. During its life, it was always a purely male domain, and very few females had ever descended the long flight of stone stairs from Oxford Street.

The Lecture Hall attached to the Carnegie Library on the corner of Finkle Street and Warwick Place, was also used as a cinema from as early as 1909. As we know the librarian, J. W. C. Purves was responsible for applying for its first Cinematograph licences. The hall was then let annually by tender to a variety of managers. The first lease was thought to have been granted to the Royal Imperial Animated Picture Company. Although it regularly changed hands each year. Following alterations in the spring of 1915 the Carnegie cinema was capable of holding 850 people.

By April 1933, the Carnegie was let to the newly formed Graves Cinemas Ltd., who also ran the Oxford and the Opera House. They were to run the cinema here for the next twenty years or so, although they still had to tender regularly to renew the arrangement. The Council minutes confirm that when the Graves lease of the Carnegie Hall was renewed in July 1953, they paid the Cor-

" I remember the safety curtain at the Carnegie Cinema being painted with advertisements for many of the town's businesses. During the interval, we would often play a game of 'ABC' using the advertisers names. "

Eric Hutton

poration £2,040 per annum. After 1963, the Carnegie Lecture Hall was no longer used as a cinema and was later converted into a conventional theatre.

In October 1936, the Borough Council approved plans for the Ritz cinema on Murray Road. This massive new 1,350 seater *"picture theatre"* was designed by local architect Thomas Nicholson [01] for Graves Cinemas Ltd. Construction work was delayed however for some months, owing to difficulties in obtaining the 300 tons steelwork for the building. This was thought to have been due to the pressure of Government armament orders, in the years preceding WW2. Eventually local firm Messrs. Drummond and Co., obtained the steel girders to form the *"skeleton of the new cinema"*.

Externally the building was built of predominately red rustic brickwork, with some large cream earthernware tiled areas. Four lock-up shops were incorporated in the scheme, along the Murray Road elevation. Entering the cinema, under the canopy on the corner of Murray Road and Upton Street, the picture-goer first stopped at a *"beautiful chromium and Empire wood pay box"* in the

[01] Architect and surveyor, Thomas Nicholson then had his office at 47 John Street, almost on the corner with Edkin Street. ■

BELOW - The Ritz cinema built in 1938, which stood on the corner of Murray Road and Upton Street.■

"The fine elevation to Murray Road was enhanced by the two large neon "RITZ" signs fixed above each side of the curved canopied entrance".

centre of the vestibule. From there visitors passed into a *"large and roomy foyer"*. The rich red carpeted staircase up to the dress circle or balcony seats rose opposite the main entrance. The ground floor of the cinema was entered through doors to the right. The Ritz had a rich and elaborate Art Deco style interior, designed by Messrs. John Alexander and Sons. These famous Newcastle based cinema interior designers, used lighting in particular to great effect at the Ritz. The new cinema was officially opened by the Mayor, Alderman James Poole on 26 September 1938.

It was common to have a organ in cinemas at this time, and the Ritz had a *"mighty wurlitzer"*, the *"Rolls Royce of cinema organs"*. During the interval at the Ritz, this very versatile organ was usually played for 15 minutes or so. It contained all the tones of a church organ together with *"many orchestral instruments such as the clarinet, flutes, piccolos, clockenspiel, tambourines, even castanets and triangles. The talented organist could also make it sound like a dance band, a drum and fife band, even bagpipes."* As the music rang out the organist could also change the lighting colour projected on the stage curtain, to reflect the mood of the music played. The first person to play the new Wurlitzer at the Ritz, is said to have been Minnie McManus, wife of one of the builders working on the new cinema. After the gigantic instrument was installed, someone was needed to play the organ, so it could be to tested and adjusted. Mrs. McManus was sent for and performed the task, playing a selection of pieces to an empty cinema.

Before the start of WW2, the town had five cinemas, the Carnegie, Opera House, Oxford, Hippodrome and the Ritz. Generally each then screened a film twice nightly, which would be changed every three nights. During the late 1940s, Joyce Burns remembers going to the Opera House almost every Monday along with other family members. Also twice a week they also went to the cinema. *"On Wednesday, it was the Ritz, and each Saturday the Hippodrome, irrespective of what was showing. I remember the cinema full of an awful lot of cigarette smoke, and the films were then obviously just black and white. Often, the films at the Hippodrome were spoiled by the loud music from dance bands playing in the dance hall below the cinema".*

In 1924, the Workington Musical Festival replaced the annual eisteddfod in the town, which was first established in 1872. Workington's eisteddfod essentially started life as a traditional Welsh music and literary festival or competition, promoting the Welsh language, literature, music and its customs. It was the brainchild of W. Ivander Griffiths [01] the owner of Barepot's Tinplate works. Initially the event was solely to provide some entertainment for his Welsh workers. During the latter half of the nineteenth century, a significant number had settled in and around Barepot, having found work with Griffiths works. In the ensuing years, the eisteddfod held every year around Christmas week, attracted more and more local entries. Gradually, the traditional Welsh influence was lost and the event evolved into a general music and literary competition. It soon became the social and cultural highlight of the year. After it became the Workington Music Festival, the final evening, gold cup night was a guaranteed sellout each year.

Over the years, it was held at many venues around the town. During the late 1930s, the Hippodrome Cinema staged the event. It's proprietors, the Williams family providing a gold cup for the best overall adult performer. The most famous winner of this prestigious cup was Kathleen Mary Ferrier (1912-53) in 1938. Lancashire born, Ferrier was 26 and married to Albert Ferrier, the manager of Silloth's Midland Bank. She would later establish herself as a leading oratorio singer, and became a huge recording star. It was her only appearance at the Workington festival, and within three years she had signed a lucrative contract with Ibbs and Tillett, and moved to London. Her best known recording is the haunting unaccompanied rendering of *Blow the Wind Southerly*. People still talk about her appearance in the festival, Dorothy Chambers remembering *"She was an unknown then, but nobody who saw her win the gold cup was surprised when she went on to great things on the concert stage"*. ∎

"In October 1945, Graves Cinemas Ltd. also proposed to build a new cinema on Weatheriggs Road, at Salterbeck. But they later abandoned the scheme."

❧ BIBLIOGRAPHY ❧

Allerdale District Council - minutes
Allen, Tom - The Team Beyond the Hills (Wingfield 1994)
Austin, John and Ford, Malcolm - Steel Town, Dronfield and Wilson Cammell (Scarsdale - 1983)
Baggley, Philip & Sanderson, Neil - Bessemer Steel, Pictorial Archive of Steelmaking at Workington (Richard Byers 2002)
Batten, Chris - NHS Ambulances, The First 25 Years (Trans-Pennine Publishing - 1998)
Bulmer - History and Trade Directory of Cumberland (1901)
Burridge, Michael - Shipbuilding in West Cumberland (1987 - unpublished notes)
Burrow, E.J (publishers) - The Seaport Town of Workington and it's development (c.1916)
Byers, Richard L. M. - History of Workington, from earliest times to 1865 (Richard Byers, Dec.1998)
Byers, Richard L. M. - Workington War Heroes (Richard Byers 2002)
Cleator & Workington Junction Railway - original minute books 1875-1923
Coleman, Terry - The Railway Navvies (Hutchinson 1965)
Cumberland Pacquet (various issues from 1866 onwards)
Cumbrian Railways Association - A History of the Furness Railway, Celebrating 150 years (CRA 1996)
Cumbrian Railways Association Journals (various issues)
Daysh, G.H.J and Watson, Evelyn M. - Cumberland, A Survey of Industrial Facilities (Cumb.Development Council 1951)
Fort Frances Times and Rainy Lake Herald (Canada - July 1936)
George, David Lloyd - War Memoirs of David Lloyd George (Odhams Press)
Gilbert, Martin - Second World War (George Weinfield and Nicholson 1989)
Green, Edwin - A History of the Midland Bank since 1900 (St. Georges Press 1979)
Grant, Dr. Ronald - The Life Story of Dr. Ronald Grant (www.simongrant.org 2002)
Gee, Majorie - Captain Fraser's Voyages (Stanford Maritime 1979)
Grocers Gazette (various issues 1930-46)
Hall, E.G. Sarsfield - A Record of the 5th Battalion Border Regiment Home Guard (1945)
Heal, David W. - The Steel Industry in Post War Britain (David and Charles 1974)
Iredale, Thomas - The Rectors of Workington (C&WAAS 1909)
Lancaster J. Y. and Wattleworth D. R. - The Iron and Steel Industry of West Cumberland (British Steel - 1977)
Lee, Norman and Stubbs, Peter - History of Dorman Smith 1878-1972 (Newman Neame 1972)
Keeling, B.S. and Wright, A. E.G - The Development of Modern Iron and Steel Industry (Longmans 1964)
Machell, Hugh W. - Some Records of the Annual Grasmere Sports (Charles Thurnam 1911)
Maryport & Workington Advertiser (various issues from 1884)
Marshall, John - Forgotten Railways, North West England (David & Charles 1981)
Mining Manual and Mining Yearbook - published in 1924.
Mordy, John - History of Workington Congregational Church (Workington Free Press, Dec.1883)
Norman, K.J - The Furness Railway (Silver Link 1994)
Our Lady & St. Michael's Church, Workington - Centenary Booklet 1876 to1976
Risman, Gus - Rugby Renegade (Stanley Paul 1958)
RNLI - Workington Lifeboat, A history (RNLI)
Schofield, Hudson - A History of Workington Savings Bank (unpublished manuscript)
Shaw, Stuart - Spotlight on Workington Reds (Soccer Star article - 10 April 1964)
Sibson, Florence - History of West Cumberland Potteries (1991)
Smith, David Burrand - Huntrods family History (1998)
Suart, George - Suart's Almamac (George Suart, Wilson Street, Workington - 1895)
Sugden, Edward Haigh - History of Arlecdon & Frizington (Richard Byers - 1997)
Thompson, Ces - Born on the Wrong Side, His Autobiography (Pentland Press - 1995)
Trinity Methodist Church, Workington - Centenary Booklet 1890 to 1900
Varty & Co. - Workington Yearbook (1908)
Walker, David - Champion of Sail, R.W. Leyland and his Shipping Line (Conway Maritime Press 1986)
Wattleworth, Douglas R. - Origin and Development of Iron and Steel Industry in West Cumberland. (paper published 1965)
West Cumberland Journal.
West Cumberland Times
Whitehaven News
Wingfield, Martin - So Sad, So Very Sad, Workington AFC. 1951-58 (Worthing Typesetting 1991)
Workington Iron & Steel Company Bulletins (c.1959-64)
Workington Reds - Official Handbook (Workington Reds Supporters Club - 1965)
Workington Star and Evening Star newspapers (various issues)
Workington Town Council (Minutes of Council and Committes)